*Cocaine*
*Politics*

University of California Press
Berkeley and Los Angeles, California

University of California Press, Ltd.
Oxford, England

© 1991 by
The Regents of the University of California

**Library of Congress Cataloging-in-Publication Data**

Scott, Peter Dale.
    Cocaine politics : drugs, armies, and the CIA in Central
America / Peter Dale Scott and Jonathan Marshall.
      p.    cm.
    Includes bibliographical references and index.
    ISBN 0-520-07312-6 (alk. paper)
    ISBN 0-520-07781-4 (ppb.)
    1. Narcotics, Control of—Central America.   2. Narcotics,
Control of—Political aspects—Central America.   3. Cocaine
industry—Central America.   4. Corruption (in politics)—
Central America.
    I. Marshall, Jonathan.  II. Title.
    HV5840.C45S36  1991
    363.4'5'09728—dc20                    90-48813
                                           CIP

Printed in the United States of America
9 8 7 6 5 4 3 2

# Contents

# Preface to the Paperback Edition

Since *Cocaine Politics* appeared in 1991, nothing has emerged to challenge our factual claims. Unfortunately, nothing has emerged, either, to suggest that the dangerous hypocrises underlying the "war on drugs" will soon be officially repudiated. Predictably, the book's appearance has evoked no response from the administration and little from the establishment media. Yet, if anything, the revelations of the last few months have added weight to our thesis that governments, very much including Washington, are a key to the worldwide drug problem, and thus to its solution.

The drug traffic should be visualized, not as a horizontal line between producers and consumers, but as a triangle. At its apex sit governments whose civilian and military intelligence agencies recurringly afford *de facto* protection to drug kingpins beneath them. In the United States as elsewhere, this vertical dimension of protected trafficking has created windows of opportunity for importing narcotics by the ton.

Our conclusion remains that the first target of an effective drug strategy should be Washington itself, and specifically its own connections with corrupt, drug-linked forces in other parts of the world. We argued that Washington's covert operations overseas had been a major factor in generating changes in the overall pattern of drug flows into the United States, and cited the Vietnam-generated heroin epidemic of the 1960s and the Afghan-generated heroin epidemic of the 1980s as analogues of the central concern of this book: the explosion of cocaine trafficking through Central America in the Reagan years, made possible by the administration's covert operation to overthrow the Nicaraguan Sandinistas.

Recent indictments, congressional hearings, and news investigations into the shadowy Bank of Credit and Commerce International indicate that the parallel we drew between Afghanistan and Central America is even prison terms and restored millions of dollars of drug profits to witnesses willing to take the stand against the man deprecated by former cartel king-pin Carlos Lehder as "just another criminally corrupt police officer."[16]

The trial, eagerly awaited by some government critics as a source of revelations about Reagan administration complicity with Noriega, has been narrowly contained by prosecutorial objections and judicial rulings barring most questions about the Contras, George Bush, and related matters. Even so, one key government witness, Floyd Carlton, testified that his associate in the cocaine trade, Alfredo Caballero, organized arms shipments to the Contras in 1983 and 1984 (see Chapters 1, 4, and 6).[17] And Lehder, who also testified to the complicity of Cuban and Nicaraguan leaders in the drug trade, admitted (over the intense objection of prosecutors) that the Medellín Cartel contributed some $10 million to the Contra cause.[18]

Meanwhile, evidence is mounting that even with Noriega removed from Panama, cocaine continues to pour through that country. One Drug Enforcement Administration agent told the General Accounting Office that the volume of cocaine transiting Panama "may have doubled since Operation Just Cause."[19] The price of cocaine reached record lows there in mid-1991.[20] Panamanian reporters have had a field day exposing the links of President Guillermo Endara (whose 1989 election campaign was financed in part by the CIA) to notorious money-laundering banks. Costa Rican authorities say that two-thirds of the cocaine transshipped through their own country goes through Panama's Chiriqui Province and is often protected by former Nicaraguan Contras.[22]

Now that the Nicaraguan civil war is over, more will surely emerge in years to come of the Contra-drug connection. In November 1991, for instance, the chief of Nicaragua's National Police Criminal Division announced the arrest of that country's leading narcotics trafficker, Norwin Meneses, known as "El Rey" (The King). Police seized 738 kilos of cocaine from the ring, which intended to smuggle it to the United States through El Salvador. The Meneses group reportedly had plans to export 4,000 kilos to the North American market.[23] As discussed in Chapter 6, Meneses was at the center of one of the most sensitive U.S. drug busts of the 1980s, the so-called Frogman seizure, which (through a press leak) exposed his role in financing elements of the Contras.

Whether new revelations will make any more difference than the old ones to Congress, public opinion or administration policy remains to be seen. Many law enforcement professionals need no persuading to accept our thesis; Dennis Dayle, former chief of an elite DEA enforcement unit, has said for the record that "in my 30-year history in the Drug Enforcement Administration and related agencies, the major targets of my investigations almost invariably turned out to be working for the CIA."[24] Yet the notion that Washington is a big part of the problem continues to meet with strong resistance in the major media, where evidence of government complicity with international narcotics traffickers is variously dismissed as unthinkable or as a mere "sideshow" to more important factors in the drug market.[25]

Signs of any new thinking about drug issues in Congress are hard to find. The U.S. Senate confirmed the nomination of Robert Gates as CIA director by a vote of 64 to 31 on November 5, 1991, despite voluminous testimony suggesting that he lied as to his ignorance of key matters in the Iran-Contra affair and that he distorted the production of intelligence esti-mates to serve the political ends of his boss, former Reagan campaign director William Casey. In this respect, one critic testified that Gates pushed the administration line on "narcoterrorism," which blamed drug trafficking on leftwing states and insurgent movements (see Chapter 2). Accusing Gates of shopping for analysts to make that case, Mel Goodman testified that "a senior analyst was called in by Bob Gates and told that Bill Casey wanted a memo that would link drug dealers to international terror-ists. This senior analyst looked at the evidence and couldn't make those conclusions. The evidence wasn't there. He was told to go back and look again. He did that. Said the evidence wasn't there. Gates took the project away from him and gave it to another analyst. I believe there is an ethical issue here." Gates admitted asking analysts to look into accusations of a linkage between traffickers and terrorists but said in his defense that three separate agency analyses concluded any such linkage was weak.[26]

Congress also shows few signs of challenging the "war on drugs," in particular, President Bush's "Andean Initiative" to send millions of dollars in aid to the militaries of Bolivia, Colombia, and Peru. Assistance to these drug-corrupted forces often goes to fight not traffickers but leftist guer-rillas and their civilian sympathizers. The program has been seriously chal-lenged only in the case of Peru, which the human rights group Americas Watch accused of having one of the worst records in the world for "disap-pearances." (The organization admits that the human rights record of the guerrilla group Shining Path, which finances its struggle in part from cocaine taxes, is at least as grisly as that of government forces.) Congress showed enough concern over official abuses in late 1991 to hold up $10 million in military aid earmarked for two army battalions combating the Shining Path.[27]

This limited dissent is not enough. The administration's disastrous drug policies must be challenged, both for traditional considerations of national security and basic considerations of humanity. The United States cannot afford to become enmeshed in counterinsurgency campaigns abroad, in

Third World jungles, nor at home in the streets of our cities. The social cost of trying to reproduce for illicit drugs the conditions of Prohibition is too high.

This book offers evidence to support changing the focus of our drug strategies away from penalizing individuals and toward curbing our own government. Ending our government's complicity in the narcotics trade and its destructive war on drugs will not solve the drug problem; the world drug traffic, and the demand that drives it, have causes and a dynamic that extend far beyond any particular covert operation or government decision. But the American people cannot begin to cope with the deeper social problems of drug abuse so long as their political representatives remain such a powerful obstacle to reform. We renew our appeal to citizens to involve themselves in this matter, at a time when both Congress and the media have largely failed to rise to the challenge. At stake is nothing less than the survival of decency in America.

NOTES

[1]*New York Times,* July 13, 1991; *Congressional Quarterly,* August 3, 1991 (quoting Jack Blum).

[2]*Wall Street Journal,* October 24, 1991.

[3]*Financial Times,* July 25, 1991, quoted in *Guardian* (New York), September 18, 1991.

[4]*Washington Post,* August 19, 1991.

[5]*Miami Herald,* August 4, 1991.

[6]*New York Times,* October 27, 1991.

[7]*Washington Post,* August 8, 1991.

[8]*New York Times,* January 19, 1991.

[9]Thus most accounts of Noriega's career agree that the CIA paid him more than $100,000 a year during the first half of the 1980s.

[10]*Washington Post,* September 6, 1991.

[11]*Wall Street Journal,* August 2, 1991; *Time,* July 29, 1991; *Village Voice,* August 6, 1991.

[12]*Wall Street Journal,* November 22, 1991.

[13]*New York Times,* October 2, 1991.

[14]*Time,* July 29, 1991.

[15]*Wall Street Journal,* October 23, 1991.

[16]Associated Press, November 19, 1991.

[17]*San Francisco Chronicle,* October 2, 1991.

[18]*New York Times,* October 26, 1991. Lehder also claimed that U.S. officials approached him in 1982, saying they would let him run drugs into the United States in exchange for his help in facilitating the flow of arms to the Contras; fearing a possible sting operation, he turned the deal down. He was blocked from answering questions about this episode (*New York Times,* October 22, 1991; *Newsday,* November 26, 1991). Nothing Lehder says should necessarily be taken at face value; he has been accused by Robert Merkel, former U.S. attorney who prosecuted him, of being "a liar from beginning to end." (*Nation,* December 2, 1991).

[19]GAO/NSIAD-91-233, "The War on Drugs: Narcotics Control Efforts in Panama," (Washington: US Government Printing Office, 1991).

[20]*San Francisco Chronicle,* July 16, 1991.

[21]Peeved by the constant criticism, Endara threw one prominent columnist, Dagoberto Franco of *El Siglo,* into jail.

[22]*Critica Libre* (Panama City), October 28, 1991.

[23]ACAN (Panama City), November 6, 1991; *San Francisco Chronicle,* December 16, 1991.

[24]Quoted in *Causes and Cures: National Campaign on the Narcotics Epidemic: Final Report* (Washington, D.C., 1991), 9.

[25]Elaine Shannon, who covers the Drug Enforcement Administration admiringly for *Time* magazine, accused the book of "neo-McCarthyism," accepting the word of "crooks," and relying excessively on "Government releases, court records and transcripts of Congressional hearings" to compile a "treasury of great conspiracy charges" (*New York Times Book Review,* July 28, 1991; for authors' reply, see *New York Times Book Review,* September 8, 1991). Another reviewer condemned the book from the opposite vantage point, for being excessively naive in finding anything surprising about CIA complicity with traffickers (David Rieff in *Newsday,* July 14, 1991). And in the pages of the *Nation,* Michael Massing took issue with what he called a "peculiar species of drug-war literature," which focuses on such "foreign sideshows" as Washington's aid to and protection of traffickers (*Nation,* December 2, 1991). With regard to Shannon's critique, a bimonthly media review published by Fairness and Accuracy in Reporting, quoted a former *Time* reporter who found "serious evidence" that Oliver North's network was bringing cocaine into the United States. The reporter quoted his senior editor as explaining why the story was killed: "*Time* is institutionally behind the Contras. If this story were about the Sandinistas and drugs, you'd have no trouble getting it in the magazine" (*Extra!,* November/December 1991, 14).

[26]Senate Select Committee on Intelligence, report, *Nomination of Robert M. Gates to be Director of Central Intelligence,* October 24, 1991, 122–123.

[27]*San Francisco Chronicle,* November 25, 1991.

# Acknowledgments

In building upon the work of many other investigators, we particularly valued the help of Jack Blum, Andrew and Leslie Cockburn, John Mattes, Robert Parry, Ted Rubinstein, Murray Waas, and Jonathan Winer. Participants at two national conferences on drugs, organized at Tufts University by Sherman Teichman and at the University of Wisconsin by Alan Block and Alfred McCoy, helped to refine our thoughts. Peter Dale Scott also wishes to thank the International Center for Development Policy in Washington, where for six months in 1987 he had the opportunity to discuss the drug-related aspects of the Iran-Contra affair with congressional staff, journalists, other researchers, and witnesses. Finally, for the index and much other help, we are indebted to the painstaking and intelligent labors of Peter Dale Scott's friend and close relative, Mary Marshall.

decisive action will tilt the balance of political power toward the president and away from Congress, just as it did at the height of the Cold War.

As Dr. Jaime Malamud Goti, former chair of the Presidential Commission on Drug Control in Argentina, observed, "The claim that national security is endangered by a vaguely defined threat to Western cultures opens the way to justifications for granting extraordinary powers to military and police forces. The portrayal of the drug problem as one of survival of Western society removes policy makers from normal legal restraints. It also justifies the argument that the problem is too urgent to submit it to domestic and international debates."[22]

His warning deserves all the more notice given the failure of Congress to tighten up presidential reporting requirements for covert operations after the exposure of the Iran-Contra scandal. During the congressional investigation, Stanley Sporkin, then the CIA's general counsel, advanced the argument that presidents could issue secret "findings" to authorize covert operations that would "override" existing laws. Sporkin claimed that as "both a statutory matter as well as a constitutional matter" presidents could decide not to notify Congress of these findings and could, in effect, unilaterally repeal the laws of the land.[23] Today Sporkin is a federal judge, and Congress has accepted his (and Bush's) contention that presidents may launch covert operations without first notifying Congress.

Would-be abusers of power may also be emboldened by the failure of the media to fully investigate the connection between the drug trade and the Reagan administration's secret deals with Iran and the Contras. Invoking the cause of drug enforcement has freed the administration from scrutiny by much of the media as well as by Congress. The scarcity of serious media dissent on waging the War on Drugs through military operations, CIA intrigues, and attacks on civil liberties confirms to presidents and their agents that foreign intervention in the name of fighting drugs will open them to few political risks.

Full exposure of the cocaine connection to the Iran-Contra case is thus vital if the nation is to avoid misuse of the drug issue for dangerous political ends. Yet full exposure is exactly what Americans have never been given. Several reporters did outstanding investigative work, but their findings were either ignored or scantily treated by major media organs like the *New York Times* and the *Washington Post*. The Iran-Contra investigating committees ducked the issue and included in their final report a mendacious memo purporting to refute the essence of the Contra-drug allegations. Only in April 1989, after intense political wrangling and crippling delays, did the Senate Subcommittee on Terrorism, Narcotics, and International Operations (the Kerry subcommittee) finally produce its own report documenting the Contra-drug connection—long after both the public and the media had lost interest in the Iran-Contra affair. With its report unread and its implications ignored, the Kerry subcommittee's efforts went largely for nought.

This book is a modest effort to set forth the facts of the Central American drug connection and to fill in the significant gaps left by the Kerry report's valuable but incomplete account. Our approach is more analytical than investigative. Interviews with current or former government officials, journalists, drug traffickers, and mercenaries inform this book, but most references are to recognized and widely accepted public sources: sworn testimony taken by committees of Congress; voluminous FBI, Customs, and other investigative records, many of them appended to the Kerry report; domestic and foreign news accounts from respected media; and official reports from abroad, such as legislative commission findings from Costa Rica.

Even the most reputable sources cannot guarantee accuracy in an area as murky as the narcotics traffic. Rather than recount some controversial stories, we have steered away from witnesses whose credibility has come into serious question. A scandal like Iran-Contra inevitably produces a large number of opportunistic superwitnesses, fantasizers, and conspiracy peddlers—not to mention conscious agents of disinformation.[24] If, despite our best efforts, history proves a few of our assertions wrong, it will hardly overthrow the larger conclusions of this study.

The first half of this work analyzes available evidence on the way corrupt military elites, Contra leaders, the CIA, and Washington policy-makers opened the door to the cocaine trade through Central America. The second half explores how administration intimidation of witnesses, congressional cowardice, and media caution allowed this alliance to persist so durably and with so little public challenge during years of great national consensus on the need to fight drugs. Jonathan Marshall is primarily responsible for the introduction, Chapters 1–4, and 10 and 12; Peter Dale Scott for Chapters 5–9 and 11.

Through this narrow but intense focus on one front in the War on Drugs, we hope to revive the debate over solutions to the nation's longstanding drug problem—and ways to avoid phony cures that only compound it.

# 1 The Kerry Report
## *The Truth but Not the Whole Truth*

*Peter Scott & Jonathan Marshall,*
*Cocaine Politics*

### *Lies, Half Lies, and Cover-ups*

In December 1985, the Associated Press scooped the world with its story that "Nicaraguan rebels operating in northern Costa Rica have engaged in cocaine trafficking, in part to help finance their war against Nicaragua's leftist government."[1] Within days, government agencies involved in the Contra war effort—the Central Intelligence Agency, the National Security Council, and the State and Justice Departments—came forth with false denials and limited admissions calculated to sidetrack media and congressional inquiries. With the efforts of the NSC, as Chapters 7–9 reveal, the administration's offensive against the truth went beyond lies to repression.

In April 1986, following a review of evidence coordinated with the Justice Department and various U.S. intelligence agencies, the State Department publicly acknowledged evidence of a "limited" number of incidents "in which known drug traffickers *tried* to establish connections with the Nicaraguan resistance groups" (emphasis added).[2] The department emphasized that if any "individual members" succumbed to temptation, it was "without the authorization of resistance leaders." And it blamed Congress for cutting off military aid and so creating "the desperate conditions" that traffickers could exploit. Any further accusations of Contra involvement with drugs, declared Assistant Secretary of State Elliott Abrams, were "simply charges whose purpose is to defeat the [Contra] aid proposals in Congress."[3]

Not until August 1987, in the midst of the Iran-Contra hearings, did Alan Fiers, head of the CIA's Central America Task Force, admit the problem went much deeper. "With respect to [drug trafficking by] the Resistance Forces," he testified, ". . . it is not a couple of people. It is a

8

lot of people." But even this apparent admission was carefully crafted for the desired political impact. Fiers emphasized that the real villains were Edén Pastora, leader of the Contras' Southern Front in Costa Rica, and his "staff and friends." With this charge, Fiers sacrificed not a friend but an enemy. It was Fiers who directed CIA officers in the field to cut off all support to Pastora in the spring of 1984, at the time of the La Penca assassination attempt against him. Fiers cracked down not because Pastora dabbled in drugs but because he refused to unite with the CIA-backed Somocista rebels in the Honduras-based Nicaraguan Democratic Front (FDN).[4]

The Meese Justice Department was even less candid. Although the FBI had significant evidence tying known drug traffickers to Contra supply and mercenary operations, the Justice Department in 1986 adamantly denied any evidence of links between the Contras and drugs. That May, a Justice Department spokesman claimed, quite falsely, that "the FBI has conducted an inquiry into all of these charges and none of them have any substance."[5] In private meetings with congressional staffers, Justice Department representatives admitted that the department's public assertions were "inaccurate." But CIA representatives continued to deny drug-linked violations of the Neutrality Act, which bars private warmaking abroad, despite evidence from multiple FBI interviews.[6]

The Justice Department's alternative tack was to admit the existence of investigations but then to suppress all information, even to Congress, ostensibly to protect the legal process. The department warned the Kerry subcommittee that its "rambling through open investigations gravely risks compromising" law-enforcement investigations, and a Miami prosecutor reported that Justice Department officials met in 1986 to discuss how to undermine Kerry's proposed hearings.[7]

## What the Kerry Subcommittee Learned

On April 13, 1989, three years after its investigation began and six months after George Bush was elected president of the United States, the Senate Subcommittee on Terrorism, Narcotics, and International Operations finally confirmed what the administration, Congress, and much of the media had attempted to dismiss: the Contra-drug connection was real.

The subcommittee's 144-page report covered drug corruption in the Bahamas, Colombia, Cuba, Nicaragua, Haiti, and Panama, but it focused on the Contras and related drug-trafficking in Honduras and Costa Rica. In several hundred pages of appendices, the report supplemented the subcommittee's four-volume hearing record with FBI and Customs Service documents, news stories, witness depositions, and a chronology of the investigation and attempts to interfere with it.[8]

The subcommittee, led by Sen. John Kerry of Massachusetts, found that drug trafficking had pervaded the entire Contra war effort. "There was substantial evidence of drug smuggling through the war zones on the part of individual Contras, Contra suppliers, Contra pilots, mercenaries who worked with the Contras, and Contra supporters throughout the region," the subcommittee concluded. Far from taking steps to combat those drug flows, "U.S. officials involved in Central America failed to address the drug issue for fear of jeopardizing the war efforts against Nicaragua," the investigation showed.[9] "In each case," the report added, "one or another agency of the U.S. government had information regarding the involvement either while it was occurring, or immediately thereafter."[10] Moreover, "senior U.S. policy makers were not immune to the idea that drug money was a perfect solution to the Contras' funding problems."[11]

The subcommittee traced the origin of the Contras' involvement in drugs to a network of mercenary pilots and arms suppliers in Central America, which in the late 1970s had served the Sandinista and Salvadoran guerrillas. One of those drug pilots, a Costa Rican named Werner Lotz, explained why this network enjoyed so much success with the Contras: "There was no money. There were too many leaders and too few people to follow them, and everybody was trying to make money as best they could."[12] That rationale fails to explain why the State Department employed the same network to supply "humanitarian" assistance to the Nicaraguan rebels. The Kerry subcommittee identified no fewer than four conduits of humanitarian aid that were "owned and operated by narcotics traffickers." Together they pulled down $806,000 in State Department contracts to help the Contras.[13]

## The Humanitarian Smugglers

One such contractor was SETCO Air, a Honduran cargo firm. A U.S. Customs report noted in 1983 that it was actually "headed by Juan Ramón Matta Ballesteros, a class I DEA violator." In other words, a kingpin. He was said to be in partnership with "American businessmen who are . . . smuggling narcotics into the United States." According to the Kerry report, the airline was "the principal company used by the Contras in Honduras to transport supplies and personnel for the FDN, carrying at least a million rounds of ammunition, food, uniforms and other military supplies for the Contras from 1983 through 1985." FDN leader Adolfo Calero testified that SETCO received funds for Contra supply operations from accounts established by Lt. Col. Oliver North. SETCO also earned $186,000 transporting humanitarian goods to the Contras on contract to the State Department.[14]

A Costa Rican seafood company, Frigorificos de Puntarenas, might have seemed an odd choice for the State Department's favors. It took in $262,000 in 1986 on the Contras' behalf. Yet, by the separate admissions of one of its founders and one of its partners, the firm was little more than a front for laundering money derived from smuggling drugs to the United States. As early as May 1983, a Cuban-American arrested for money laundering, Ramón Milián Rodríguez, told federal authorities about the hidden criminal life of Luis Rodríguez (no relation), a fellow Cuban-American and one of the seafood company's principals.[15] In the spring of 1984, Luis Rodríguez took the Fifth Amendment when questioned by the Internal Revenue Service about his involvement with drugs. Later that year, the Miami police passed a report to the FBI that Rodríguez was funding the Contras through "narcotics transactions." The State Department either ignored or dismissed this information when it moved a quarter of a million dollars into the account of Frigorificos in 1986. A year later, Luis Rodríguez was finally indicted on major drug charges.[16]

Another Cuban-American, Bay of Pigs veteran Alfredo Caballero, also profited from the State Department's program. His Miami-based airplane dealership and parts supply company, DIACSA, earned more than $41,000 in the humanitarian supply program. Previously, the company had lent its services to the Contras to launder deposits arranged by Oliver North. The Kerry subcommittee noted that Caballero "was under DEA investigation for cocaine trafficking and money laundering when the State Department chose the company to be a . . . supplier. Caballero was at that time a business associate of Floyd Carlton—the pilot who flew cocaine for Panama's General Noriega." But Caballero was more than a business associate of Carlton: according to one informant, he supplied the planes Carlton used to move his drugs and was "the man in charge of operations" for the whole smuggling ring. And the State Department not only overlooked a quiet DEA investigation of the man; it continued to do business with DIACSA six months after the indictment of the firm's top officers on cocaine and money-laundering charges. Each of those defendants was later found guilty of importing cocaine.[17]

A fourth State Department contractor, the Miami-based air supply company Vortex, consisted largely of two cargo planes formerly used for drug smuggling by the firm's vice president, Michael Palmer. It won more than $317,000 worth of business from the federal government. At the time the contracts were signed, the Kerry report notes, "Palmer was under active investigation by the FBI in three jurisdictions in connection with his decade-long activity as a drug smuggler, and a federal grand jury was preparing to indict him in Detroit."[18]

State Department officials told congressional investigators, in the words of the Kerry report, "that all the supply contractors were to have been screened by U.S. intelligence and law enforcement agents prior to their receiving funds from State Department on behalf of the Contras to insure that they were not involved with criminal activity."[19] Yet in all four of these cases, the Reagan administration chose to do business with individuals and companies already known for their role in the narcotics trade. The Kerry investigation, therefore, tells of more than the Contras and drugs; it tells the story of the U.S. government and drugs.

The subcommittee could not determine with certainty just how the State Department had selected this rogues' gallery of firms, but testimony before the Iran-Contra Committees indicated that North had instructed the department to continue "the existing arrangements of the resistance movement" when selecting contractors—in other words, to use those already approved by the CIA and NSC. "At best, these incidents represent negligence on the part of U.S. government officials responsible for providing support to the Contras," the subcommittee concluded. "At worst it was a matter of turning a blind eye to the activities of companies who use legitimate activities as a cover for their narcotics trafficking."[20]

## The Southern Front

The subcommittee also explored several case studies of drug involvement by foes of the Sandinistas. Its first example focused on members of Edén Pastora's guerrilla movement in Costa Rica. A State Department report quoted by the subcommittee cited CIA information that

> a senior member of Eden Pastora's Sandino Revolutionary Front (FRS) agreed in late 1984 with [Colombian trafficker George Morales] that FRS pilots would aid in transporting narcotics in exchange for financial assistance. . . . The FRS official agreed to use FRS operational facilities in Costa Rica and Nicaragua to facilitate transportation of narcotics. [Morales] agreed to provide financial support to the FRS, in addition to aircraft and training for FRS pilots. After undergoing flight training, the FRS pilots were to continue to work for the FRS, but would also fly narcotics shipments from South America to sites in Costa Rica and Nicaragua for later transport to the United States. Shortly thereafter [Morales] reportedly provided the FRS one C-47 aircraft and two crated helicopters. He is reported to have paid the sum of $100,000 to the FRS. . . .[21]

One of Pastora's former pilots, Gerardo Duran, was arrested in January 1986 in Costa Rica for flying cocaine destined for the United States.[22]

Marcos Aquado, a top Pastora aide who dealt with Morales, later told the subcommittee that the traffickers "took advantage of the anti-communist sentiment which existed in Central America . . . and they undoubtedly used it for drug trafficking." And he claimed, somewhat less persuasively, that the traffickers "fooled people" in Pastora's movement by claiming they were flying arms when their real cargo was cocaine.[23]

The more explosive finding of the subcommittee concerned the CIA's role in this affair. Pastora's political ally Octaviano César had informed his CIA control officer about Morales's offer and the fact that he was a drug dealer. The response: Go ahead, "as long as you don't deal in the powder." The CIA's involvement didn't stop there. After the agency dropped Pastora in the spring of 1984, it continued to fund Contra leaders who collaborated with Morales and Duran. Morales was thus fully equipped to implicate the CIA when he was finally arrested in June 1986. He offered to talk, but the U.S. Attorney in Miami and his chief drug prosecutor refused to deal. The two prosecutors impugned Morales's credibility and tried to block him from testifying before Congress. Only in November 1988 did the DEA give Morales a polygraph exam and pronounce truthful his testimony about making guns-for-drugs deals with the Contras and the CIA.[24]

The CIA's own station chief in Costa Rica admitted that another drug suspect, American rancher John Hull, had worked with the Agency on "military supply and other operations on behalf of the Contras," besides receiving a $10,000 monthly retainer courtesy of Oliver North.[25] (Hull, who lived in Costa Rica until 1989, told an interviewer that from 1982 to 1986 he was the CIA's chief liaison with the Nicaraguan rebels in Costa Rica.)[26] The subcommittee found no fewer than five witnesses who testified to Hull's involvement in the narcotics traffic, including one who personally saw cocaine being loaded in Hull's presence for air shipment to the United States.[27]

When Hull came under investigation by the U.S. Attorney in Miami in 1986 with regard to a Neutrality Act case, U.S. embassy officials in San José warned him not to talk and did their best to get witnesses to recant their statements. To bolster his case, Hull prepared affidavits that the Justice Department concluded had been forged. He was also implicated in criminal fraud regarding a $375,000 loan from the Overseas Private Investment Corporation, a U.S. government entity. Yet, the Kerry report notes, the Justice Department has taken no action against Hull either for obstruction of justice or for fraud, much less for narcotics trafficking.[28]

Costa Rican authorities finally arrested Hull in January 1989, charging him with drug smuggling, arms trafficking, and other violations of Costa Rica's security.[29] Although a superior penal court dismissed the case as defective in its presentation, a prosecutor charged him once again with permitting 2,500 kg of cocaine to pass through his ranch.[30] After being declared persona non grata, Hull left the country for Miami.[31]

## Cuban Exiles: Guns and Drugs

The subcommittee also explored the role of right-wing Cuban-Americans in providing "direct and indirect support" for the Contras in Costa Rica after Congress cut off military aid to the Nicaraguan resistance. A State Department report to Congress in July 1986 stated flatly that "there is no information to substantiate allegations" that Miami-based Cuban exiles had "been a source of drug money for . . . any . . . resistance organization."[32] In response to further congressional inquiries, the Justice Department first withheld information, then insisted that allegations had been fully investigated and refuted. The CIA went even further, declaring that any reports of Cuban exile involvement in weapons shipments, much less drug smuggling, were the result of a disinformation campaign.[33]

FBI reports made public by the subcommittee exposed those official claims as outright lies. Far from having "no information" to back up the allegations, the FBI had direct substantiation in September 1984 from José Coutin, a Cuban American actively involved in the Contra support effort. Coutin declared that fellow exile Francisco Chanes was "a narcotics trafficker" who was "giving financial support to anti-Castro groups and the Nicaraguan Contra guerrillas . . . from narcotic transactions." In an interview, Coutin accurately placed Chanes with the Miami branch of the Costa Rican drug front and State Department contractor, Frigorificos de Puntarenas. Coutin also passed along information that another Cuban exile, Frank Castro, was seeking to finance the Contras with proceeds from the drug business.[34]

The FBI also interviewed an exile, Rene Corvo, who stated that "the only crimes" he had committed were "United States neutrality violations for shipping weapons from South Florida to Central America," giving the lie to the CIA's denials. Without discussing drugs, Corvo indicated that "paramilitary supplies were stored at the residence of Frank Chanes in Southwest Miami as well as Corvo's own garage," thus implicating this suspected narcotics trafficker in gun-running plots to help the Contras.[35] Corvo also told the FBI he had given military training to Moisés Nuñez, who was "assisting the anti-Communist cause in Central America." Nuñez was a partner with Chanes in Frigorificos de Puntarenas.[36]

If the CIA had any remaining credibility on this topic, it was destroyed by the testimony of North's aide Robert Earl about CIA worries in 1986 that "disreputable characters in the Cuban-American community . . . are sympathetic to the Contra cause but causing more problems than help and that one had to be careful in how one dealt with the Cuban-American community and its relation to this, that although their motives were in the right place there was a lot of corruption and greed and drugs and it was a real mess."[37]

In contrast to its detailed treatment of the Southern Front, the Kerry subcommittee paid little attention to Honduras and the main Contra movement based there, the Nicaraguan Democratic Front (FDN). But the report does briefly summarize the case of José Bueso Rosa, a Honduran general implicated in a drug-financed plot to murder the elected civilian president of his country. After Bueso Rosa's conviction in federal court, North and other administration officials arranged an extremely lenient sentence on grounds that he "had been a friend to the U.S." and was "involved in helping with the Contras." The report also explores, without resolving, the mystery of why the DEA closed down its critical Honduras station just as the CIA was escalating the war against Nicaragua from Honduran bases. And it notes Washington's failure to seek the extradition of Honduran drug kingpin Juan Ramón Matta Ballesteros until April 1988, after he had ceased to be of use in the Contra supply operation.[38]

On the basis of this evidence, the subcommittee reached some tough conclusions. It condemned the refusal of intelligence agencies to cooperate with law enforcement in bringing to justice individuals associated with the Contra cause. It criticized the widespread practice of "ticket punching" by which notorious traffickers buy immunity under the cloak of national security by allying themselves with U.S. covert operations. It found that "in the name of supporting the Contras, we abandoned the responsibility our government has for protecting our citizens from all threats to their security and well-being." And it warned that "the credibility of government institutions" had been jeopardized by the administration's decision to turn "a blind eye to domestic and foreign corruption associated with the international narcotics trade."[39]

## Beyond the Kerry Report

If the Kerry subcommittee's report had been definitive, this book would not have been written. Unfortunately, constraints of time, resources, and politics cut the report short. Staff and committee disputes, editing decisions, and stonewalling from the executive branch also took their toll. The result was a nearly unassailable, but incomplete, account. For example, the subcommittee failed to pursue (even if only to refute) intriguing allegations in the foreign media of other Contra-drug links. The Bolivian and Spanish press, for example, gave considerable attention to reports that a notorious cocaine factory near Bolivia's border with Brazil was financing the Nicaraguan resistance. The story received a remarkable boost when the son of Bolivian drug lord Roberto Suarez charged that the factory was actually controlled by the DEA and challenged Bolivian authorities to let journalists see for themselves.[40]

The subcommittee also overlooked the case of Manzer al-Kassar, a Syrian arms dealer and drug trafficker with terrorist connections who supplied North's operation with $1.5 million worth of Eastern bloc weapons.[41] U.S. intelligence officials believe al-Kassar sold weapons to Abu Abbas, head of the Palestinian Liberation Organization faction responsible for the *Achille Lauro* hijacking, and to Abu Nidal, mastermind of the Rome and Vienna airport massacres in December 1985.[42] But Manzer al-Kassar's business is not limited to arms and terrorism: he belongs to what is reputedly "the largest drug-and-arms dealing family in Syria."[43] In 1977, he was sentenced in England to two and a half years in prison for smuggling hashish. According to one investigator, al-Kassar has been connected to major deals "involving up to 100 kilos (220 pounds) of heroin."[44] In 1987, he also met with a leader of the Medellín cartel, Jorge Ochoa, to discuss dividing up the European cocaine market.[45]

In at least one case, political concerns persuaded the subcommittee to limit its discussion of the CIA's involvement with a drug pilot who flew supplies to the Contras on government contract. As Senator Kerry declared at one subcommittee hearing, "I have been very, very careful here. . . . I have stayed away from naming any companies that are [CIA] proprietaries . . . because I have an agreement with Senator Boren," chair of the Senate Intelligence Committee.[46]

The net effect of these many gaps in the subcommittee report was to downplay evidence linking the CIA to individuals and companies implicated in drug trafficking. For example, the Kerry report notes that the drug-linked airline Vortex was selected by the State Department for the Contra supply program after consultation with one Pat Foley, identified only as "the president of Summit Aviation."[47] But it did not address reports that Foley was a CIA agent who had sold warplanes and guns to the Somoza dictatorship; that Summit had outfitted special planes "used by high-ranking members of the Thai military in northern Thailand to protect illegal drug activity"; and that it had equipped three planes with rocket launchers for use by the Contras.[48] Nor did the subcommittee cite a memorandum produced by Oliver North's field representative, Robert Owen, about the CIA-drug link to Foley and the Contra supply operation: "No doubt you know the DC-4 Foley got was used at one time to run drugs, and part of the crew had criminal records," Owen related. "Nice group the Boys [CIA] choose. The company is also one that Mario [Calero] has been involved with using in the past, only they had a quick name change."[49] Kerry acknowledged only (during the hearings, not in the subcommittee's final report) that Vortex had an aviation maintenance contract with a CIA proprietary.[50]

Although the Kerry subcommittee remained mum, unnamed sources told the Los Angeles Times that "the State Department's Nicaraguan Humanitarian Aid Office awarded the contract to Vortex Aircraft Sales and Leasing because it was on a CIA list of suggested vendors." According to the paper, Palmer "indicated that he had sold one of the firm's DC-6 aircraft to a CIA proprietary company in 1986 for $320,000, turning a profit of more than $100,000." Perhaps a small sum for a pilot who smuggled more than $30 million worth of marijuana into the United States, but substantial nonetheless.[51]

The report was also remarkably reticent about Felipe Vidal, a Cuban-born CIA contract agent who played a major role on the Contras' Southern Front. Among other jobs, he undermined Pastora's position when the CIA turned on him in early 1984. Vidal laundered humanitarian aid funds into military supplies for the anti-Sandinista Indian group Kisan through the Miami account of Frigorificos.[52] A public advocate of international terrorism against pro-Castro targets, Vidal has reportedly been arrested at least seven times in Miami on narcotics and weapons charges.[53] An official report by a Costa Rican legislative committee noted that of the emergency telephone contacts Vidal gave Hull, "the first four had been formally accused of drug trafficking in the United States."[54] A staff investigation by the House Select Committee on Narcotics Abuse and Control turned up allegations that he used Contras to guard cocaine shipments.[55] Even his CIA control officer, the station chief Joseph Fernandez, admitted Vidal had "a problem with drugs."[56] Nonetheless, Fernandez tried to protect Vidal from Justice Department investigators in 1986.[57]

The subcommittee report was also silent about drug allegations against Southern Air Transport, a Florida-based cargo airline once controlled by the CIA. Southern Air provided the Contra supply plane whose downing in October 1986 helped unravel the secret of covert White House support for the Nicaraguan rebels. Flight logs found in the plane's wreckage indicated that it had made trips to the Colombian city of Barranquilla in 1985. An FBI informant, the wife of a Colombian drug trafficker, claimed to have seen Southern Air Transport planes being loaded with cocaine that year in Barranquilla. She also asserted that a plane with the airline's markings had been involved in a guns-for-drugs swap at an airfield there in 1983.

The story gets even more complicated. According to *Newsday*, "The woman has also said that drug kingpin Jorge Ochoa, a Colombian fugitive from U.S. drug charges, told her that he was working with the CIA to get illegal cocaine into south Florida. The informant also alleged that a federal judge, a U.S. Customs official, and an air traffic controller in Miami were taking bribes from the drug dealers. Department of Justice spokesman Patrick Korten said the results of a lie detector test given to her were inconclusive. However, Senate sources claim that she passed the polygraph tests."[58]

Another news report added further suggestions of cover-up: "Initial disclosure of the witness' claim was made by the *Miami News* on October 30. That day, Associate Attorney General Stephen Trott, acting at the behest of Attorney General Edwin Meese, told FBI Director William Webster to delay the bureau's investigation of Southern Air. The request for a delay came initially from Vice Admiral John Poindexter, then national security adviser, to Meese."[59]

Southern Air Transport officials have vigorously denied any involvement with the illegal drug trade. No one has taken any official action against the firm. It may thus have been only a coincidence that a Southern Air Transport vice president used Banco de Iberoamerica, an institution deeply implicated in laundering drug money (for a founder of Frigorificos, among others), to move funds from North and Secord's "Enterprise" to the Contra air-supply operation.[60]

The Kerry subcommittee explored none of these allegations and coincidences in its public report. "There are inevitably loose ends," explained its former chief counsel, Jack Blum. "There would be regardless of the investigator. But how much do you need to know to make public policy decisions? What we did was to make it very clear that the administration's priority decision to defrock the Sandinista government was much more important than trying to deal with the drug problem. Ultimately money was so powerful that anyone in the region got involved in it up to their armpits."[61]

The report's silence with respect to some details did not diminish its tremendous contribution to the public's knowledge of this basic issue.

By ignoring most of the historical context, however, it left the false impression of a problem limited to a few years of the Reagan era. On the contrary, as the next chapter will show, the Contra-drug connection was deeply rooted in other covert operations and political intrigues in the Western hemisphere extending back many years.

Part I

# RIGHT-WING NARCOTERRORISM, THE CIA, AND THE CONTRAS

# 2   The CIA and Right-Wing Narcoterrorism in Latin America

*Narcoterrorism as Propaganda*

President Reagan came to office with a mission: to roll back the frontiers of world communism, especially in the Third World. Almost from the start he singled out Nicaragua as a dangerous base of Soviet bloc operations in the Western Hemisphere. But with the American public's anticommunist sentiments dulled by a decade of détente and memories of Vietnam, how could his administration revive support for combating the Nicaraguan challenge to U.S. power and credibility?

One answer was to invent a new threat, closely associated with communism and even more frightening to the public: narcoterrorism. The term, rarely well defined by its users, encompasses a variety of phenomena: guerrilla movements that finance themselves by drugs or taxes on drug traffickers, drug syndicates that use terrorist methods to counter the state's law enforcement apparatus, and state-sponsored terrorism associated with drug crimes.[1] But in the hands of administration officials, the epithet served a more political than analytical purpose: to capitalize on popular fear of terrorists and drug traffickers in order to mobilize support for foreign interventions against leftist regimes.[2] As two private colleagues of Oliver North noted in a prospectus for a propaganda campaign to link the Sandinistas and drugs, "the chance to have a single issue which no one can publicly disagree with is irresistible."[3]

Administration spokesmen drove the lesson home through sheer repetition. In January 1986, President Reagan said, "The link between the governments of such Soviet allies as Cuba and Nicaragua and international narcotics trafficking and terrorism is becoming increasingly clear. These twin evils—narcotics trafficking and terrorism—represent the most insidious and dangerous threats to the hemisphere today." A year and a half earlier, Secretary of State George Shultz decried the "complicity of communist governments in the drug trade," which he called "part of a larger pattern of international lawlessness by communist nations that, as we have seen, also includes support for international terrorism, and other forms of organized violence against legitimate governments."[4] Elliott Abrams, assistant secretary of state for Inter-American Affairs, told a meeting of the Council on Foreign Relations in 1986 that "sustaining democracy and combatting the 'narcoterrorist' threat are inextricably linked."[5]

The term "narcoterrorism" also soon became an essential adjunct to the doctrine of national security developed by right-wing Latin American military forces to rationalize their repressive domestic activities and seizures of power. At the Fourteenth Bilateral Intelligence Conference of the general staffs of the Argentine and Bolivian armies, held in Buenos Aires in late August 1988, military leaders concluded that "the relationship between drugs and subversion, which generates narcoterrorism, has become part of the East-West confrontation, with a real impact on the national-international security of the West." They declared that "narcoterrorism now constitutes a means of Revolutionary War" and that "the MCI [International Communist Movement] uses narcoterrorism as a socio-ideological procedure for provoking social imbalances, eroding community morale, and corrupting and disintegrating Western society, as part of the strategic objective of promoting the new Marxist order." Combating narcoterrorism would justify repressing a whole range of familiar enemies: "trade unions, religious, student groups, etc." Above all, it would require granting more resources and political power to military elites: "The intervention of the armed forces in this context has been considered necessary, given that the increase in drug trafficking surpasses individual action."[6]

The Reagan administration's calculated use of the term was often challenged by leftist critics, academics, and even the Drug Enforcement Administration, which cautiously demurred from the most inflammatory accusations against Nicaragua, Cuba, and Latin American guerrilla movements. But White House officials went beyond exaggerating the truth to make their case against Marxist movements and regimes: they sponsored narcoterrorists of their own within the Contras in the course of waging a "covert" war against Nicaragua.

The distortion of the Contras' ostensibly democratic cause by drugs and terrorism owed much to the practices of three important influences on the anti-Sandinista rebels: militant CIA-trained Cuban exiles, the Mexican drug Mafia, and Argentine military intelligence agents. Their methods, both in war and in crime, indelibly tainted the Contras' own cause. In short, the Contra-drug link, supported by Washington, exemplified the very narcoterrorist threat that Assistant Secretary Abrams called an enemy of democracy.

A brief career résumé of one obscure individual who personified the narcoterrorist impulse in the Contra movement will illustrate this point. The CIA-trained Cuban exile Frank Castro, a significant figure in the Costa Rican-based Southern Front, has received scant mention by any of the official congressional investigations of the Contras, including the Kerry subcommittee's. Yet he brought together the intelligence, terrorist, and criminal forces in the Contra movement.

A veteran of the CIA's abortive Bay of Pigs invasion of Cuba in 1961, Castro later trained at Fort Jackson to continue the war against communism. He then joined the guerrilla camp of Manuel Artime, political head of the Bay of Pigs operation, in Central America.[7] With CIA support, Artime's group attacked Cuban economic targets, including sugar mills and freighters. From these efforts, it was only a small step to outright terrorism. As head of the Cuban National Liberation Front, Castro became one of the most militant of the exile terrorists. In 1976, he helped found a new terrorist front uniting the most extreme organizations. Known as CORU, it unleashed a wave of bombings, kidnappings, and assassinations throughout the Americas in the late 1970s.[8]

Castro also apparently began another line of work on the side: trafficking in drugs. According to federal prosecutors, he joined some of the biggest cocaine and marijuana rings of the mid- and late 1970s. Castro was indicted for smuggling more than a million pounds of marijuana into the United States.[9]

Despite—or because of—Castro's narcoterrorist record, he found a significant role with the Contra movement in Costa Rica, with the knowledge of the National Security Council and the approval of the CIA station chief, Joseph Fernandez. Oliver North's personal representative on the scene, Robert Owen, reported back to Washington in November 1984 that "several sources are now saying [Southern Front Contra leader Edén] Pastora is going to be bankrolled by former Bay of Pigs veteran Frank Castro, who is heavily into drugs. It was Castro who gave Pastora the new DC-3 and has promised the planes. The word has it Pastora is going to be given $200,000 a month by Castro."[10] Less than a year later, Owen told his boss that the CIA's Fernandez believed Castro and his fellow Cubans "can be helpful."[11] Castro visited the Costa Rican farm and Contra staging area of CIA agent John Hull, with another former drug defendant in tow, to assist other Cubans fighting on the Contras' behalf.[12]

Castro and yet another former Cuban-American drug defendant financed a Contra training camp in the Florida Everglades. Yet they were indicted for this apparent violation of the Neutrality Act only in 1988, after Washington had essentially abandoned its commitment to the Contras.[13]

Through it all, Castro stayed one step ahead of the law. Charges against him in a 1983 Texas drug arrest were dropped in June 1984, just when he began operating his Florida-based Contra training camp. In 1989, a federal judge dismissed the Neutrality Act case against him, ruling that the law did not apply given the hostile relations between Nicaragua and the United States.[14]

Castro would appear to be one of the many "disreputable characters in the Cuban-American community" whose involvement in "corruption and greed and drugs" worried the CIA. Yet Castro's name received not a mention in the report of the Iran-Contra investigating committees of Congress and only a single, passing mention in the Kerry subcommittee's report.[15] As we shall see, however, Castro's career intersects many of the historical intrigues that fostered the narcoterrorist apparatus in the Contra movement: the widespread involvement of CIA-trained Cubans in drug trafficking, CORU's alliance with Mexico's chief drug protector, and the CORU connection to Argentine death squads that later worked with Bolivia's cocaine lords and the Contras. Together, these strands, unexplored by Congress and largely ignored by the media, suggest that the Contra-drug connection was not merely an isolated incident but rather part of an ongoing history of illegal activities that enjoyed at least some official protection from U.S. intelligence agencies.

### The CIA-Cuban-Drug Connection

On June 21, 1970, agents of the federal Bureau of Narcotics and Dangerous Drugs (BNDD) arrested 150 suspects in cities around the country. The agency termed it "the largest roundup of major drug traffickers in the history of federal law enforcement."[16] Attorney General John Mitchell announced at an unprecedented Sunday morning press conference that the Justice Department had just broken up "a nationwide ring of wholesalers handling about 30 percent of all heroin sales and 75 to 80 percent of all cocaine sales in the United States."[17]

The syndicate smashed in "Operation Eagle" was remarkable not only for its size but also for its composition. As many as 70 percent of those arrested had once belonged to the Bay of Pigs invasion force unleashed by the CIA against Cuba in April 1961.[18] The bust gave a hint of evidence that would accumulate throughout the coming decade of the dominance of the U.S. cocaine and marijuana trade by intelligence-trained Cuban exiles.

Chief among those arrested in Eagle was Juan Restoy, a former Cuban congressman and member of Operation 40, an elite CIA group formed to seize political control of Cuba after the Bay of Pigs landing.[19] His attorney, Frank Ragano, had also served the powerful Tampa Mafia boss Santos Trafficante;[20] the drug ring was, in fact, an outgrowth of Trafficante's crime empire, which had flourished in Cuba before the revolution as it did in Florida thereafter. Trafficante enjoyed a privileged position in the underworld, having been recruited by the CIA in the early 1960s to mount assassination attempts against Fidel Castro using his Cuban contacts.

Restoy's major accomplice was a fellow Cuban exile and career drug trafficker, Mario Escandar. Restoy was killed by federal drug agents after escaping from jail, but Escandar (along with other defendants) had his case thrown out on a technicality. Becoming a valued police informant and then corrupting officers to whom he reported, Escandar went on to become one of Miami's most powerful and untouchable traffickers. He used Miami detectives to arrest his enemies, collect debts, and avoid judicial sanctions.[21]

Until Colombian traffickers finally wrested control of the trade in the late 1970s by monopolizing sources of supply, Cuban exiles like these had an advantage over other trafficking groups: their CIA training and the protection that came with involvement in national security operations.

Former CIA commando leader Grayston Lynch noted that his trainees "were actively sought out by other people in the drug trade, because of their [smuggling] expertise. When I'm talking about expertise, let me put it this way: Some of them made over 100, 200, 300 missions to Cuba." He added, "They [had been] going in against the most heavily patrolled coast that I've ever heard of. . . . These people came out knowing how you do it. And they found it absolutely child's play when they started in [with drug smuggling] over here, because we [U.S. law enforcement] didn't have that type of defense. They didn't even need most of their expertise."[22]

Many of these traffickers, like Escandar, also traded on their government connections to become privileged informers, snitching on their rivals in return for protection from federal narcotics officers. No one employed this technique better than Ricardo Morales, a veteran of CIA operations in the Congo and a trained paratrooper and demolitions expert. Morales informed on exile activities to the CIA, on exile terrorism to the FBI, and on smuggling by fellow exiles to the BNDD and its successor, the DEA.[23] Despite his record as a longtime drug trafficker, enforcer for the Mafia, terrorist bomber, and murder suspect, he enjoyed near-immunity from prosecution.[24]

Many other traffickers went the same route, even if few achieved Morales's notoriety. A joint CIA-DEA intelligence program, which Morales himself may have joined, provided a protected route for some exile smugglers to achieve prominence in their business.

In October 1972, CIA Director Richard Helms offered to provide the BNDD with "several former CIA assets to obtain strategic and operational intelligence for BNDD on Cuban drug trafficking in the Caribbean."[25] The CIA assistance was channeled to a new BNDD intelligence office established under Lucien Conein, a veteran CIA covert operations specialist who boasted of the trust he enjoyed in the Corsican underworld. As Conein saw it, his mission was to recruit drug agents from the CIA and "to develop individuals for clandestine operations."[26]

Conein established a tightly compartmentalized, secret unit within the drug agency. Its Miami operation, known as DEACON 1, recruited only "former Central Intelligence Agency assets who operated in the Miami area during the 1960s," a description that fit Morales and his peers.[27] Originally it targeted the Trafficante organization, based on leads from Operation Eagle. But its focus quickly shifted to a much broader look at political intelligence of greater interest to DEACON's CIA patrons, including "violations of neutrality laws, extremist groups and terrorism and information of a political nature" as well as information "of an internal security nature."[28] DEACON 1's principal agent was said to be "reporting on civic and political groups" as well as supervising other agents.[29]

By the end of 1974, Conein's operation had not contributed to the bust of a single drug ring. But it had apparently sanctioned drug smuggling by its own agents, as indicated by an official review of DEACON 1 that suggested the DEA promulgate regulations regarding "the level of drug trafficking permissible for an asset."[30]

One of Conein's assets was the CIA-trained Bay of Pigs veteran Carlos Hernandez Rumbaut. Arrested in 1969 in Mobile, Alabama, with 467 pounds of marijuana, he was recruited by the BNDD as a "class I cooperating individual." State authorities were not so generous, and he was convicted of the crime in state court. However, he received help in posting bond from another DEACON informant and CIA veteran, Guillermo Tabraue. Hernandez Rumbaut fled to Costa Rica, where he soon became second-in-command of the Costa Rican narcotics police and a bodyguard to President José Figueres. Far from showing any displeasure toward Hernandez Rumbaut for smuggling drugs and flouting justice, the U.S. government reportedly allowed him to reenter the country bearing a U.S. diplomatic passport. He continued to work with the DEA through its Mexico City office, which agreed to cover the bail Tabraue forfeited on his behalf. And he continued to smuggle drugs to the United States as late as 1976, working with Ricardo Morales.[31]

As for Tabraue, the DEA increased his informant payments to compensate him for the lost bail money. He made as much as $1,400 a week for his work. Tabraue and various relatives went on to become class I traffickers on their own, even while working for the DEA. According to charges filed a decade later, Tabraue's syndicate earned $79 million from importing marijuana and cocaine between 1976 and 1987. It imported no less than 500,000 pounds of marijuana and 95 kg of cocaine in that period and enjoyed protection from the deputy police chief of Key West and various Miami police officers.[32] When prosecutors learned, to their amazement, that Tabraue had begun trafficking under government protection, the judge declared a mistrial. Tabraue later pleaded guilty to income tax evasion.[33]

Both Tabraue and Hernandez Rumbaut got their start in the drug trade under the wing of Bay of Pigs veteran and anti-Castro activist José Medardo Alvero Cruz, whose pioneering use of "mother ships" to offload large volumes of marijuana was "something he picked up from the CIA," according to Grayston Lynch.[34] Alvero Cruz also employed Morales to handle collections and security.[35] One exile active in the Contra support effort told federal investigators in 1984 that Alvero Cruz had "provided large sums of money to the anti-Castro cause."[36]

By the late 1970s, Frank Castro had joined another drug kingpin and graduate of the Alvero Cruz network, José Antonio Fernandez. Fernandez, according to his own testimony in a later drug trial, had been sent into Cuba by the CIA to handle communications for the Bay of Pigs invasion. His smuggling organization included a host of CIA veterans from that era.[37] According to a DEA report, two of the ex-CIA agents in the Fernandez organization conspired in 1979 to import drugs with Gustavo Villoldo, a Cuban-born CIA officer sent four years later into Central America by Vice President Bush's national security adviser Donald Gregg to advise the Contras on military strategy.[38] Villoldo was an investment partner of a former president of Brigade 2506 (the Bay of Pigs veterans' group) convicted of laundering drug money.[39]

Fernandez bought much of his marijuana from DEACON 1 agent Tabraue.[40] He also bought drugs from a fellow CIA-trained exile whose business partners included Contra supporter Luis Rodríguez. Rodríguez's indictment on drug charges was mysteriously held up for four years in the mid-1980s after federal authorities received hard information of his crimes. During much of this time, as we noted in Chapter 1, Rodríguez was receiving State Department contracts to help the Nicaraguan resistance.[41]

Frank Castro did not remain loyal to Fernandez; around 1980, he and another Bay of Pigs veteran kidnapped his boss and hauled him to Colombia, where the ring's marijuana supplier extorted a huge ransom. Eventually Fernandez, Castro, and several other CIA-trained Cubans were indicted as a result of Operation Grouper. But Castro's associate Ricardo Morales escaped unscathed.[42] In 1980, he became the informer in Operation Tick-Talks, a Miami investigation that implicated Castro and other Bay of Pigs veterans in a huge conspiracy to import cocaine from the new military rulers of Bolivia.[43]

## CORU: Drug-financed Terrorism

Frank Castro and Ricardo Morales were linked by terrorism as well as drugs; their violent records stretched back into the 1960s. But their anticommunist efforts reached a climax in 1976, when Frank Castro joined several other Cuban exile leaders in founding CORU, an umbrella organization for terrorism against Cuban installations and against the persons and property of countries deemed overly sympathetic to Fidel Castro's regime. Morales gave sanctuary to some CORU agents in Venezuela, where he had become a high-ranking officer in the intelligence service, DISIP.

"The story of CORU is true," one of its leading organizers told an interviewer in 1977. "There was a meeting in the Bonao mountains [of the Dominican Republic] of 20 men representing all different activist organizations. It was a meeting of all the military and political directors with revolutionary implications. It was a great meeting. Everything was planned there. I told them that we couldn't just keep bombing an embassy here and a police station there. We had to start taking more serious actions."[44] The organization took credit for the October 1976 explosion of a Cuban passenger jet and fifty other bombings in Miami, New York, Venezuela, Panama, Mexico, and Argentina in the first ten months of its existence. In a CBS News interview, one member explained, "We use the tactics that we learned from the CIA because we—we were trained to do everything. We are trained to set off a bomb, we were trained to kill . . . we were trained to do everything."[45] Five of CORU's founders, including Frank Castro, later joined the Contras.[46]

Financing for CORU operations allegedly came from WFC, a Florida-based financial conglomerate and drug-trafficking front closely associated with the Restoy-Escandar-Trafficante organization exposed in Operation Eagle. An unpublished congressional staff study of the company found that it encompassed "a large body of criminal activity, including aspects of political corruption, gun running, as well as narcotics trafficking on an international level."[47] The WFC empire was led by CIA-trained Bay of Pigs veteran Guillermo Hernandez Cartaya, whom federal authorities suspected of working with the Contra backer and former CIA officer Gustavo Villoldo.[48] The head of the Dade County investigation of WFC later said he found that one company subsidiary was "nothing but a CIA front."[49]

Indeed, knowledgeable exile and law-enforcement sources said the same of CORU, according to journalists John Dinges and Saul Landau. CORU was said to have "the active support of the CIA and at least the acquiescence of the FBI" and "was allowed to operate to punish Castro for his Angola policy without directly implicating the United States government." One Miami police veteran added, "The Cubans held the CORU meeting at the request of the CIA. The Cuban groups . . . were running amok in the mid-1970s, and the United States had lost control of them. So the United States backed the meeting to get them all going in the same direction again, under United States control. The basic signal was, 'Go ahead and do what you want, *outside* the United States.' "[50] The CIA director and deputy director at the time of CORU's founding were George Bush and Vernon Walters, later key figures in the Reagan administration's Contra support program.

Perhaps CORU's single most notorious act was the midair bombing of a Cuban passenger jet in October 1976 that killed all seventy-three passengers. Venezuelan authorities arrested, among others, Luis Posada, a longtime agent of both the CIA and Venezuela's DISIP. (Years later, Ricardo Morales himself took credit for the airline bombing, saying he planned it at the CIA's instigation.)[51] Posada also had materials in his possession linking him to the assassination of former Chilean ambassador Orlando Letelier in Washington, DC, a month before the Cubana Airlines bombing.[52] In 1985, Posada bribed his way out of jail and was recruited into the Contra logistics network by fellow CIA agent and Bay of Pigs veteran Félix Rodríguez.[53] From the Ilopango Air Force Base in El Salvador, Posada handled both military supply flights and shipments flown by drug-linked airlines hired by the State Department's Nicaragua Humanitarian Assistance Organization.[54]

Another CORU crime was the botched kidnapping of the Cuban consul (and the murder of his chauffeur) in Merida, Mexico, on July 23, 1976, only a month after the group's founding. WFC's drug money financed this operation, and WFC's founder, Hernandez Cartaya, may even have helped plan it.[55] One of those implicated was Gustavo Castillo, a close friend of Frank Castro and a member of his Cuban National Liberation Front.[56] Later intelligence linked another exile to the plot: Armando López Estrada. He was military coordinator of Brigade 2506 (one of CORU's component groups) and a CORU organizer. However, during the 1970s López Estrada enjoyed official protection from the CIA, which had a role in undermining his prosecution on weapons and Neutrality Act charges in 1977. López Estrada turned up a decade later in Costa Rica, along with three other CORU terrorists. He claimed then that "The U.S. government sent me to Costa Rica to do intelligence work and serve as liaison to . . . the Nicaraguan Contras with the purpose of providing them with advisors and military equipment."[57]

Yet another conspirator in the Merida case, according to at least one informant, was the Mexico City–based Cuban exile Francisco Manuel Camargo.[58] Camargo, who headed intelligence operations in Mexico for Brigade 2506, had received a message from López Estrada to "take care of" one of two other Cuban-Americans who actually pulled off the job. Camargo's role and connections made the whole operation almost untouchable. Married to the daughter of a Mexican general, he was also rumored to be "in regular contact with the Mexican national police, narcotics officers, and also the CIA," according to a former Justice Department prosecutor.[59] Camargo allegedly enjoyed protection from an American working under cover in the U.S. embassy in Mexico City, who had taken part in at least two terrorist bombings himself.[60]

Perhaps the most deeply drug-linked of all CORU's members were those involved in the Cuban Nationalist Movement (CNM), a small neo-fascist group with bases in both Miami and Union City, New Jersey. Their exploits ranged from a 1964 bazooka attack on the United Nations to a 1974 conspiracy to bomb the Cuban consulate and trade commission in Montreal.[61] Despite its limited membership, the CNM enjoyed international influence owing to its connections with DINA, the Chilean secret police. The organization received training in Chile, took credit (to throw off the police) for an assassination attempt by DINA contract agents in Rome against a prominent Chilean exile, and carried out the car bombing of former Ambassador Letelier in September 1976. Three CNM members attended the founding meeting of CORU.[62]

But the CNM was more than an extremist political sect; it was a gang that derived income from extortion and drug trafficking. Those who stood in its way or threatened to expose its operations, including several prominent exile leaders, it murdered in the name of "Cero" or "Omega 7."

The CNM reportedly got its start in drugs through Juan Restoy, the CIA veteran and leader of the drug syndicate busted in Operation Eagle; the brothers Ignacio and Guillermo Novo allegedly acted as drug runners for his organization in New Jersey.[63] Later Guillermo Novo was linked to the Alvero Cruz organization.[64] The group appears to have profited directly from drug smuggling organized by DINA.[65] A congressional staff investigation determined that the CNM's northern branch, Omega 7, was in contact with Alvaro Carvajal Minota, believed to be the leader of a drug ring busted in San Francisco that allegedly helped finance the Contra cause.[66] More recently, two CNM militants implicated in the Letelier assassination, Virgilio Paz and José Dionisio Suarez, resurfaced as hit men for the Colombian drug Mafia, based in Barranquilla. (Suarez, as we shall see, also had a brief stint training the Contras under Argentine auspices.) Both are suspected of drug trafficking in Florida and of collecting drug debts for the Colombians.[67]

## The Mexican Connection

The 1978 arrest in Miami of two CNM members and Letelier assassination suspects, Alvin Ross and Guillermo Novo, was the first public indication of the group's narcoterrorist operations (although the FBI suppressed the evidence). Police discovered in Ross's possession a large bag of cocaine.[68] And they discovered in Novo's company one Manuel Menendez, a notorious heroin dealer. Although wanted on federal charges, Menendez was allowed to walk out of jail, supposedly because nobody checked his record.[69]

Menendez was both a major East Coast retailer of Mexican heroin and an employer of Omega 7 members. His main supplier was another Cuban exile, Antonio Cruz Vasquez, who operated out of Las Vegas.[70] Cruz Vasquez looked in turn for his heroin to the Zambadas of Mexico, a family of Cuban exiles into which he married and who reemerged in the late 1980s as drug traffickers. When Cruz Vasquez was finally sentenced in 1978, federal authorities called him one of the largest heroin retailers in the country, responsible for supplying about six hundred pounds a year to New York City and New Jersey. He also had intelligence connections in Somoza's Nicaragua, but whether to the CIA or to Fidel Castro's secret service, law enforcement authorities did not know.[71]

Cruz Vasquez appears to have been part of a network of CIA-protected Mexican traffickers that started with the precocious Cuban exile drug king Alberto Sicilia Falcón. In his late twenties, Sicilia came from nowhere after the bust of the French Connection in 1972 (marked also by the killing of the French heroin trafficker Lucien Sarti in Mexico) to head a

Tijuana-based organization that moved Mexican marijuana, Andean cocaine, and European heroin in vast quantities to the United States.

Sicilia and his people, like Cruz Vasquez, were given lavish compli-
mentary rooms and services by Armando Campo, the chief liaison to
wealthy Latin American gamblers at Caesar's Palace in Las Vegas. Rumored to be a "Cuban Mafia" leader (a charge he denied), Campo pleaded
guilty to income tax evasion after being arrested for possessing a large
amount of cocaine. Campo was also a close friend of Sicilia's close associate, the CIA-trained intelligence officer José Egozi.[72]

Egozi provided one of Sicilia's many apparent links to the CIA. In
1974, Egozi lined up CIA support for a right-wing plot to overthrow the
Portuguese government that involved a quarter-billion-dollar arms shipment arranged by Sicilia. Sicilia claimed to have engaged in CIA commando raids against Cuba and was also suspected by one of his close
aides of acting as a conduit for CIA shipments of arms to Central America
in the 1970s. DEA agents in charge of the case soon realized that not
only was the CIA station in Mexico City thoroughly familiar with Sicilia,
but his name also produced strange pressures from Washington. Federal
drug agents speculated that the CIA had recruited Sicilia in Miami and
assisted his rise but that he ultimately "got too big for his britches" and
thus had to be brought down.[73] (As we shall see, one of Sicilia's men who
took his place as a leader of the Mexican drug trade also appears to have
enjoyed CIA protection, in part because of his support for the Contras.)

Aside from the CIA, Sicilia also had ample support from top politicians,
intelligence agents, and law-enforcement officials in Mexico. One of the
most important of these was the head of the powerful Dirección Federal
de Seguridad (DFS), Miguel Nazar Haro. After Sicilia was recaptured
following an escape from prison, Nazar intervened to protect him from
torture—and thus from possibly spilling embarrassing information.[74]

Nazar was one of the most powerful men in Mexico in this period.
The DFS, a sort of combined FBI and CIA with broad national security
functions, played a central part in Mexico's fight against left-wing subversion, both directly and through a death squad organized under Nazar's
supervision, the "White Brigade." The strategic role of the DFS also
attracted a host of foreign interests: Nazar provided a key point of intersection for anti-Castro Cubans, the DEA, and the CIA in Mexico.

Nazar is known to have been close to several CORU Cubans implicated
in the Merida case, including Francisco Manuel Camargo and Armando
López Estrada. Camargo, as we noted, was rumored to be in contact with
the Mexican police, narcotics officers, and the CIA. Another of Nazar's

Cuban-American contacts, Bernardo de Torres, reportedly provided Nazar's death squad with weapons. He worked for the DEA as an informant while also, according to federal sources quoted by former *Newsday* reporter John Cummings, running "guns into Mexico and drugs out with Nazar's knowledge. In fact, it was common knowledge that when de Torres went to Mexico he was picked up at the airport by Nazar's personal limousine—without having to go through customs or immigration—and swiftly taken to Nazar's office." Nazar protected the operations of these Cuban terrorists, not least by seizing and destroying evidence of their culpability in the Merida case and possibly by helping one of the perpetrators to escape from prison.[75]

The DEA also had ties to Nazar. One DEA agent said to be in contact with him was Tucson-based Hugh Murray. A former CIA officer, Murray ran the Bolivia station during the campaign to capture the pro-Castro guerrilla leader Ernesto Che Guevara, a mission accomplished in 1967 with the help of Cuban-born CIA officers Félix Rodríguez and Gustavo Villoldo.[76] Murray was recruited into the DEA in 1974 by the former CIA officer and DEACON 1 leader Lucien Conein. One DEA informant later testified that Murray used his DEA job as a cover for running political intelligence operations within the Mexican government. Such activities would explain his alleged contacts with Nazar and with the corrupt police chief of Mexico City, Arturo Durazo, who reportedly made a fortune from the drug trade.[77]

Political espionage is, of course, the job of the CIA, not the DEA. But the line between the two agencies has often been blurred, and nowhere more so than in Mexico, where the CIA required the drug agency in the 1970s to hand over a list of all its Mexican assets and coordinate operations.[78] And if Nazar was a sometime DEA asset, he was indisputably the CIA's "most important source in Mexico and Central America" by the agency's own admission.[79]

As Elaine Shannon has observed:

> DFS officials worked closely with the Mexico City station of the US Central Intelligence Agency and the attaché of the Federal Bureau of Investigation. The DFS passed along photographs and wiretapped conversations of suspected intelligence officers and provocateurs stationed in the large Soviet and Cuban missions in Mexico City. This information was of crucial importance to US counterintelligence specialists at the CIA and FBI. . . . The DFS also helped the CIA track Central American leftists who passed through the Mexican capital. Finally, the DFS provided security details for the US ambassador and other American dignitaries.[80]

The CIA's loyalty paid off for Nazar when FBI agents began investigating a stolen car ring that moved no fewer than 4,000 "hot" autos across the border from the United States into Mexico. Bureau informants named Nazar Haro as one of the ringleaders. An FBI affidavit produced in the case reported that in June or July 1979 one of the car thieves "traveled to DFS headquarters in Mexico City and obtained orders for stolen vehicles. . . . The vehicles were subsequently stolen in California and delivered to DFS headquarters in Tijuana. Miguel Nazar . . . inspected the stolen vehicles and had a number of his DFS agents accompany the stolen vehicles to Mexico City."[81]

A United States grand jury indicted Nazar, but officials in the Mexico City embassy balked at any attempt to bring the highest-ranking career officer at the DFS to justice. The FBI legal attaché Gordon McGinley wrote to the Justice Department that "CIA station and legat [legal attaché] believe our mutual interests and as a consequence the security of the United States, as it relates to terrorism, intelligence, and counterintelligence in Mexico, would suffer a disastrous blow if Nazar were forced to resign." In another cable he referred to Nazar as "an essential repeat essential contact for CIA station in Mexico City." When Associate Attorney General Lowell Jensen (now a federal judge) refused to permit Nazar's indictment, U.S. Attorney William Kennedy publicly exposed the CIA's role in obstructing justice and was summarily fired.[82]

Nazar Haro plays a critical role in the story of U.S. government tolerance and support for international drug smuggling. Trafficking in stolen cars was the least of the crimes in which he was implicated—and for which the CIA and DEA covered his tracks in order to win his continued cooperation. U.S. authorities knew by the early 1970s that DFS was implicated in serious drug trafficking, yet they continued to defend and protect the agency.[83] This pattern emerges again in the Contra period, and indeed some DFS-protected drug kingpins implicated in the Contra effort trace their roots to Nazar's tenure in Mexico.

### The Mexican Snow Job

The years of Nazar Haro's reign at DFS (1977–82) have been praised by U.S. drug enforcement officials and State Department spokesmen as the golden age of Mexican drug enforcement. In 1978, Peter Bourne, director of White House Office of Drug Abuse Policy, told a Senate subcommittee, "The ongoing activities of the Mexican and American governments in the field of drug control must rank among the most exemplary forms of international cooperation in the world today."[84] By 1980, U.S. and Mexican officials were boasting that "The success of Mexico's program to eradicate opium poppies, from which heroin is processed, and marijuana is more than evident in the scarcity, inaccessibility and tiny size of the fields being sprayed in the inhospitable mountains east of Culiacan, near the Pacific coast 650 miles northwest of Mexico City."[85]

As late as 1983, the House Select Committee on Narcotics Abuse and Control could report back after a study trip that "since 1975 Mexico has been successful in virtually eliminating marijuana production and has substantially reduced opium cultivation." It also had high praise for the Mexican government's success in building "the world's finest aerial crop-eradication program. Its size, professionalism, competence, performance, and experience make it the world leader in this technique."[86]

In retrospect, such assessments were not merely ludicrously wrong; they represented one of the greatest cover-ups in the history of U.S. drug enforcement. Government officials knew the Mexican enforcement effort was a sham but chose to disguise that fact until the brazen murder of DEA agent Enrique Camarena in February 1985. Only then did DEA Administrator Francis Mullen, Jr., startle the public with his revelation that "Mexico hasn't arrested a major drug trafficker in eight years."[87]

DEA and other agencies had known for most of that time that the Mexican miracle was really a nightmare. As early as 1980, for example, the DEA was aware that the city of Guadalajara had been taken over by international drug traffickers like Miguel Angel Félix Gallardo, Rafael Caro Quintero, and Ernesto Fonseca Carrillo.[88] In 1982, the DEA learned that Félix Gallardo was moving $20 million a month through a single Bank of America account, but the CIA would not cooperate even marginally with the investigation.[89] By then U.S. officials also knew that Mexico had replaced Colombia as the major supplier of marijuana to the United States and that it transshipped at least 30 percent of the cocaine consumed in America.[90] In November 1984, Mexican police raids turned up 10,000 tons of marijuana growing on slave plantations in Chihuahua— eight times as much as the United States officially estimated was produced in all of Mexico in a year, and nearly as much as estimates of America's entire annual consumption. (Ironically, those consumption figures had been calculated on the basis of phony Mexican production estimates.)[91]

The key to the public deception was the much-vaunted Mexican enforcement campaign known as Operation Condor. It began in 1975 with a two-pronged emphasis on aerial spraying of drug crops and military operations against traffickers in remote mountain areas, particularly in the state of Sinaloa. It succeeded in filling the jails with hapless peasants accused of growing marijuana on their tiny plots—or suspected of political organizing in the countryside—but failed to arrest a single important trafficker.[92]

The drug chiefs were similarly untouched by the bogus aerial drug-eradication program funded by the United States, which supplied seventy-six planes and other aid worth at least $115 million. Although the State Department's narcotics office had official responsibility, the CIA also had a hand in this program. To fly the planes and train Mexican pilots, Mexico contracted with Evergreen International Aviation. The deal was arranged by two CIA members, one of whom had flown for the agency in Laos. The year Condor began, Evergreen acquired most of the assets of a CIA proprietary airline, Intermountain Aviation. It also put the former head of all CIA air operations, George Doole, on its board of directors.[93] The company with the contract for all airplane maintenance for the program in Mexico was E-Systems, which acquired the CIA proprietary Air Asia and which has three former top CIA officers among its senior executives.[94]

For whatever reason, these contractors and their State Department overseers failed to get the job done. They did not sound the alarm when it became evident that a bad drought, rather than herbicidal spraying, was the major cause of the short-term decline in Mexico's drug production in the late 1970s.[95] As early as 1978, when Mexican authorities refused to permit the United States to fly over the spray zones to verify eradication of the drug crop, the DEA learned that pilots were either spraying fields with water or unloading their herbicides in the desert. Informants reported that some Mexican officials used the planes for joy rides and pleasure trips, while other officials shook down drug cultivators in exchange for protection from spraying. Reports of this fraud made it into occasional press reports, but these were buried under the State Department's press releases about the Mexican miracle. "We're perpetuating a fraud just by being there," one frustrated DEA official finally told a reporter in disgust.[96]

Only in February 1985, after DEA agent Camarena's murder, did a congressional staff mission report that the State Department's drug eradication program in Mexico was:

> in a shambles. . . . There are no adequate records to indicate how funds have been and are being spent, where commodities have gone and whether they are being used properly. Until recently, the eradication program had no independent verification to indicate whether eradication had actually been carried out, and thus the Mexican statistics provided annually are largely meaningless. Furthermore, much of the eradication which has

taken place has consisted of eradicating the same areas over and over again each year. . . . The study mission was informed that no evaluation had ever been conducted of the Mexican eradication program.[97]

But even this report left the impression that the heart of the problem was incompetence, not corruption.

Such failures were inevitable given the records of the two Mexican presidents who oversaw Condor. Luis Echeverría, under whom the program began, appears to have been linked to Sicilia Falcón through his wife, whose family members had suspected ties to the European heroin trade.[98] And José López Portillo, who took charge in 1976, reportedly "amassed hundreds of millions of dollars in criminal profits" and bought large estates in Spain with the proceeds.[99] One of the officials who ran the eradication program under them, and then rose to become minister of defense for President Miguel de la Madrid, allegedly supplied military credentials to a major border trafficker and took $10 million from the drug mafia to protect the 10,000-ton Chihuahua marijuana complex.[100]

Condor's primary focus on Sinaloa, home of many of Mexico's traditional trafficking families, may well have been inspired by Sicilia, who was based in Tijuana. He paid huge bribes to direct the operation against his competitors in order to obtain a monopoly on the Mexican marijuana trade.[101] But with his arrest in 1975, the plan backfired. Instead, Condor began working to his competitors' advantage. The main Sinaloa traffickers simply moved to Guadalajara (a city Sicilia once owned) and strengthened their grip. "In a way," notes Elaine Shannon, "Operation Condor/Trizo did them a great service by winnowing out the competition."[102]

Nazar Haro's DFS speeded up that process by protecting the chiefs of the Guadalajara cartel. In 1985, shortly after the murder of DEA agent Camarena, a top U.S. investigator complained that the DFS was "a very big problem. Every time we grab someone, they're carrying a card from the DFS. A lot of people have been issued badges who are not really on the payroll."[103] DEA agents considered the DFS badge a "license to traffic." Badge holders could carry machine guns, install wiretaps, and interrogate suspects. DFS agents "rode security for the traffickers' marijuana-laden truck convoys, used the Mexican police radio system to check border crossings for signs of American police surveillance, and ferried contraband across the Rio Grande by boat."[104] Ernesto Fonseca even employed DFS agents as his chauffeur and bodyguards.[105] In the months after Camarena's murder, under pressure from the United States, Mexican authorities fired a fifth of the organization's 2,200 agents and replaced nineteen of its thirty-one state directors.[106]

But the DFS did much more than simply protect the most notorious traffickers. It brought them together as a cartel, centralized and rationalized their operation, snuffed out competitors, and, through its connections with the CIA, provided the international protection needed to ensure their success. No wonder Mexican trafficker Carlos de Herrera called the DFS one of the "most strong mafias in Mexico."[107]

A former DFS consultant disclosed the existence of a vast smuggling operation called "La Pipa" (The Pipe) orchestrated by the DFS. According to this informant, the DFS

> in the late 1970s acquired about 600 tanker trucks, ostensibly for ferrying natural gas from the US for sale in Mexico. On the northbound leg of the trip, DFS men packed the empty trucks with marijuana provided by Mexican dealers and ran ten to twelve trucks a day into Phoenix and Los Angeles. At the border, several Mexican officials and US Customs personnel were bribed $50,000 a load to let the trucks pass. . . . The relationship between the traffickers and the Mexican government agency began in the mid-1970s. Two DFS commanders persuaded the leading smuggling families to settle a bloody feud over control of drug production in the Sierra Madre highlands and to unite against the antinarcotics campaign being waged by Mexico and the US. The DFS helped the families relocate to Guadalajara, introduced them to local officials and assigned them bodyguards. In the meantime, the agency, which, among other duties, is charged with keeping tabs on political subversives and works in close contact with the CIA, went after minor traffickers, winnowing down competition to the new Guadalajara cartel. In exchange, the cartel handed over 25% of all its profits to the DFS.[108]

The Mexican agency also oversaw the $5 billion marijuana plantation in Chihuahua whose bust by rival federal police in 1984 apparently led to Camarena's murder.[109]

This collaboration between DFS and the traffickers continued after Nazar Haro left the agency in 1982 with the change of Mexican administrations; so did the collaboration of DFS and the CIA. The CIA station in Mexico City maintained close contact with Nazar's successor, José Antonio Zorrilla Perez, despite overwhelming evidence of his agency's responsibility for the drug traffic. "They don't give a damn," said one DEA agent of the CIA. "They turn their heads the other way. They see their task as much more important than ours."[110]

Yet the DEA itself, at least at higher levels in Mexico City and in Washington, contributed to the cover-up of information ferreted out by brave field agents in dangerous local offices like Guadalajara. It followed embassy orders not to brief congressional missions on the true state of the drug trade in Mexico in the early 1980s.[111] As late as 1984, when the power and scope of the Guadalajara cartel was evident to the field agents, "their superiors in Mexico City and Washington seemed not to notice. Cables to the embassy or DEA headquarters went unanswered, requests for reinforcements were ignored, calls for diplomatic intervention were ignored. . . . The prevailing attitude among many diplomats, and some DEA officials as well, was that corruption and duplicity had to be suffered for the sake of preserving the 'special relationship' between the United States and Mexico."[112]

One can only speculate whether this special relationship also encompassed the help that two of Mexico's most notorious smugglers were giving the Nicaraguan Contras in this same period. Mexico's single biggest smuggler, Miguel Félix Gallardo, responsible for moving four tons of cocaine every month into the United States, was also "a big supporter" of the Contras, according to his pilot Werner Lotz.[113] Lotz told the DEA that his boss advanced him more than $150,000 to pass on to the Contras. Attorneys for another Mexican trafficker who stood trial in the United States charged that "from an examination of all the available evidence, it is apparent that various agencies of the federal government, including the CIA, were aware of Félix Gallardo's cocaine smuggling activities and have purposefully ignored them due to Félix Gallardo's 'charitable contributions' to the Contras." An assistant U.S. attorney did not dispute Lotz's claim, but only argued that it had no bearing on the government's failure to indict Félix Gallardo for the murder of Camarena.[114]

A prosecution witness in a subsequent Camarena murder trial claimed that Félix Gallardo had boasted of supplying arms to the Contras, and of rounding up other traffickers to finance their cause during 1983 and 1984, in exchange for protection.[115] The same witness also described hearing of a training camp established by Mexican law enforcement agencies at a ranch owned by Rafael Caro Quintero in Veracruz. Some Contras had apparently been trained there as well. The CIA ran the facility, he told DEA agents at one point, using DFS "as a cover, in the event any questions were raised as to who was running the training operations."[116] The CIA denied the story, but the Justice Department took it seriously enough to ask for an investigation by Iran-Contra special counsel Lawrence Walsh.[117] In evaluating the story, it may be significant that another acquaintance of Félix Gallardo, a military veteran of Operation Condor, boasted to a DEA undercover agent of helping to train the Contras in Honduras.[118]

Félix Gallardo's main partner and cocaine supplier, Juan Ramón Matta Ballesteros, had Contra connections of his own through SETCO, which ferried supplies for the FDN and State Department in Honduras even after Matta came under investigation for his involvement in the Camarena murder. Matta rose to prominence in the drug trade as Sicilia's pipeline to Andean cocaine. After Sicilia's downfall, Matta joined Félix Gallardo in the same capacity, racking up a fortune estimated at $2 billion. In 1985, *Newsweek* described Matta as the "boss of bosses of Mexico's cocaine industry" and cited official estimates that his organization supplied "perhaps one-third of all the cocaine consumed in the United States." As one DEA agent said, "He is the kind of individual who would be a decision-maker of last resort. He is at the same level as the rulers of the Medellín and Cali cartels."[119] As we shall see in Chapter 3, Washington's protection of Matta and the Honduran connection was a direct product of its single-minded commitment to the proxy war against Nicaragua.

## The Argentine Connection

To further understand why the Contras gravitated toward drugs to finance terrorist operations, one must understand the narcoterrorist methods of their original patrons, the Argentine military junta that took power in 1976. Its brutal methods at home were responsible for the "disappearance" of at least 9,000 civilians. Some of those victims were suspected of leftist subversion; others were simply targets of criminal vendettas by gangsters who rose to positions of authority in the security services. The same criminality was reflected in the regime's support of state-sponsored narcoterrorism abroad, particularly in Bolivia, a major cocaine producer.

The Argentine junta, like the Chilean dictatorship of Gen. Augusto Pinochet, exported its methods. Argentina and Chile were founding members of Operation Condor, not the Mexican eradication program but an alliance of Latin American military regimes dedicated to wiping out communism through joint intelligence operations and assassinations of opposition figures. Among those killed by its hit teams were former Chilean ambassador Orlando Letelier in Washington, DC, former Chilean commander-in-chief Gen. Carlos Prats, former Bolivian President Juan José Torres, the Uruguayan politicians Hector Gutierrez Ruiz and Zelmar Michelini in Argentina, and Col. Ramón Trabal of Uruguay in France. These killers were also responsible for the attempted murder of Chilean opposition leader Bernardo Leighton in Italy. A classified U.S. Senate report indicates that the CIA was aware of Condor as early as 1974 but intervened only to prevent Miami from becoming its main base of operations.[120] From Miami and offshore havens, however, CORU Cubans became essential instruments of Condor, often acting as the hit men for jobs within Argentina.[121]

Even more than Pinochet's regime in Chile, which confined itself mainly to murdering dissident Chilean exiles abroad, Argentina's military waged an ideological struggle against its enemies on a broad front, from Mexico to the southern tip of Latin America. Its theorists called their ideology the doctrine of "ideological frontiers." "The idea," said Leandro Sanchez Reisse, a veteran military intelligence agent, "is that frontiers don't terminate with the individual geography of each state but that it is necessary to defend Western politics wherever necessary. That is to say, if subversion fights internationally there must be an international defense. It is therefore necessary to act against those who could become a second Cuba, and to collaborate with the United States directly and indirectly."[122]

According to Sanchez Reisse, "The idea was born in the First Army Corps and then went to the presidency. . . . All the leadership came from the First Army Corps."[123] The head of that unit was Gen. Carlos Guillermo Suarez Mason, one of the most notorious practitioners of the "dirty war" against Argentine civilians in the late 1970s. (In 1989, a United States judge ordered him to pay $60 million in compensation to families of three who disappeared in that gruesome period.) The well-known Argentine newspaper editor Jacobo Timerman accused Suarez Mason of ordering his imprisonment and torture for two and a half years.[124]

Suarez Mason owed his ascendancy to the secret Italian Masonic lodge known as "Propaganda Due" or P2. Its goal in Italy was the creation of a secret, authoritarian state through the recruitment of top politicians, business tycoons, military leaders, and intelligence chiefs; in Latin America, it created a parallel network concentrated in Argentina and Uruguay. In 1986, Argentina's interior minister branded the P2 group "an enormous criminal conspiracy which aimed to take power in the country."[125] The P2 network reportedly raised money from the South American drug traffic and other criminal sources.[126]

Suarez Mason was a member of this exclusive secret society; so was José López Rega, a Rasputin-like figure who returned from Spain to Argentina with Juan Perón in 1973. López Rega took over the powerful Ministry of Social Welfare, which put him in charge of the police and, unofficially, of the Argentine Anticommunist Alliance (AAA), a notorious death squad that collaborated with Omega 7, the drug-linked

Cuban exile terror organization, and later contributed personnel to the Contra training teams.[127] The same year, Suarez Mason was promoted to general and put in charge of Army intelligence.[128]

When a coup ousted the Perónist government in 1976, López Rega went back into exile amid charges that he had financed his conspiratorial activities through wholesale trafficking in cocaine.[129] Suarez Mason, however, kept rising. In 1976 he was appointed commander of the First Army Corps in Buenos Aires. By the end of the 1970s he had become head of the Joint Chiefs of Staff. He retired from the military in 1981 and ran the state oil monopoly, YPF, until 1982.[130]

Suarez Mason put his doctrine of ideological frontiers into practice through what became known as the Andean Brigade. "It was a sort of secret foreign legion whose job was rooting out Communists wherever they happened to be, especially the Montoneros guerrillas and those assisting them," says Jack Blum, former chief counsel of the Senate subcommittee on terrorism and narcotics. "The Argentine military became convinced the Montoneros were doing business with drug traffickers, so they moved in to establish their own connections with the traffickers and to finance their operations out of drugs. The Bolivian cocaine coup helped fund their Andean Brigade."[131]

That coup took place in July 1980, toppling a short-lived civilian government. Argentina's president, General Videla, hailed the takeover for preventing a "situation in the heartland of South America that would amount to what Cuba represents in Central America." Argentina moved almost instantly to recognize the new military regime.[132]

And no wonder. Argentina had infiltrated agents into Bolivia to work with military plotters and with Klaus Barbie, the escaped Nazi war criminal and former U.S. intelligence agent who was their close ally. Suarez Mason and his fellow officers put an Argentine intelligence specialist in charge of the operation.[133] One of his key agents on the scene was an adviser at Bolivia's military intelligence school.[134] In all, the Argentines had as many as two hundred military personnel in Bolivia to coordinate the seizure of power.[135]

One of the more significant Argentine military intelligence officials was Alfredo Mario Mingolla. Trained by the Israelis, he had worked for the right-wing military intelligence services of Honduras and Guatemala between 1976 and 1980. After helping to overthrow the Bolivian government, he stayed on in that country as an adviser to the military junta on "psychological operations." After a stint in Guatemala working primarily with the North Americans, he returned to Bolivia, where he was arrested in November 1982 for plotting to assassinate the Bolivian vice president. In 1987, he was again arrested, this time by Brazilian authorities in São Paulo for carrying 357 kg of cocaine.[136]

Yet another Argentine agent involved in the Bolivian coup was Stefano delle Chiaie, an Italian fugitive wanted for numerous bombings and political killings at home. A Condor assassin for Chile, Argentina, and possibly other governments, delle Chiaie had organized for DINA the attempted murder of former Chilean opposition politician Bernardo Leighton in Rome in 1975—an act for which the drug-trafficking Cuban exile group CNM, which also worked for DINA, claimed credit.[137] By the late 1970s, delle Chiaie had moved to Argentina, with whose AAA death squad he had long collaborated, to work full-time for its military regime. He hoped to make Buenos Aires, Suarez Mason's base of operations, an international neofascist center.[138]

Along with several other European extremists enlisted in the cause of preparing a coup in Bolivia, delle Chiaie assumed the guise of an Argentine intelligence officer and began working with Bolivian Col. Luis Arce Gomez. Delle Chiaie called his international team of assassins the "Phoenix Commando." The Argentine junta backed them by increasing the size of its military mission in the Bolivian capital to seventy, "including in their number several notorious veterans of Argentina's dirty war," according to one book.[139]

On June 17, 1980, a month before the coup, six of Bolivia's biggest traffickers met with the military conspirators to work out a financial deal for future protection of their trade.[140] This collaboration was no secret even then. One remarkably prescient news account reported later that month, "A leading businessman in La Paz has suggested that the possible army takeover next month should be called the Cocaine Coup."[141] And indeed that name branded the July takeover for all time.

The coup itself, on July 17, 1980, was a bloody affair, marked by mass arrests, beatings, and torture. Such tactics bore the stamp both of Argentina's military, which prepared computerized lists of opposition figures to imprison, torture, and kill,[142] and of the foreign mercenaries who stayed on to advise and train paramilitary security squads for the government. These mentors continued to influence the new regime's course. "At least 40 Bolivian officers have traveled to Argentina to study 'anti-subversive techniques,' " *Newsweek* reported in late 1981, "and Argentinians practiced in torture [are serving as] interrogators."[143]

The repression was organized by Interior Minister Luis Arce Gomez, the same colonel who had employed delle Chiaie to prepare for the coup. Arce Gomez became notorious for his ruthless methods against political opponents and quickly gained further infamy for his open collaboration with Bolivia's cocaine lords.

Within days of taking power, Arce Gomez, a cousin of Bolivia's premier cocaine trafficker, Roberto Suarez, began releasing convicted smugglers from prison and recruiting them into his paramilitary squads. He went into direct partnership with some of the biggest smugglers and taxed others for protection.[144] (One alleged buyer of his cocaine was the drug ring implicated in Operation Tick-Talks, including three Cuban exiles who later threw their support behind the Contras.)[145]

Arce Gomez delegated his neofascist militants, under the leadership of Klaus Barbie, to protect Bolivia's major cocaine barons and transport their drugs to the border. These mercenaries proudly called their criminal strong-arm squad the "Fiancés of Death."[146] One of their number, a German neo-Nazi, later testified that delle Chiaie also acted as a liaison between the Bolivian military and the Sicilian drug Mafia.[147]

Only a month and a half after Bolivia's Cocaine Coup, many of its chief organizers celebrated Argentina's successful export of drug-financed, military-style revolution. The venue for their victory party was a meeting of the Latin American Anticommunist Confederation (CAL), held on September 2, 1980, in Buenos Aires. Hosting the conference was General Suarez Mason himself; in attendance were his agent delle Chiaie and the man they had just put in charge of Bolivia, Gen. Luis Garcia Meza. Also on hand were the godfather of Guatemala's death squads, Mario Sandoval Alarcón, and his Salvadoran protégé Roberto d'Aubuisson, who only six months earlier had apparently ordered the assassination of Archbishop Oscar Romero.[148] For d'Aubuisson and his Argentine hosts, the meeting proved fruitful: "Within two months, at least fifty Argentine unconventional warfare advisers were dispatched into El Salvador to assist their anti-communist compatriots. They helped their students perfect the counterterror tactics so well that the extent of the 'dirty war' in Argentina would be dwarfed by that in El Salvador."[149]

For both Suarez Mason and delle Chiaie, the victory was short-lived, however. In July 1982, just as a new civilian government was coming to power in Bolivia, delle Chiaie fled before Italian authorities could have him arrested for acts of terrorism in Europe. He crossed the border into Argentina and came under Suarez Mason's protection in Buenos Aires, where he reportedly teamed up with another emigré, Arce Gomez, who had fallen in a recent coup. Later that year delle Chiaie reportedly visited Miami with a heroin-trafficking leader of the

Gray Wolves, a right-wing Turkish organization. In 1987, delle Chiaie was arrested by the Venezuelan secret police, DISIP, who stumbled across him while looking for some cocaine traffickers. In his Caracas apartment the agents reportedly found evidence linking him to drugs and international terrorism.[150]

Suarez Mason, too, was forced into exile when Argentina's military regime crumbled after its humiliating defeat in the Falklands War. With the election of a new, democratic government in December 1983, Suarez Mason fled. Four months later, according to a sworn deposition by his wife, he was granted an interview with the State Department. In November 1984, Argentina's civilian government issued an international warrant for his arrest, accusing him of working with drug and arms traffickers in a conspiracy to overthrow the new government.[151] In 1985 he was reported by the Italian press to be "entrenched in Miami" and to have become "one of Latin America's chief drug traffickers," along with Bolivia's former president, General Garcia Meza.[152] U.S. authorities finally arrested him in 1987 and, after a long extradition proceeding, deported him in May 1988. (His attorney in that case, Josue Prada, was indicted a few months later in a huge drug conspiracy case with Pablo Escobar and José Gonzalo Rodríguez Gacha, two leaders of the Medellín cocaine cartel.)[153]

By the time he fell, however, Suarez Mason's narcoterrorist methods had left an indelible mark on the Contras and the Reagan administration's approach to the covert war against the Nicaraguan Sandinistas. In the late 1970s, as part of Argentina's war of ideological frontiers, Suarez Mason began exporting "dirty war" veterans to several Central American countries to provide leadership to local military death squads. Argentina's involvement included "the training of more than 200 Guatemalan officers in 'interrogation techniques' (torture) and repressive methods"; the creation, with Israeli specialists, of a computerized intelligence center in that country; and the dispatch of similar "consultants" to Honduran security units led by Col. Gustavo Alvarez Martinez, who had studied military doctrine in Argentina.[154]

Having also worked with the tough National Guard of Nicaragua's Anastasio Somoza, the Argentine military was a natural ally of those National Guard veterans, some of them also graduates of Argentina's military academies, who formed the fledgling Contra movement in Guatemala and Honduras in 1981. In Central America, this aid was coordinated with CAL by death squad leaders Mario Sandoval Alarcón of Guatemala and Roberto d'Aubuisson of El Salvador, both of whom attended the September 1980 CAL convention in Buenos Aires with Suarez Mason.[155] (One particularly close ally of both d'Aubuisson and the Argentine secret police was right-wing Salvadoran businessman Francisco Guirola Beeche, who was suspected by U.S. Customs of smuggling cocaine and arms and laundering money. Yet in a deal that has never been fully explained, the U.S. government dropped most of the charges against him in a 1985 money-smuggling case—supposedly to avoid jeopardizing his future chances of emigrating to North America.)[156]

In the United States, support for the Argentine connection was encouraged by two associates of Sen. Jesse Helms, Republican of North Carolina: Nat Hamrick, a former business partner of the Somoza family, and John Carbaugh, a Helms aide who also attended the Buenos Aires meeting. (Helms was an outspoken supporter of both the Argentine and Bolivian military governments.)[157]

As early as July 1980, Hamrick was paving the way for a U.S.-Argentine alliance behind the Nicaraguan counterrevolution by escorting an Argentine diplomat, who had served in both Guatemala and Bolivia, around the Republican convention that nominated Ronald Reagan. On the other end of the continent, he was urging Argentina's President Roberto Viola to step up his country's support for a movement against the Sandinistas. And he took former Somoza National Guard Col. Enrique Bermúdez to Argentina in April 1981 to line up the military's support for his cause.[158] Bermúdez brought back at least $50,000 in seed money, with promises of more to come if he followed Argentina's direction. That money put Bermúdez and a band of seventy followers in a commanding position in the fledgling Contra movement.[159]

Carbaugh worked closely with Hamrick on this effort.[160] He was responsible for the inclusion of a call for overthrowing the Sandinistas in the 1980 Republican Party platform, and he helped swing the new Reagan administration's invitation to General Viola for a White House visit in March 1981 to organize help for the Contras. He also helped orchestrate the visit of Ambassador-at-Large Vernon Walters to Buenos Aires in June 1981 for the same purpose.[161]

In August 1981, the newly appointed chief of Latin American operations for the CIA, Duane Clarridge, went to Honduras to discuss the Contras with President Policarpo Paz Garcia, the military intelligence boss Col. Leonides Torres, and the Argentine-trained police chief, Col. Gustavo Alvarez Martinez. (All three Hondurans, as we shall see later, had ties to the drug trade.) Clarridge returned to Honduras later that August with Col. Mario Davico, vice chief of

Argentine military intelligence, to pledge Washington's support for the Contras and to urge Honduran cooperation with Argentina's training and supply mission. These assurances helped seal Honduras's commitment of support for the Nicaraguan couterrevolution.[162]

The Washington visit of Gen. Leopoldo Galtieri, head of Argentina's military junta, the same August helped confirm that country's own commitment. With Argentine and U.S. money behind them, the Argentine-trained former Somoza National Guards led by Bermúdez also came together in August 1981 to form the Nicaraguan Democratic Front (FDN), the main coalition of Contra forces.[163]

John Prados describes what happened next: "Fifty Contras were sent to Argentina for training, subsequently to become instructors at camps in Honduras. [Col. José Ollas or Hoyos, alias Julio Villegas] became chief of Argentine logistics; another colonel named Osvaldo [Ribeiro] became the chief of operations, supervising a cadre of about fifty advisers in Honduras and Costa Rica."[164] Argentina appointed its army intelligence chief as ambassador to Panama to coordinate the Central America operation.[165] In each of the countries where they set up training units, the Argentine advisers encouraged violence and political assassinations.[166]

Still other Argentine personnel, according to one of their number who defected, went to Miami, "where other companions of theirs [were] trained in the same way in paramilitary [anti-Castro] Cuban–North American camps."[167] At least two Argentine military intelligence officials were assigned to Miami. Leandro Sanchez Reisse, a leading member of the Argentine intelligence unit known as Battalion 601, was put in charge of financing and currency exchange, "buying special equipment that couldn't be acquired through normal channels" and making contact with "anti-Sandinista groups in Florida," in particular Alpha 66 and Omega 7.[168] (The far-right Alpha 66, which ran two Florida guerrilla training camps, was regularly represented at conferences of the Latin American Anticommunist Confederation.)[169]

Sanchez Reisse may thus have played a role in recruiting, among others, two key anti-Castro Cubans into the Argentine training apparatus: José Dionisio Suarez, the fugitive accused killer of Orlando Letelier, who reportedly became a hit man for the Colombian cocaine mafia; and Félix Rodríguez, a former CIA security adviser to Bolivia and Argentina's First Army (Suarez Mason's unit) and confidant of George Bush's former national security aide Donald Gregg.[170]

Sanchez Reisse also audited the finances of the Argentine Special Tasks Group in Honduras; his contact there reportedly was Oliver

North's representative Robert Owen.[171] Sanchez Reisse denied accusations by the Argentine press and government that he financed some of his activities, with the help of other Battalion 601 officers, through the kidnappings and ransom of wealthy Latin businessmen.[172]

His superior in the Miami-Honduras operation was Raul Guglielminetti, who took an intelligence course with Sanchez Reisse in the United States in 1976. Guglielminetti reportedly established cover through a coin and pawn shop in Miami called the Silver Dollar that was later sold to a CIA-connected Cuban exile. He put Sanchez Reisse in charge of administering the business and its covert weapons-purchasing arm.[173]

Through such channels, Argentina played the dominant role in directing the Contras through 1982, despite the strain in U.S.-Argentine relations during the Falklands War and the subsequent decrease of support from Buenos Aires. FDN leaders have said that "decisions on timing, training, logistics, and targets were made by the Argentines. The Argentines were also the paymasters." Argentina also trained and built bases for the Miskito Indians in their struggle against Sandinista domination.[174] Not until mid-1983 did the CIA buy in to the Argentine operation to the point where Washington gained full control over the rebel army.[175] Early in 1984, after the Alfonsin government took charge, Argentina finally wrapped up its aid program. Its review of military records indicated that "unbelievable sums of money" had been sent into the Special Tasks Groups in Central America without any accounting.[176]

The operation was not easy to dismantle, however. The same intelligence units put into play for repression in Honduras, Guatemala, and Nicaragua came back to threaten Alfonsin once he withdrew them from Central America. Guglielminetti, for example, organized former military intelligence and AAA death squad veterans into an antigovernment conspiracy. After a wave of bombings and kidnappings that threatened to destabilize the new democracy, police raided Guglielminetti's house and discovered high explosives, napalm-tipped rockets, and sophisticated radio transmitters.[177] Similar intelligence veterans played a part in the cocaine-financed coup attempts of Col. Aldo Rico in 1987 and 1988.[178] Thus, the Argentine counterrevolution against Sandinismo in Nicaragua turned into a counterrevolution against democracy at home, much as the Reagan administration's own covert war came to threaten the rule of law in the United States.

# 3   Bananas, Cocaine, and Military Plots in Honduras

In no Central American country did Argentine military intelligence have a tighter grip than in Honduras. There its agents enjoyed a symbiotic relationship with the CIA, the Contras, and the Argentine-trained chief of police Col. Gustavo Alvarez Martinez. Argentine units trained the Honduran national police in interrogation and torture while building up the country's first death squads. When Argentina's Honduran protégés weren't kidnapping or torturing suspected leftists, they were helping former officers of Nicaraguan President Somoza's National Guard regroup as a rebel guerrilla force. By 1982, Alvarez had been promoted to general and army chief of staff in Honduras. He soon became notorious as leader of the country's death squads.[1] Military corruption and drug trafficking flourished on his watch.[2]

## The Roots of Corruption

Alvarez invented neither repression nor corruption in his desperately poor country; he merely built on a long and ignoble tradition established by the collaboration of domestic power brokers and military caudillos with powerful North American interests. Until 1975 Honduras was the classic banana republic, dominated by two giant U.S. companies, Standard Fruit and United Fruit, whose practices fostered corruption as a way of life in the country.

By the late nineteenth century, Honduras meant bananas. Soon much of the Honduran economy was controlled not from Tegucigalpa but from New Orleans, the capital of the banana trade. And as the New Orleans banana market, in turn, came under the domination of organized criminal gangs, established banana trade routes also became drug routes.

The history of the New Orleans Mafia thus sheds light on the long-standing importance of drugs to the Honduran economy. One historian of organized crime records that by 1890, "No banana freighter could be unloaded until a fixed tribute was paid by the importer to the firm of Antonio and Carlo Matranga, originally of Palermo. No Negro or Italian longshoreman would move unless he had orders from one of their appointed bosses."[3] Fruit shippers were particularly vulnerable to extortion since their expensive cargo would rot after a few days' delay on the docks. Large banana merchants had an incentive to form alliances with waterfront gangsters to protect their investment and muscle out business competition.

The reputed boss of organized crime in New Orleans in the 1870s, Joe Macheca, was one of the first Americans to exploit Central America's banana trade. In 1900, his successful shipping line merged with the United Fruit Company, one of whose founders later employed Italian criminals from New Orleans to build a railroad empire in Central America.[4] Macheca's successor as head of the New Orleans underworld, Charles Matranga, remained close to United Fruit, whose executives paid their respects at his funeral in 1943.[5]

United Fruit's major competitor, Standard Fruit, was founded by four New Orleans–based Sicilian immigrant brothers named Vaccaro. The firm had similar ties to criminal circles in that city and beyond. Perhaps the most telling evidence was the presence on its board of directors of Seymour Weiss, who managed the Roosevelt Hotel, in which the Vaccaro brothers had a major interest.[6] Weiss was a former New York bootlegger and chief bagman for corrupt Louisiana governor Huey Long. In the mid-1930s, Weiss arranged payoffs to Long at the hotel from three leaders of the national crime syndicate, Frank Costello, Jake Lansky, and "Dandy Phil" Kastel. Together, those senior underworld figures built a Louisiana slot machine empire under Long's protection.[7] The local New Orleans mob, then coming under the sway of a rising criminal named Carlos Marcello, got its own lucrative cut from that racket: the gift of 250 slots, which Marcello put into operation on the west side of town.[8]

A biographer of Marcello notes that by the 1930s, the New Orleans Mafia was "heavily into smuggling narcotics."[9] A major source for those narcotics, including morphine and cocaine, was Honduras. In 1932 and 1933, Honduras imported from Europe eighty-seven kg of morphine, enough to satisfy the country's own legitimate needs for a century. Most of it was reexported illicitly to the North American market, primarily New Orleans.[10] The future head of Marcello's narcotics operations was arrested for his role in a Honduran arms-for-drugs deal in 1934.[11]

The Honduran drug trade flourished in the 1930s under the leadership of President Tiburcio Carias Andino, who had the backing of United Fruit. One U.S. Narcotics Bureau informant accused Carias of authorizing drug shipments on the American-run Honduran cargo airline TACA.[12] His long rule (1933–49) was marked by "suppressed civil rights, restrictions on political activity, elimination of both national and local elections and imposed authority," according to one student of Honduran politics.[13] Perhaps Carias had some justification for playing politics by ruthless gangland rules; he had to fight off at least two serious coup attempts in the mid-1930s, both led by one of the country's leading morphine traffickers.[14]

One group suspected by U.S. authorities of involvement in the illegal trade under Carias included his vice president, the Honduran consul in New Orleans, the owner of TACA, and a soldier of fortune and sometime New Orleans police chief named Guy Maloney.[15] Maloney had an important link of his own to the banana trade: in 1911 he helped lead an invasion of Honduras, financed by the American banana entrepreneur Samuel Zemurray, to topple President Miguel Davila. Davila was unsympathetic to Zemurray's desire for port, rail, and land concessions and was unpopular in some quarters for enforcing anti-smuggling laws. Zemurray's mercenary revolt succeeded, and he soon won a twenty-five-year concession from the new president. In 1930 Zemurray sold out to United Fruit, becoming its largest shareholder. Within a couple of years, he returned to take charge of United Fruit's operations in Central America. His arrival coincided with a new mercenary operation by Maloney to install Carias in power.[16]

This pattern of banana-republic politics and corruption went virtually unchallenged until the mid-1970s, when the power of both the drug networks and the fruit companies was shaken by a series of scandals. In 1974, the Honduran consul in Miami, a Cuban exile named Enrique Argomaniz, pleaded guilty to income tax violations after coming under prolonged investigation for narcotics trafficking. His associates included Mario Escandar, the Bay of Pigs veteran and target of Operation Eagle. His employer was another CIA-trained veteran of the Bay of Pigs, Guillermo Hernandez Cartaya, proprietor of the money-laundering front WFC (see Chapter 2). The same year, investigations exposed the Honduran drug connection of the Cuban exiles' main patron in Central America, Nicaraguan dictator Anastasio Somoza. Somoza was a partner of a major U.S. marijuana smuggler, Raymond Grady Stansel, Jr., in a Honduras seafood company. Court testimony established that Somoza made airplanes available to the smuggler, who in turn boasted to one associate, "Our greatest protection is in having General Somoza on our side."[17]

The fruit companies suffered damaging exposure at the same time. Standard Fruit was revealed to have been making illegal payoffs to leaders and right-wing movements in Central America; the company was also accused of plotting the assassination of Panamanian strongman Omar Torrijos.[18] United Fruit took a serious blow, too. The Honduran president, General Oswaldo López Arellano, was overthrown in 1975 after the revelation that he had taken $1.5 million in bribes from the company to save it $7.5 million a year in export taxes.[19] The coup against him was headed by Humberto Regalado Lara, a young officer who was arrested in 1988 for importing large amounts of cocaine. López Arellano retired after the coup with a reported fortune of $25 million to become head of the national airline Tan-Sahsa, which flew Regalado's cocaine into the United States.[20]

López Arellano's successor was a more senior officer, Juan Alberto Melgar Castro. Under his leadership, the banana companies enjoyed renewed prosperity. Standard Fruit, for instance, got help from the army to take over a business set up by peasants on lands the company had abandoned in 1974. The leader of the army attack, who received special payments from the firm prior to the raid, was Lt. Col. Gustavo Alvarez, the Contras' future patron.[21]

President Melgar lasted only until August 7, 1978, when he was ousted in a coup that brought to power General Policarpo Paz Garcia. It appears that the key financier behind the overthrow of Melgar was Juan Ramón Matta Ballesteros, a leader of the Mexican connection. The rise of Paz Garcia cemented the power of the cocaine lords in Honduran politics and paved the way for an alliance of the military, the drug leaders, and the CIA to support the Contras from bases in Honduras. This "cocaine coup," which preceded by two years the more famous coup in Bolivia, has been neglected by historians. Yet it is of central importance for understanding the corrupting power of drugs in Honduran politics. The events that precipitated the Paz coup began in the spring of 1978. Melgar, who had ambitions to run in elections scheduled for 1980, began pressuring his right-wing military rivals in the newspaper *La Prensa*. Its news pages started linking senior officers to gold and gem smuggling.

The paper also began publishing revelations about the 1977 murder of two members of a drug smuggling ring, Mario and Mary Ferrari. Matta, who was even then known as "chief of the Honduran mafia," was eventually charged with the crime.[22] But the chief representative of Interpol in Honduras, Lt. Juan Angel Barahona, also implicated several unnamed top military officers, adding that they were turning Honduras into a major transit station for cocaine to the North American market. General Paz Garcia, acting as president while Melgar Castro recuperated from an illness in the United States, had Barahona arrested for slander. He then set up a commission under his own leadership to probe evidence of involvement by the armed forces.

But Paz was too close to Matta for a genuine investigation. Melgar's press organ *La Prensa* reported that Paz and Matta were joint owners of a sizeable rural estate northeast of the capital. Melgar's failure to suppress such damaging information cost him his job. That summer, Paz overthrew his fellow officer.[23] Around this time, the DEA learned that Matta was financing a coup in Honduras—almost certainly this one.[24]

The DEA knew all about Matta by the time of the 1978 coup. Arrested at Dulles Airport in 1970 for importing fifty-four pounds of cocaine, he was marked as a major cocaine trafficker long before most of the Colombian families arrived on the scene.[25] In 1973, the DEA considered Matta an important enough target to try entrapping him in a sting.[26] By 1975, U.S. drug agents knew he had teamed up with Alberto Sicilia Falcón's successor, the Mexican drug king Miguel Félix Gallardo, as a prodigious supplier of drugs to the U.S. market through his Colombian and Peruvian connections.[27]

Jimmy Carter's administration chose to overlook its knowledge of Matta's role, perhaps because Paz, unlike Melgar, supported Somoza in his struggle against the Sandinistas. Indeed, Carter overlooked considerations of human rights as well, despite the new regime's repression of labor unions. Economic assistance to Honduras tripled from 1978 to 1980, making it the largest recipient of U.S. aid in Central America. In 1979, Carter sent a special envoy to confer with Paz in Tegucigalpa. In March 1980, Carter hosted Paz at the White House.

Even before the coup, Honduras was a transfer point for half a billion dollars' worth of drugs bound for the United States each year.[28] For the next three years, Matta worked hand in hand with the army to build Honduras up as an even larger cocaine trafficking center.[29] His key contact in 1978–81, besides Paz, was the head of military intelligence (G-2), Col. Leonides Torres Arias.[30]

Paz and Torres were, in turn, the two key contacts of the CIA's chief of Latin American operations, Duane Clarridge. As noted in Chapter 2, he visited them in August 1981 with the vice chief of Argentine military intelligence in order to establish Honduras as a sanctuary for the Contras.[31] Several successors to Torres as head of G-2, who acted as military liaison to the Contras, also had reported ties to the drug trade. (One of them was appointed in 1988 to head a new antidrug unit in the armed forces.)[32] In fact, the CIA relied totally on the cocaine-trafficking military of Honduras to back its plans to overthrow the Sandinista regime in Nicaragua.

The CIA also began relying on Matta in 1983, when his airline, SETCO, began providing air transport for the Honduran-based FDN Contras (see Chapter 1). By 1984, the airline had become the CIA-backed Contra group's chief mover of supplies and personnel, including ammunition, uniforms, and food. The FDN paid for these services through bank accounts established by Oliver North.[33]

Matta's control of SETCO was no mystery to the U.S. government; a Customs report confirmed it as early as May 1983. The CIA may have had even more intimate knowledge; Honduran military sources told two American reporters in 1984 that the airline was "set up by the CIA to carry contra forces and supplies."[34]

Nor was the Honduran military's role in the drug trade any secret from Washington. In 1981, the DEA opened up its first station in Tegucigalpa, reflecting the country's growing importance as a transit point for Colombian cocaine. The agent who staffed the office was Thomas Zepeda. During his two years in the country, Zepeda was able to document the role played by Colonel Torres and other high-ranking Honduran officers with Matta in the drug traffic.[35] When he sought cooperation from the Honduran Navy to catch smugglers' boats, he later recalled, officers would "stall for time, identifying a number of problems, lack of fuel, the boat would be unable to operate." When he finally got official authorization for a patrol run, the smugglers were usually long gone. "It was difficult to conduct an investigation and expect the Honduran authorities to assist in arrests when it was them we were trying to investigate," he observed.[36]

Zepeda's job was doubly difficult. Not only did DEA need the military to help make arrests, but the CIA also needed them to support the Contras. This dependence forced an inevitable showdown between the conflicting U.S. goals of drug enforcement and covert operations. Zepeda and other agents familiar with the Honduran situation proposed empaneling a grand jury to investigate corruption in the military, but the CIA reportedly blocked the move because of its interest in maintaining Contra bases in the country.[37]

As one U.S. official explained bluntly, "If we move against these guys on drugs, they can screw us on the Contras."[38] A DEA agent recalled, "The Pentagon made it clear that we were in the way. They had more important business."[39] Or as a former high-level American diplomat in the region told a reporter, "Without the support of the Honduran military, there would have been no such thing as the Contras. It's that simple. If evidence were developed linking the Honduran military to cocaine trafficking, the administration would have to take action—causing an immediate and conclusive end to the Contras—or purposely turn a blind eye to what was going on. Neither alternative was particularly appealing. So they got rid of [the DEA station] before they were forced into taking a serious look in the first place."[40]

The DEA office in Tegucigalpa was shut down in June 1983, only two years after it opened. The order to close it—without consulting and indeed against the judgment of the agent in charge[41]—was nothing short of astonishing, considering what the DEA knew of Matta's enormous drug business and of the Honduran military's rampant corruption. At a time when the CIA station in Tegucigalpa was being doubled in size, the DEA claimed it did not have sufficient funds to keep its own tiny office open.[42]

The timing of the drug agency's sudden austerity measure is telling. In May 1983, only a month before the DEA moved Zepeda out of Honduras, Customs asked him to investigate Matta's airline SETCO, which was then gearing up to fly supplies for the FDN.[43]

## Drug Airlines, the Calero Family, and the "Arms Supermarket"

The choice of SETCO came shortly after the CIA established a new Contra leadership structure in early 1983, in the wake of the Argentine withdrawal. As part of that changeover, Adolfo Calero, the former manager of Coca-Cola's bottling plant in Nicaragua, joined the political directorate of the FDN as the CIA's favored leader. His brother Mario assumed major responsibility for the Contra supply operation.

Mario had his own special relationship with SETCO and its offshoots. The Kerry report noted that

> One of the pilots selected to fly Contra supply missions for the
> FDN for SETCO was Frank Moss, who has been under
> investigation as an alleged drug trafficker since 1979. . . . In
> addition to flying Contra supply missions through SETCO, Moss
> formed his own company in 1985, Hondu Carib, which also flew
> supplies to the Contras, including weapons and ammunition
> purchased from R. M. Equipment, an arms company controlled
> by Ronald Martin and James McCoy. The FDN's arrangement
> with Moss and Hondu Carib was pursuant to a commercial
> agreement between the FDN's chief supply officer, Mario Calero,
> and Moss, under which Calero was to receive an ownership
> interest in Moss's company. The Subcommittee received

documentation that one Moss plane, a DC-4 N90201, was used to move Contra goods from the United States to Honduras.[44]

The Calero family's link to Hondu Carib was more incriminating than this passage indicates. Hondu Carib was not formed in 1985 by Moss, as the report claims. Instead, his DC-4 was listed to Hondu Carib in a 1983 Customs report that linked the aircraft to several individuals said to be "involved in large-scale narcotics smuggling."[45] The plane was also being watched because an informant said it dropped narcotics on the isolated Louisiana farm of Adler "Barry" Seal, an American who managed the Colombian cartels' shipping operations into the United States (see Chapter 5).[46]

Mario Calero's interest in the same DC-4 and in Hondu Carib became known in 1987 when a second Moss-controlled plane was impounded and searched in Charlotte County, Florida, after dumping what appeared to be a load of drugs. The DEA asserted that the plane was "purchased with drug money for the intent of smuggling drugs." Besides showing signs of having carried marijuana, the plane yielded up documents showing Mario Calero's ownership interest in Hondu Carib, evidence of his involvement in arms exports to Honduras, and a notebook containing the telephone numbers of other Contra leaders and of Robert Owen.[47]

Some indication of the intrigue surrounding this operation comes through in the private memos of Robert Owen to Oliver North. In one memo of February 10, 1986, Owen referred to a DC-4 "used at one time to run drugs," part of whose CIA-selected crew "had criminal records." Owen added, "The company is also one that Mario has been involved with using in the past, only they had a quick name change."[48] In another memo, Owen complained to North about the "liars and greed motivated" people around Adolfo Calero, lamented that Adolfo would not respond to U.S. government attempts to remove his brother Mario, and transmitted unconfirmed reports that both Adolfo and Mario Calero had bank accounts in Switzerland.[49]

R. M. Equipment, the American arms company that used Hondu Carib's DC-4 to export war supplies from Miami to the Contras, was also touched by accusations of involvement in the drug traffic. Ronald Martin had been an associate of the CIA station in Miami since the anti-Castro operations of the 1960s, and his partner James McCoy was a former U.S. military attaché in Managua under Somoza and a close friend of Adolfo Calero from that period.[50] Martin responded to the Boland Amendment that cut off CIA aid in October 1984 by organizing in Honduras what North called a "munitions 'supermarket,' " which North soon bypassed by forcing Adolfo Calero to receive arms only from Richard Secord.[51] Although Calero's records showed purchases of $2,095,000 in arms from Martin and McCoy, Martin's attorney later confirmed to the *Washington Post* that the two weapons brokers accumulated "$15 million to $20 million" in undelivered arms and ammunition in a warehouse in Honduras.[52]

Where did they get the money? North recorded in his diary that "$14 million to finance" the Martin-McCoy arms supermarket "came from drugs."[53] Assistant Secretary of State Elliott Abrams and CIA officer Alan Fiers passed the same allegation to the House and Senate intelligence committees, according to a *Newsweek* source.[54]

North and other administration officials probably heard this gossip from Secord, Martin's rival for the lucrative Contra arms trade. Martin's goal, according to Secord, was to monopolize arms shipments to Honduras. "Martin bought Honduras," Secord told author Leslie Cockburn. "It only takes a few million dollars to buy Honduras." Wondering where the money came from to establish Martin's "thirty-million-dollar supermarket," Secord said he "sent investigators to check it out. They thought some of the money was coming from drugs."[55]

Martin vigorously denied the allegation to a Senate investigator, raising the possibility that Secord's information was incorrect and even intended to damage Martin.[56] Rob Owen's memos to Oliver North corroborate a growing fight in 1986 between one team led by Martin and McCoy and another led by Secord for control of the arms trade. In March 1986, Owen told North that a number of people were talking about Secord's arms sales, "in all probability . . . because they want a part of the action." He added that Adolfo Calero "may even have thought Seacords [*sic*] was the one behind his not being able to buy from the [Martin-McCoy] Supermarket in Honduras."[57]

Martin and McCoy did not give up easily. They had a well-connected "arranger" in Honduras, Mario Dellamico, who gave Secord a run for his money. In June 1986, North referred in his diary to a connection between Dellamico and former CIA agent Gustavo Villoldo, who North had previously heard was "involved with drugs" (see Chapter 2).[58] (The next day, North met with DEA Administrator Jack Lawn to discuss ways in which two drug agents, then assigned to North for covert duties in the Middle East related to hostage rescue efforts, could deal with Villoldo, possibly to take Dellamico out of the picture.)[59] In September 1986, retired general John Singlaub warned North that Dellamico was also close to Villoldo's former CIA partner Félix Rodríguez, a fierce critic of Secord's arms procurement practices.[60]

These connections made Dellamico a formidable arms agent. Singlaub reported that Dellamico's Honduran friend and military intelligence chief, Col. Hector Aplicano, had a stranglehold on military business with the Contras. After arranging an arms shipment to the Contras in the spring of 1986, Secord heard from the Honduran chief of staff: "From now on you will buy from us," he said, which Secord took to mean Martin.[61]

Whatever the truth about the arms supermarket, drug money injected into some branch of the Contra arms pipeline would explain the discrepancy in 1984 and 1985 between acknowledged sources of cash for the anti-Sandinista movement and its actual expenses. The U.S. Ambassador to Honduras, John Ferch, suspected at the time that drugs were financing the shipments of Contra arms that suddenly began arriving in Honduras around the time of the U.S. cutoff in military aid in October 1984. But because the DEA had shut down its station in mid-1983, there was no agent to investigate.[62]

### Bueso Rosa and the Cocaine Coup of 1984

The DEA station closing was only one indicator of where Washington's priorities lay. Between 1982 and 1987, the Reagan administration lavished more than $335 million on the Honduran military for equipment and training, on top of $836 million in economic aid. This avalanche of dollars signaled to the military that Washington would "just forget about questions about drug trafficking," as one Christian Democratic member of the Honduran congress complained.[63]

Much as they wanted to, however, top Reagan administration officials could not forget about Honduran officer Gen. José Bueso Rosa, convicted on charges of conspiring to murder the president of Honduras with financing from a huge cocaine shipment. But senior members of the NSC, the Pentagon, and the State Department arranged a lenient sentence at a minimum-security prison to honor his services to the Contras.

On October 28, 1984, FBI agents seized 763 pounds of cocaine, worth more than $10 million wholesale, at a remote airstrip in southern Florida. A successful sting operation rounded up the entire gang, which included one of the richest men in Honduras, the international arms dealer Gerard Latchinian, and the former chief of staff of the Honduran army, General Bueso Rosa, who had a reputation among drug traffickers as a man who would provide security in Honduras for a price.[64]

Both of these defendants had ties to the Contras or their direct supporters. Bueso Rosa had been instrumental in setting up the CIA's logistics and training support for the rebels. Latchinian was a former business partner of Félix Rodríguez, who took charge of the Contra supply line in El Salvador, and an associate of Pesakh Ben-Or, an Israeli arms dealer based in Guatemala who shipped weapons to the Contras.[65]

The purpose of the drug shipment was to finance a coup and assassination plot against the elected president of Honduras, Roberto Suazo Cordova. Bueso Rosa and his coconspirators apparently hoped to reinstate retired Gen. Gustavo Alvarez Martinez, Bueso's former boss and patron of the Contras, who had been forced into retirement that March.[66] Alvarez had left the country for the United States, where he stayed for a time in Latchinian's Miami home.[67] Although implicated in Argentine-inspired death squad killings from his days as head of the police and army, Alvarez for a time found a comfortable niche in exile, working as a consultant to the Pentagon.[68]

The Honduran coup plotters approached two former U.S. Army commando leaders to organize the hit team, promising them $300,000, twenty pounds of cocaine, a jet, and all manner of high-tech weapons. Unfortunately for the ringleaders, these recruits went to the FBI and turned them all in.[69]

The cocaine to finance this plot, according to Latchinian, came from the chief of police of Honduras, who had approached one of the coconspirators for advice on how to dispose of more than a ton of the drug in the United States.[70]

Bueso Rosa was convicted in 1986 on murder-for-hire conspiracy charges. The Justice Department called his plot "the most significant case of narco-terrorism yet discovered."[71] Yet one current and one retired senior U.S. government official testified in his behalf at the sentencing, and the administration filed a sealed deposition to urge leniency.[72] "General Bueso Rosa has always been a valuable ally to the United States," it read. "As chief of staff of the Honduran armed forces he immeasurably furthered the United States' national interest in Central America. He is primarily responsible for the initial success of the American military preserve in Honduras. For this service, he was awarded the Legion of Merit by the president of the United States, the highest award that can be presented to a foreign military officer."[73]

This information prompted the judge to give Bueso what one senior Justice Department official termed a "lenient sentence." He was made eligible for immediate parole despite conspiring to assassinate a foreign head of state.[74] Yet Oliver North at the National Security Council urged that the administration intervene to make the sentence lighter still.

In a note to National Security Adviser John Poindexter, North pointed out the "problem" with the Bueso case: the general had been the man with whom four senior administration officials, including North himself, had "worked out arrangements" for logistics, training, and other support of the Contras.[75] During the trial, North observed, Bueso's lawyer had prepared subpoenas for all four officials but never issued them because Bueso pleaded guilty, believing that he would be going to a minimum security facility "for a short period [days or weeks] and then walk free."[76] "Our major concern," he continued, ". . . is that when Bueso finds out what is really happening to him, he will break his longstanding silence about the Nic[araguan] Resistance and other sensitive operations."

North added that he and other officials planned to "cabal quietly in the morning to look at options: pardon, clemency, deportation, reduced sentence. Objective is to keep Bueso from feeling like he was lied to in legal process and start spilling the beans."[77] Poindexter replied, "You may advise all concerned that the President will want to be as helpful as possible to settle this matter."[78]

Despite pressures from the CIA and the Pentagon, the State and Justice Departments blocked efforts to grant Bueso immediate parole. In the end, the Justice Department refused to agree to clemency or deportation, but it did arrange for Bueso to be housed in the minimum-security facility at Eglin Air Force Base in Florida, where he apparently decided not to talk.[79]

No less a figure than former Ambassador to Costa Rica Francis McNeil has concluded from this extraordinary attempt at cover-up that "the circumstantial evidence is such that one has to wonder if there is not a narcotics angle" behind the administration's back-room maneuvering. McNeil added, "Colonel North is quoted as saying in his note to Poindexter about the subject of getting Bueso Rosa off from serving any time that Bueso Rosa could sing songs we don't want to hear. And my question is, What were those songs? Were they about narcotics or possibly something else?"[80]

## Capturing Matta, Sparing the Military

Corrupt officers who stayed on Honduran soil, unlike Bueso, had nothing to worry about. In return for various forms of aid and protection from harassment by local U.S. drug agents,[81] Honduran military commanders gave the CIA carte blanche. By 1988 the U.S. embassy in that tiny, impoverished country had swollen to more than three hundred employees, making it one of the largest diplomatic outposts in the world. (To meet the needs of all those personnel, the embassy rented two houses owned by Matta.)[82] "Its principal tasks are to direct the Contra war and to insure that Honduras cooperates fully with United States strategy in Central America," observed the *New York Times*. "American diplomats exercise more control over domestic politics in Honduras than in any other country in the hemisphere, and in private that fact is universally acknowledged here."[83]

Since no one bothered to exercise any control over drug corruption in those years, however, smuggling activity picked up markedly.[84] After Matta returned to Honduras in 1986, having spent $2 million to bribe his way out of a Colombian prison, there followed what one scholar called an "explosive growth of [cocaine] shipments through Honduras into Mexico."[85] In 1987 U.S. officials confiscated two shipments of cocaine from Honduras totalling 6.7 tons. The second, amounting to more than 8,000 pounds, was "the largest such seizure ever made in the United States" at that time.[86] U.S. government investigators determined that it went "right to the doorstep of the Honduran military."[87] The cocaine in turn came from the leaders of Colombia's Cali cartel, with whom Matta dealt directly.[88] By 1987, Honduras accounted for anywhere between a fifth and a half of all the cocaine entering the U.S. market, a staggering record. The banana republic had become a cocaine republic.[89]

In November 1987, the Honduran military attaché to Colombia, an officer distinguished for his services to the Contras, was implicated as a close associate of the Medellín cartel leader Jorge Ochoa. The officer, Col. William Said Speer, had been a prominent backer of the Contras' chief Honduran goods supplier, the Hermano Pedro Supermarket. Its multimillion dollar business with the rebels, paid for out of humanitarian funds from Washington, offered ample resources for commissions and bribes. Rival officers organized a police raid on the owner's house in August 1986. They succeeded in forcing him to sell out and move to Miami, even though Said tried to intervene on his behalf. As a result of this power struggle, Said lost his command in a shakeup orchestrated by the new chief of staff, Gen. Humberto Regalado, and the chief of police, Col. Leonel Riera Lunati.[90]

The two Honduran officers responsible for the ouster of Ochoa's friend Said may not have been any cleaner. Regalado and Riera frequently socialized with Matta, who lived in an opulent mansion in Tegucigalpa under their protection. Although Assistant Secretary of State Abrams, a Contra supporter, praised their extensive record of cooperation against drugs, another official in the department charged that Regalado "turned a blind eye to drug shipments" for a price and that "all of the senior officers" were "reaping the profits." At least two convicted cocaine smugglers, including Regalado's own half-brother, linked him to drugs. Regalado himself vigorously denied the charges. But his denial leaves the question of how Matta managed, under the military's eye, to buy a security company, hire retired Honduran officers as bodyguards, and acquire a permit to carry automatic weapons.[91]

A subsequent report of the Honduran Special Drug Traffic Investigation Commission explained how Matta and other drug traffickers befriended top commanders: "They propose business partnerships with them, they obtain credentials as collaborators of the security corps, and even get their wives to make false friendships with the officers' wives."[92]

The U.S. embassy had no illusions about these relationships. According to accounts from Honduras, the DEA had information linking five top members of the armed forces with the drug traffic but was "persuaded not to act on its information" in late 1987 "so as not to endanger Honduran cooperation in the contra war."[93] However, faced with enormous cocaine seizures from Honduras, the DEA did make preparations to reopen its office in Tegucigalpa early the next year.[94]

The CIA had independent confirmation of these facts. One of its Honduran informants, the brother of one of Matta's front men in SETCO, was arrested in Texas on cocaine-smuggling charges in January 1987. He told the court, "Colombia and Nicaragua are flying loads of drugs to Honduras. They're paying off officials, military officials, to allow this exchange of one plane for a clean plane of Honduras so that then they can transport drugs over into this country." These transactions occurred, he intimated, at Honduran bases thick with U.S. military personnel. After CIA intervention, a federal prosecutor dropped charges against this informant in a closed court hearing.[95]

Not until April 1988, after Congress had terminated military assistance to the Contras, did Washington finally move to force the extradition of Matta, who had been wanted since 1985 for the murder of Mexico-based DEA agent Enrique Camarena.

Although General Regalado received a medal for "extraordinary leadership" from the U.S. Marshal Service for Matta's capture, he and Riera reportedly acted only in order to keep their names and those of other officers from being publicly linked with drug trafficking.[96] If that allegation is true, Washington in effect sanctioned continued high-level Honduran drug corruption in return for the capture of a single important but ultimately replaceable smuggler.

# 4  Noriega and the Contras
## *Guns, Drugs, and the Harari Network*

Regional influences, both political and criminal, fueled the explosive growth of drug trafficking through Honduras in the early 1980s. In 1980 and 1981, for example, the head of military intelligence in Panama, then-Col. Manuel Noriega, teamed up with his counterpart at the head of the Honduran G-2, Colonel Torres, to smuggle first arms (on behalf of Marxist rebels in El Salvador) and then drugs.[1] Torres, as we noted, became one of the Contras' most important patrons.

Noriega's malign influence spread to Costa Rica as well. A Costa Rican legislative commission concluded in 1989 that Noriega helped install in that country at least seven pilots who ran guns to the Contras and drugs to North America. "More serious still," it added, "is the obvious infiltration of international gangs into Costa Rica that made use of the [Contra] organization. These requests for Contra help were initiated by Colonel North to General Noriega. They opened a gate so their henchmen utilized the national territory for trafficking in arms and drugs."[2]

As that finding suggests, Noriega's reach extended far beyond Central America to Washington. Indeed, his relationship with U.S. intelligence helps account both for his own long-standing immunity from American law enforcement and for his ability to promote corrupt elements of the Contra support movement.

Noriega was first recruited as an agent by the U.S. Defense Intelligence Agency in 1959, while still a young military cadet studying in Peru. He went on the CIA's payroll in 1967. The next year, a military coup assisted by the U.S. Army's 470th Military Intelligence Group gave Noriega his opportunity to take charge of Panama's own G-2. His new job made him a priceless source for the American services, which used Panama as a listening post for much of Latin America.[3]

Before long, however, Washington discovered its protégé's criminal bent. As early as May 1971 the Bureau of Narcotics and Dangerous Drugs heard serious allegations of Noriega's involvement in trafficking. A former chief of staff to Gen. Omar Torrijos, Panama's military ruler, settled in Miami after botching a coup attempt. He revealed to U.S. authorities that Noriega had "overall operational control" of the officially sanctioned narcotics trade in Panama. The BNDD actually amassed enough evidence to indict him in a major marijuana smuggling case, only to run up against practical objections from the U.S. Attorney's office in Miami: no one in those days could imagine invading Panama to bring a senior officer to justice.[4]

In January 1972, BNDD director John Ingersoll asked his staff to evaluate alternative means of taking action against corrupt Panamanian leaders, particularly Noriega. According to an unpublished report of the Senate Select Committee on Intelligence, five major options emerged for cracking down on him: "linking the official [Noriega] to a fictitious plot against General Torrijos; leaking information on drug trafficking to the press; linking his removal to the Panama Canal negotiations; secretly encouraging powerful groups within Panama to raise the issue; and 'total and complete immobilization.' " Although this final option was quickly rejected, "some were put into action," according to the Justice Department. Indeed, one top BNDD official, who had proposed that Noriega be killed, passed reports of a plot against Torrijos on to the CIA for transmission to Panama. The motive may have been to discredit Noriega and let Torrijos do the dirty work of removing him.[5]

Intent on negotiating a new Panama Canal treaty, however, the State Department put other foreign policy objectives ahead of law enforcement and persuaded BNDD to back off.[6] A long honeymoon began—and Panama's economy boomed under the stimulus of drug dollars attracted to its modern and secretive banking sector.

By 1976, Noriega was fully forgiven. CIA Director George Bush arranged to pay Noriega $110,000 a year for his services, put the Panamanian up as a houseguest of his deputy CIA director, and helped to prevent an embarrassing prosecution of several American soldiers who had delivered highly classified U.S. intelligence secrets to Noriega's men.[7]

Republicans had no monopoly on covering up for the Panamanian colonel. The Carter administration, although it dropped Noriega from its payroll, did its best to suppress any public disclosure of the Torrijos regime's involvement in the drug trade in order to salvage a Panama Canal treaty. But the truth was no secret to government officials. A former Senate Intelligence Committee member recalled from that period, "We had a very complete picture. We knew about the drug problem. And the Panamanians knew we knew it. Once we ratified the treaty, the Panamanians got the word that the United States was open for the drug business."[8]

If Carter needed friends in Panama to smooth the way to a canal treaty, Reagan (who strongly opposed that treaty) needed them to support the Contra cause. Noriega's intelligence and smuggling facilities could be useful, as could his influence on other Central American military leaders. CIA payments to Noriega resumed when Reagan took office in 1981, starting at $185,000 a year. At their peak, in 1985, Noriega collected $200,000 from the Agency.[9] The CIA deposited the money in Noriega's account at the Bank of Credit and Commerce International, two of whose units later pleaded guilty to laundering drug money.[10] CIA Director William Casey frequently met with Noriega alone in Washington.[11]

Noriega earned his pay. He supplied pilots who helped smuggle weapons to the Contras. He tried, at the CIA's urging, to persuade Southern Front Contra leader Edén Pastora to unite with the main FDN Contra faction. In July 1984, he contributed $100,000 to Contra leaders based in Costa Rica. In March 1985, Noriega helped Oliver North plan and carry out a major sabotage raid in Managua, using the services of a British mercenary. In 1985, responding to pleas from Casey, he promised to help train Contra units and let them use Panama as a transit point. In September 1986, North met Noriega in London; the two discussed further sabotage against Nicaraguan economic targets, including an oil refinery, an airport, and the electric and telephone systems. North's diary indicates that Noriega offered the aid of skilled (probably Israeli) commandos, including one who "killed head of PLO in Brt [Beirut]." The two men also considered setting up a school for commandos that could "train experts" in such matters as "booby traps," "night ops," and "raids."[12]

Noriega also allowed members of North's Enterprise to set up Panamanian corporate fronts to disguise the financing of Contra supplies. As noted in Chapter 1, one such front, Amalgamated Commercial Enterprises, used the services of the drug-linked Banco de Iberoamerica. A related dummy company, which did business with the same bank, purchased arms for the Contras through Manzer al-Kassar, the Syrian arms and drug broker, who also dealt with leaders of the Medellín Cartel.[13] Noriega's personal lawyer and business representative in Geneva also set up a front to establish an airfield in Costa Rica for supplying the Contras.[14]

Evidence gathered by Costa Rican judicial authorities suggests that Noriega's intelligence operatives also helped the CIA and its allies in the Costa Rican security services obstruct the investigation of an assassination attempt against Pastora by peddling disinformation about the main suspect's background. The bombing of Pastora's press conference at La Penca on May 30, 1984, which killed several journalists and an aide to Pastora but missed the rebel leader himself, was most likely planned by hard-liners in the Contra movement close to the CIA, according to an official Costa Rican probe. The Noriega connection to the La Penca cover-up is significant since, according to Floyd Carlton, his former friend and drug partner, "there are some officers who are connected to the intelligence services of Costa Rica which to a certain extent are the creation of General Noriega. They have been trained in Panama . . . and these people keep a certain . . . loyalty to General Noriega."[15]

Carlton's allegation of Panamanian influence in Costa Rica received support from another Noriega confidant, José Blandón. Blandón testified before Kerry's subcommittee that Noriega bought influence in Costa Rica's National Liberation and Social Christian Unity parties. In 1985, according to Blandón, Noriega paid $500,000 to the presidential candidate of the anti-Sandinista Social Christian Unity Party because "it was very important to control the government of Costa Rica."[16] A Noriega-controlled Panamanian political party reportedly gave some $54,000 to the rival National Liberation Party at the same time, perhaps as insurance.[17] The question arises of whether Noriega coordinated this alleged electoral operation and intelligence penetration with the CIA; as yet, it is unanswerable.

Even as he was serving Washington's interests, Noriega was also doing business with major traffickers. One of them was Steven Kalish, who smuggled hundreds of tons of marijuana into the United States. (His network included Michael Palmer, arrested by Michigan authorities in 1986 while holding a State Department contract to assist with humanitarian aid to the Contras.)[18] In September 1983, Kalish flew to Panama and made contact with César Rodríguez, Noriega's personal pilot and a successful businessman. Rodríguez offered corporate, banking, and investment services to launder the huge sums of cash that Kalish generated—enough to fill entire rooms. Rodríguez introduced Kalish to Noriega as his partner. After leaving Noriega a suitcase filled with $300,000 cash, the first of several such payments, Kalish became a full partner in Servicios Turisticos, an airline owned by Rodríguez, Noriega, and another smuggler. He also got special military protection for shipments of money into the country and a Panamanian diplomatic passport. Kalish claimed that in 1984 he won the trust of the Medellín cartel by arranging to free some Colombians jailed in Panama after police raided a cocaine processing plant in Panama's Darién province. But that July, before the relationship could blossom,

Kalish was arrested in Tampa. He asserted that he made hundreds of thousands of dollars in payoffs to Noriega in less than a year.[19]

A more direct link between Noriega, drugs, and the Contras can be found in the careers of Floyd Carlton, also a Noriega confidant, and Alfredo Caballero, a Miami-based Cuban exile, Bay of Pigs veteran, and friend of Mario Calero, the chief supply officer for the Honduras-based Contras.[20]

Carlton's first contact with Noriega came in 1966, when the young Panamanian officer offered him a bribe to fix some court records. Twelve years later, the powerful intelligence chief recruited Carlton along with Rodríguez to fly weapons into Nicaragua for the Sandinistas. In 1982, a Colombian trafficker named Francisco Chavez Hill offered Carlton a deal. "He wanted to introduce me to some very powerful individuals from Colombia," Carlton testified. "The deal which he proposed was that I would take money from the United States to Panama. They had seen we enjoyed a certain type of 'immunity.' " Carlton went with Chavez to Medellín, where he met drug lords Pablo Escobar and Gustavo Gaviria in person. They talked cocaine, not money. Carlton begged off, saying he would have to consult his boss—whom the Colombians knew to be Noriega. Noriega, angry at first, soon agreed to let Carlton fly drugs, but only in non-Panamanian aircraft and only for a cut. Noriega's starting fee for using Panama as a drug base was $100,000 per trip, according to Carlton; the sum quickly climbed to $200,000. Carlton received $400 per kilogram to fly loads from Colombia into government-controlled airstrips in Panama.[21] His main Colombian connection was Fabio Ochoa, a leader of the Medellín cartel.[22]

In 1984 Noriega ordered an end to the flights through Panama. Carlton then went into business elsewhere, first in Nicaragua (where he was arrested and deported) and subsequently in Costa Rica, using remote airstrips to accommodate his loads. Between October 1984 and June 1985, his ring moved at least 4,000 kg of cocaine through Costa Rica. One Costa Rican member of Carlton's network, Eduardo Zapparolli, was described in court testimony by Edén Pastora as an important "collaborator" who helped his Contra group locate supply airstrips. Another Carlton associate, Edwin Viales, was a colonel in the Costa Rican rural guard who tried to bribe a fellow officer to leave a secret Contra airstrip unguarded two days a week (whether for drugs or other purposes remains unclear). Viales told a Costa Rican judge, "The politics of the government were totally open to help the Nicaraguan counterrevolution. . . . I had higher orders to directly help everyone who was providing humanitarian aid for the Contras." Both Zapparolli and Viales eventually received ten-year sentences in Costa Rica for their drug crimes.[23]

Business went well for Carlton in Costa Rica until mid-1985, when he suffered the first of several setbacks. One of his pilots and a $3 million shipment of cocaine simply disappeared in Costa Rica. Carlton's Colombian suppliers accused him of theft and dispatched a hit man; only Escobar's timely intervention saved him. Carlton himself concluded that Zapparolli had probably killed the pilot, flown the drugs to John Hull's farm, and used the proceeds to buy arms for the Contras (see Chapter 6).[24]

Carlton was ultimately arrested in Costa Rica in 1986 after his former chief of operations in the cocaine transportation business, Alfredo Caballero, began cooperating with law enforcement authorities. As Chapter 1 shows, Caballero's airplane supply company DIACSA, partly owned by Costa Rican interests, laundered funds for the FDN Contras, strongly suggesting that it had ties with the CIA. It also earned more than $41,000 from the State Department's Contra supply program even while under investigation for drug crimes. Caballero was indicted in January 1986 for helping to import 900 pounds of cocaine to the United States and launder $2.6 million in drug proceeds. He was sentenced to only five years' probation in return for his cooperation.[25]

The Reagan administration may not have known every detail of these and other transactions, but it surely knew the general outlines long before it stopped conspiring with Noriega against the Sandinistas. As former National Security Council official Norman Bailey testified, "Clear and incontrovertible evidence was, at best, ignored, and at worst, hidden and denied by many different agencies and departments of the government of the United States in such a way as to provide cover and protection for [Noriega's] activities."[26]

Some of the information even leaked into the public record. Senate investigators reported in late 1982 that Panama's National Guard had "ties to and income from various traffickers in drugs, arms and other contraband, as well as fugitives." They also disclosed that the Guard "provides warehousing for narcotics on their way north, assures the release, for bribes received, of drug traffickers arrested, guarantees the non-arrest of offenders wanted elsewhere who have paid a kind of local 'safe conduct' fee, [and] supervises the air transport of gold, arms, spies bound to and from North America, Cuba and Central America."[27] By 1983, according to former Customs Commissioner William Von Raab, U.S. agencies had "more than enough evidence of General Noriega's involvement in the narcotics trade."[28]

In early 1985, the House Foreign Affairs Committee staff reported, "Corruption continues to be one of the biggest obstacles to effective anti-narcotics action in Panama. As one knowledgeable US source put it, 'the Panamanian Defense Force is the axle around which the wheel of corruption turns.' This corruption is endemic and institutionalized; in fact, under previous governments members of the PDF were encouraged to take second 'jobs,' including drug trafficking, to supplement their income. Allegations persist that high-ranking military officers are involved in protection or actual trafficking themselves."[29] In June 1986, the *New York Times* and NBC News ran lengthy and sensational exposés of Noriega's corruption and brutality, based largely on administration sources.[30]

None of these allegations apparently made any impression on Vice President George Bush, coordinator of the Reagan administration's War on Drugs. Bush claimed during the 1988 presidential campaign to have known little or nothing of Noriega's narcotics dealings. Perhaps he was kept in the dark by his top drug aide, Adm. Daniel Murphy, who declared in September 1988, "I never saw any intelligence suggesting General Noriega's involvement in the drug trade. In fact, we always held up Panama as the model in terms of cooperation with the United States in the war on drugs."[31] Murphy may have seen only what he wanted to see. In 1987, as a private but well-connected businessman, he visited Noriega with Tongsun Park, notorious for his role in a Korean influence-peddling scandal on Capitol Hill, to discuss ways of smoothing over relations between Panama and the United States. The outcome was disastrous; Noriega understood Murphy to be conveying a message from the White House, the Pentagon, and the CIA that with cosmetic reforms he could stay in power. That misunderstanding stiffened Noriega's resolve to remain in Panama and turned the Reagan administration irrevocably against him.[32]

Nor did the steady stream of facts and allegations against Noriega matter to officials spearheading the Contra operation. In August 1986, only two months after Noriega's battering in the American media, North and the CIA's Duane Clarridge discussed a request from Noriega for help in countering his bad publicity in return for assassinating the Sandinista leadership. Far from recoiling at the proposition, North recorded in his diary that they talked of "five steps . . . to clean up image."[33] Within days, North gave his approval for a public relations firm, which handled much of North's fund-raising for the Contras, to represent Panamanian government interests. And as noted above, North did meet with Noriega that September, with National Security Adviser John Poindexter's approval, to review sabotage missions in Nicaragua.[34]

The allegations against Noriega mattered least of all to the CIA, which prized him as an asset.[35] In 1986, author James Mills revealed that "When the DEA boss in Panama City suggested an SFIP (Special Field Intelligence Program) to unravel the shadowy background of billions of dollars of Panama-stashed drug money, he sought necessary approval from the CIA station chief. The station chief agreed, but with an interesting reservation. If the SFIP developed any information involving Panamanian government officials, that particular aspect of the investigation must be immediately dropped."[36]

Noriega lost his most ardent defenders within the administration, North and Casey, when the Iran-Contra scandal blew up in November 1986. As the whole White House program of covert support for the Contras came crashing down, Noriega suddenly became expendable. In January 1987, the Costa Rican government extradited Floyd Carlton to the United States, triggering the events that led to Noriega's indictment in Miami in early 1988. Prosecutors charged Noriega with accepting millions of dollars in bribes to facilitate cocaine shipments and money laundering by the Medellín cartel.

The political intrigues that first attracted the administration to Noriega and ultimately repelled it will take years to uncover fully. The CIA never turned over its files on Noriega to federal prosecutors. The National Security Council ordered agencies to refuse congressional requests for information that would illuminate the policy debates.[37] However, it seems clear that official approval of Noriega's indictment and subsequent military capture had as much to do with politics as with law enforcement.[38] After the June 1986 media revelations about Noriega, an interagency meeting of senior administration policy makers decided to "put Noriega on the shelf until Nicaragua was settled."[39] After Noriega's indictment in early 1988, one State Department official commented, "We don't know anything today about Tony Noriega that we didn't know a year ago. What's changed is politics and Panama, not Tony Noriega."[40] And as the *New York Times* observed (almost four years to the day after it branded him Central America's leading criminal), Noriega's alleged drug dealing was "relatively small scale by Latin American standards. . . . American officials strongly suspect high-ranking military officers in Honduras, Guatemala and El Salvador of similar, and in some cases even greater involvement in drug dealing—yet have not taken harsh action against them."[41]

Perhaps the most striking evidence of a political double standard was the silence of the Bush administration on the composition of the postinvasion regime. The U.S.-installed president of Panama, Guillermo Endara, had been a director and secretary of Banco Interoceanico, targeted by the

FBI and DEA and named by Floyd Carlton as a major front for laundering Colombian drug money.[42] The bank reportedly served both the Cali and Medellín cartels.[43] Endara's business partner Carlos Eleta, who reportedly laundered CIA funds into Endara's presidential campaign in the spring of 1989, was arrested in April of that year in Georgia for allegedly conspiring to import more than half a ton of cocaine into the United States each month. Prosecutors dropped the indictment following the invasion, citing lack of evidence.[44]

Washington issued no public protest when Endara appointed to the key posts of attorney general, treasury minister, and chief justice of the supreme court three former directors of First Interamericas Bank, an institution controlled by the Cali cartel and used to wash its drug money. Panamanian authorities took over the bank in 1985 and liquidated its assets—an action hailed by U.S. authorities as the government's first major action against a money-laundering operation.[45] Noriega's move against the bank may have been less than altruistic, however; a lawyer for the Cali interests complained that Noriega made a practice of turning in rivals of the Medellín cartel.[46]

## The Harari Network

One of the deepest mysteries surrounding Noriega and the Contras regards the so-called Harari network, named after a senior Israeli intelligence officer and Noriega confidant, Michael Harari.

Harari has become a lightning rod for rumors and conspiracy theories regarding all manner of Central American intrigues. In the early 1970s, as the number-three man in Mossad (the Israeli intelligence agency), he helped lead Israel's effort to assassinate suspected Palestinian terrorists.[47] After a foul-up in which he had the wrong man killed, Harari transferred to Mexico, where he reportedly became Mossad's station chief for Latin America. Later he "retired" and went to Panama, where he became a trusted security adviser to General Noriega and a trainer of his elite personal bodyguard unit, UESAT. Most authorities believe he never retired at all, but remained an unofficial agent of Israeli influence (and arms sales) in Panama.[48] Shortly before the U.S. invasion, he was reported to be supervising a group of at least ten other Israelis involved in "security assistance and counseling to Noriega."[49] Despite official U.S. complaints to the Israeli government about his role in Panama, Harari reportedly received the honorary rank of colonel in the Israeli army.[50] He escaped Panama during the U.S. invasion, apparently with American help, and returned to Israel.[51]

José Blandón told the Kerry subcommittee that Harari arranged arms purchases in Europe on Noriega's behalf to help the Sandinistas in their struggle against President Somoza in the late 1970s. From this experience, the subcommittee concluded, Noriega expanded his lucrative sales and became a major arms conduit first to the Salvadoran rebels and then to the Contras. "Noriega put his pilots to work flying weapons from Panama to Costa Rica for the Contras. . . . Many of the pilots moved mixed cargoes of guns and drugs to the bases in Costa Rica, dropped off the guns and flew on to the United States with drugs."[52]

Blandón also testified that "convincing evidence . . . links the Harari network" to Central American airstrips used by the traffickers. "The Harari network," he explained, "is a network that was established with Israeli citizens, Panamanians, and United States citizens for arms supply purposes" between 1982 or 1983 and 1986. He agreed with Senator Kerry that through the Harari network, "guns would go in one shipment and drugs would come out in another."[53]

Blandón and another "senior Panamanian official" told reporter Frederick Kempe that "Noriega's political adviser at the time, Michael Harari, made contacts through CIA Latin American directorate chief Duane Clarridge and President Bush's National Security Adviser Donald Gregg to establish a network of airfields and support for the Contras." Gregg, however, denied any involvement in the operation or that he ever met Harari.[54]

Blandón's story received substantial elaboration from Richard Brenneke, a self-styled arms dealer from Portland, Oregon. Brenneke told the subcommittee that he "was asked by Mossad agents to act as a purchasing agent for the operation, and brokered purchases of East-bloc weapons out of Czechoslovakia." He also claimed that "the same planes used to ship the arms were then used to fly cocaine from Colombia through Panama to the United States in an arrangement with the Medellín cocaine cartel in Colombia." Brenneke asserted that he had been recruited for this work in 1983 by the Guatemala-based Israeli arms dealer Pesakh Ben-Or, who in turn put him in touch with Gregg.[55]

An investigative report by ABC News fleshed out the story, adding that Israel had put up $20 million to finance the Harari operation. It quoted one anonymous pilot who allegedly flew arms into Costa Rica and El Salvador and drugs back to the United States: "I guess you'd have to say at that time, I felt my primary employer was Israel. Secondarily, my employer was the U.S. of America." Brenneke, interviewed on the same newscast, explained, "Typically, the drugs were run through Panama and into the United States. The pilots were in most cases working for the cartels. If the shipments were extremely sensitive, you'd see Israeli pilots and aircraft."[56]

Later Brenneke told yet another interviewer that Harari had instructed him to go to Medellín to "pay my respects" to the drug lords. He claimed to have told Gregg all about the drug problem in late 1985, only to be reminded to "do what you were assigned to do. Don't question the decisions of your betters."[57]

Brenneke's ambiguous record justifies special caution toward such sensational allegations. When the Kerry subcommittee undertook an "exhaustive effort" to assess his credibility, it didn't like what it found. Careful analysis of government files indicated that "he spent considerable effort unsuccessfully in trying to become an intelligence agent and when that failed, an arms dealer." Contrary to his claims, the subcommittee observed, "The records show that Brenneke was never officially connected to U.S. intelligence and that he was never tasked by a U.S. intelligence agency to gather information." Although Brenneke did develop a wealth of international contacts while trying to break into the arms business, "he did not produce any evidence of any business transacted" nor even "any evidence that he was reimbursed for any of the expenses he incurred while trying to arrange arms deals."[58]

Other independent bits and pieces of evidence, however, suggest that stories of Israeli agents and drugs in Central America may contain some truth. Military special operations veteran and mercenary trainer Frank Camper shed some light on the matter in his testimony before the Kerry subcommittee. In early 1984, according to Camper, a Panamanian agent approached him to purchase equipment for General Noriega's UESAT unit. Camper said he discovered that "the Israeli Mossad had primary responsibility for training and equipping the unit with some special equipment they couldn't obtain from the United States." The same UESAT agent who recruited Camper then asked him to meet some representatives of the Medellín cartel who were staying at the same hotel in Panama. "I was being requested to provide shoulder-fired heatseeking antiaircraft missiles for the use of the Medellín [cartel]," Camper recalled, "and also an illegal helicopter, which would have been a Bell 212 or 412 type. And I was shown $4 million cash in American dollars as evidence that these people had the means to pay and were serious about doing business." In the course of the same mission, Camper said he heard "military representatives from across Central America" discuss "drug trafficking and weapons shipments in and out of Panama and Costa Rica . . . connected with the Contra resupply effort."[59]

Other odd connections prove nothing but remain suggestive. In Honduras, Gerard Latchinian, the arms dealer convicted of a cocaine-financed assassination plot against President Suazo (see Chapter 3), brought the

Israeli security firm ISDS into the country to train bodyguards for Army Chief of Staff Gen. Gustavo Alvarez Martinez, and, according to Alvarez's successor, members of a Contra death squad.[60] Honduran military sources said that one Israeli principal of ISDS, Emil Saada, supplied Israeli arms to the Contras.[61] Saada also had business ties to Honduran Vice-President Jaime Rosenthal, who resigned in April 1988 to protest the extradition of Juan Ramón Matta Ballesteros to the United States.[62] In Costa Rica, the pro-Contra drug enterprise Frigorificos de Puntarenas made unexplained payments to an account in Israel of the Israel Discount Bank.[63]

Stories about the Harari network and the Israeli connection received a big boost in credibility after the sensational murder of Colombian presidential candidate Luis Galan in August 1989. Colombian government investigators put the spotlight on Israeli (and other) mercenaries who had trained drug-cartel assassins and drug-financed paramilitary squads responsible for much of the political terrorism in that country.[64] Colombia's top drug investigator, Gen. Miguel Maza Marquez, blamed Yair Klein, the chief Israeli hired gun, of training terrorists who blew up a Colombian commercial airliner in November 1989, killing 117 people: "He is the person who trained these people in the making of bombings and is responsible for this aggression."[65]

After they finished their contract with associates of the Medellín drug bosses, some of the Israelis were scheduled to begin assignments in Honduras and Costa Rica for the benefit of Contra forces.[66] One member of Klein's firm implicated in the Colombia operation had previously trained Contras in Honduras and claimed to have instructed most of Guatemala's high-ranking officers through a contract arranged by Brenneke's alleged controller Pesakh Ben-Or.[67]

Klein was reportedly in contact with Harari.[68] When this news broke, a former Mossad chief commented that "one would have to be crazy to connect Harari with drug dealing."[69] Yet within days the Israeli newspaper *Hadashot* declared that Harari was "wanted by U.S. authorities," who consider him "one of the world's biggest drug lords."[70] And Colombia's chief narcotics investigator reported a few weeks later that the Israeli mercenaries smuggled their weapons into Colombia through Panama, a sign that Harari was probably involved.[71]

Given Klein's status as a reserve colonel with a high-level position in the war room of the Israeli chief of staff, it is hard to imagine that the Israeli government was truly ignorant of his business with representatives of the Medellín cartel.[72] The prestigious Hebrew daily *Ha'aretz* reported that Colombian authorities had complained to the Israeli government as early as February 1989 about mercenary activities. Although Israel followed up by sending a Mossad agent and foreign ministry official to discuss the situation, for months it took no action against Klein, who, like other Israelis working in the security field, depended on licenses from the Defense Ministry to stay in business.[73]

Klein then became the center of another scandal involving a large shipment of Israeli arms to the Medellín cartel leader José Gonzalo Rodríguez Gacha, overseer of the foreign mercenaries. The weapons traveled via the Caribbean island of Antigua. Klein claimed that he had ordered the arms on behalf of a group of CIA-backed Panamanian exiles who intended to train on Antigua under Klein's supervision to "neutralize Mike Harari" and overthrow Noriega. He asserted further that the CIA called off the Panamanians, who then disposed of the weapons on their own.[74] His story made no sense; the Antiguan government turned down the proposal for a training camp long before the arms arrived. The Israelis could not have intended the arms for any activity on the island. Antigua was simply a convenient destination of record to disguise the true buyer.[75]

The leader of the Panamanian dissidents, who became head of Panama's police force after the invasion, said he did hold discussions with Klein regarding a possible Antigua training camp. But he discounted Klein's story and declared, "Col. Mike Harari, who is now in Israel, is behind all this." Agents of Colombia's Department of Administrative Security (DAS) have confirmed that Harari, like Klein, indeed entered Colombia to train mercenaries under the command of Rodríguez Gacha.[76] A British television report identified Pesakh Ben-Or and a retired Israeli general as key figures in the arms deal. A high-ranking Colombian official told *Newsday*, "All the information obtained . . . permits one to declare unequivocally that officials of the Israel government knew of and consented to the sale of the arms shipment to Colombia, up to the point of expediting a vessel to complete the first step of the route."[77]

Only after the Antigua scandal broke and Colombia suspended an immigration treaty with Jerusalem did an Israeli court finally charge Klein with illegally supplying military expertise and equipment to a Colombian "farmers' organization."[78] But Colombian investigators continued to complain that Israeli authorities were providing no real help in tracing arms shipments.

Other Israeli mercenaries served a similar function for drug-linked paramilitary groups in both Peru and Bolivia. Israel, in connection with Argentina, provided mercenary and diplomatic support for the Bolivian Cocaine Coup of 1980.[79] *Hadashot* reported that "elements linked to the drug growers" in Peru "spent approximately $9 million on military equipment from Israeli arms dealers in 1987." The arms were allegedly sent via Mexico and Guatemala.[80] Israeli arms deals in Guatemala are a monopoly of Contra supplier Pesakh Ben-Or.

Rafael Eitan, former chief of staff of the Israeli army, hardly softened the blow of all these revelations when he told the *Jerusalem Post*, "Someday, perhaps, if it's decided that the stories can be told, you'll see that the state has been involved in acts which are a thousand times more dirty than anything going on in Colombia. As long as the government decides to do something, something that the national interest demanded, then it is legitimate."[81]

Israel's true role in this trade may not be made public for a long time. Both Congress and the Reagan and Bush administrations suppressed the facts, especially as they pertain to the Contras. Senior sources in both branches of government told the London *Sunday Telegraph* that

> hundreds of documents revealing Israeli work on behalf of the
> Contras were so sensitive they were not declassified. They were
> not even shown to members of the congressional committees
> which investigated the Iran-Contra scandal in 1987, it is said.
> The documents contained information about Israeli mercenaries
> who, with the knowledge of the Israeli and U.S. governments,
> flew weapons and ammunition to Tegucigalpa, the Honduran
> capital, at a time when Congress had banned military aid. The
> arms were then distributed to Contra bases on the Nicaraguan
> border.[82]

One congressional source who saw the documents called them "crucial to understanding the whole scandal" and added, "The American public never knew. It is a cover-up."[83]

All this mystery and intrigue should not inflate Israel's role nor suggest that Jerusalem had any single or simple policy goal. Israel had multiple interests, such as expanding arms markets, cultivating local diplomatic support, pleasing Washington by supporting the Contras, and avoiding scandal by minimizing its involvement. And Mossad, like most successful intelligence agencies, played both sides; in Panama, for example, it had its hooks not only into Noriega, through Harari, but also into Noriega's chief adversary, Eduardo Herrera Hassan, a PDF officer whom Noriega made ambassador to Israel to get him out of the country.[84] After the U.S. invasion, with Harari back in Israel, Herrera became had of the new Public Force, successor to the PDF. Thus, Israeli agents, like Noriega and his own clique, must be seen not as hidden puppet-masters but rather as important actors in a larger milieu of mercenaries, drug smugglers, arms salesmen, and intelligence agents who helped shape Central America's political evolution in the 1980s.

# 5 The International Cali Connection and the United States

*Milieu, Networks, Syndicates, and Cartels:*
*From Unity to Diversity*

The convergence of international drug-trafficking networks on Honduras and the Matta organization was not merely a consequence of the Contra operations of the 1980s. On the contrary, as we have seen, Juan Ramón Matta Ballesteros had risen to prominence as the local representative of a much older network that involved some of the same international elements (Cuban, Israeli, and American) as the Contra connection.

When the Reagan administration closed down the Honduras DEA office in 1983, Matta was a principal beneficiary, but by no means the only one. Matta by then was known to U.S. Customs and the DEA as a smuggler of cocaine from a much larger international network, one large enough to merit, in the DEA's opinion, its self-selected title of "International Narcotics Organization." At one point its Peruvian cocaine source, a former Honduran, supplied (in the words of a DEA analyst) "all the key traffickers in Colombia, all the people in Mexico, most of the United States, and a lot of Europe."[1]

Traffickers based in Cali (the forerunners of the so-called Cali cartel) were the senior Colombian members, who may well have supplied the initiative to organize the group around its refining capacity. In this chapter we shall use the name "International Connection" for the international network that James Mills discusses in *The Underground Empire*. In the early 1980s the Colombian element of this international network articulated into a more complex and Mafia-like scene of national cartels (the Cali and Medellín cartels), sometimes allied and sometimes at war, much like the Mafia families in New York.

Chapter 2 explored the pervasiveness of diverse cocaine connections (Cuban-American, Mexican, Argentine, etc.), with the CIA, and their contribution to the genesis of the Contras. This chapter focuses on the international Cali network, its governmental origins and relations, and its relationship to the United States. The two pictures, one stressing diversity, and the other coherence, are complementary.

Mills's book, to which this chapter frequently refers, stresses the organizational coherence of the International Connection in the 1970s, its continuity with older networks like the Auguste Ricord syndicate, and above all its dependence on governmental protection in Peru, Honduras, and elsewhere for its survival. A more scholarly work, Rensselaer Lee's *White Labyrinth*, has a much more pluralist picture of the drug scene in the 1980s:

> Five loosely organized syndicates headquartered in Medellín and Cali control an estimated 70–80 percent of the cocaine exported from Colombia and about 60–70 percent of all cocaine sold in the United States. Bolivia's cocaine trade is controlled by some 12 to 25 families. . . . In Peru, on the other hand, the industry is highly fragmented and disorganized and, to a large extent, dominated by Colombian traffickers. Colombia is clearly the linchpin—the *país clave*—of the cocaine industry. . . . The big Colombian syndicates do not form a cartel in the sense of being able to maintain prices. . . . [they] probably do not control more than 70 percent of the total world trade in cocaine. . . . There is bad blood between the Medellín and Cali groups, stemming from Medellín's attempts to poach on Cali's sales territory in New York City. Yet, there is considerable business collaboration within each group: Traffickers cooperate on insuring cocaine shipments, engage in joint ventures, exchange loads, and jointly plan assassinations. Moreover cocaine barons share a common political agenda that includes blocking the extradition of drug traffickers, immobilizing the criminal justice system, and selectively persecuting the Colombian left.[2]

Although he does not use the word, Lee in this paragraph has given a sensitive portrait of the international cocaine milieu, where ad hoc deals and transient partnerships can be concocted by disparate groups. Its portrait of diversity is, as far as it goes, entirely accurate. Where there is systematic political corruption, however, the pluralism of competing drug rings often operates within the single on-going governmental connection permitting them to operate.

High-level corruption and protection, particularly if it is sanctioned by CIA and other dominant intelligence agencies, may confer a systemic unity upon a milieu that is otherwise competitive and diverse. We shall see that the Peruvian cocaine industry, which Lee describes as fragmented and disorganized, has benefited over decades from symbiotic governmental protection, dominated by the corruption by Colombian traffickers of the Peruvian Investigative Police (PIP), Peru's top drug police. This corruption appears to have endured the rise and fall of individual drug lords who benefited from it, thus supplying a unifying theme to an otherwise diverse story. Such continuity contradicts the DEA assumption that the key to destroying a drug network is to eliminate its kingpin. Too often the kingpin is simply the man with the key governmental connection; and it is the connection that generates the kingpin, not vice versa. Thus to get rid of the kingpin means little: the kingpin is dead, long live the kingpin!

Mills alleges that such high-level political protection and immunity are secured by "the participation in the drug traffic of high officials in at least thirty-three countries." He sees in this systematic corruption the further unifying traces of the CIA, and speculates that the CIA may dirty itself "in the narcotics industry because that is where it finds the leaders of nations it seeks to comprehend and influence."[3] A key clue to the difference between Mills's book and Lee's is that the former has some two dozen references to the CIA in its index, and the latter has none.

The International Connection's relations to the United States, though polymorphous and difficult to describe in the abstract, involved more than the CIA. Traffickers in Cali appear to have developed organized, institutional channels for importing cocaine into the United States, by (for example) corrupting corporate officers of at least one major U.S. airline (Eastern). Their money launderers banked in Miami with a network of banks linked both to past CIA-drug bank scandals and to the State Department's "humanitarian assistance" for the Contras.[4]

There are other signs that, as former DEA agents and informants have alleged, the United States, even before Reagan, chose not to prosecute members of this International Connection for political reasons. And the Reagan and Bush administrations appear to have used one member of the International Connection, Barry Seal, to blame the huge flow of cocaine into the United States on a "narcoterrorist" conspiracy, allegedly centered on the Medellín cartel and directed by Castro's Cuba and the Sandinistas of Nicaragua.

The notion of a communist narcoterrorist conspiracy, which CIA Director William Casey appears to have imposed on his intelligence analysts, reached a national audience with President Reagan's charge "that top Nicaraguan government officials are deeply involved in drug trafficking" and Vice President Bush's charge that Nicaragua had joined the Medellín cartel to inspire a 1985 attack by M-19 guerrillas against the Colombian Supreme Court. Bush's charge in 1986 was no simple matter of electoral rhetoric; it was the rationale for an important National Security Decision Directive making drugs a national security matter, which helped generate the 1989 Bush drug strategy. In Chapter 11 we shall see that the DEA carefully declined to endorse these propagandistic charges.

Thanks to the Kerry subcommittee's publication of a Customs report naming Barry Seal and Juan Ramón Matta Ballesteros, we know now that as late as 1983, DEA and the Customs Service still linked Matta to Cali veterans Santiago Ocampo and Isaac Kattan of the International Connection. The use of Seal against the Medellín cartel raises the question of whether in targeting Medellín, the United States had not returned to protecting high-level traffickers in Cali, a practice that would mirror Noriega's practice of setting up Cali traffickers for arrest to please their Medellín competitors.[5]

## The Matta Network, the Cali Connection, and International Political Protection

The 1983 Customs report released by the Kerry subcommittee shows that the Reagan administration had ranked Matta among the highest-level drug traffickers of which it was then aware. Among Matta's associates, the report listed (from DEA records) the senior Colombian trafficker Santiago Ocampo Zuluaga, who had been indicted by a U.S. court in 1980 as the head of the "biggest cocaine ring in U.S. history," and also the American pilot John Clary Allen, who worked for Ocampo.[6] The report noted that in January 1982 Matta "provided 850 kilos of cocaine to the organization of Isaac Kattan Kassin," a Syrian-born Jew in Cali, whom the U.S. Attorney in Miami called "the biggest drug financier in South America."[7]

The report also recorded an informant's tip on a plan to airdrop marijuana and cocaine from Honduras, flown on a DC-4 (N90201) that would subsequently fly supplies for the Contras (see Chapter 3). The drop was to be made at an isolated farm belonging to Barry Seal and Wendell K. Seal, both allegedly major narcotic smugglers and distributors throughout the eastern and southern United States.[8]

In brief, the 1983 Customs report confirms Matta's links to the network described by James Mills as the principal target of the special drug Task Force Centac 12 (later Centac 21). It was a network with the highest political connections, not just in Honduras, but in every country where it chose to operate. Santiago Ocampo, for example, had secured the cooperation of General Omar Torrijos, the strongman of Panama in the 1970s, not only by giving him a Paso Fino racehorse, but also by investing with the general's brother, Hugo Torrijos, in a Colombian airline that moved cocaine from Colombia into Panama. (The airline, misleadingly called Aerolineas Medellín, was based in Cali.) A highly reliable DEA informant later told the drug agency that in exchange General Torrijos had granted Ocampo "free access to Panama for his aircraft and vessels."[9]

Mills identifies both Matta and the pilot John Clary Allen as the go-betweens who arranged the smuggling of Ocampo's cocaine to the Mexican networks of Alberto Sicilia Falcón and, following Sicilia's arrest in 1975, Miguel Félix Gallardo.[10] As already noted, both Sicilia and Félix enjoyed the necessary government protection in Mexico from the DFS secret police chief Miguel Nazar Haro, whom the CIA once identified as its "most important source in Mexico and Central America."[11]

But Mills also roots the Ocampo-Matta-Mexico connection in still higher and older networks about which the Customs report is silent. For example, John Allen's introductions to Ocampo, Matta, and the Sicilia network had been arranged through future Cali cartel kingpin Giovanni Caicedo Tascón, the nephew of Eduardo Tascón Morán. And Tascón Morán, who became known as the senior Cali cartel leader, shipped cocaine not only to the United States but also to Italy and even to Thailand. He was said to have on his payroll almost every public official of the Colombian cities Cali and Tulua, and he was the brother-in-law of the governor of the Colombian department of which Cali is the capital.[12] Together with two other Ocampo associates, Gilberto Rodríguez Orejuela and José Santacruz Londoño, Tascón Morán and his nephew provided the early leadership for the Cali cartel.[13]

Soon afterwards Ocampo arranged for Allen to pick up cocaine from his source in Peru, a former Honduran (and friend of Matta) called Alfonso Rivera. DEA informants described Rivera as *el hombre*, "Mr. Big," of a self-styled "International Narcotics Organization," a major coalition formed in 1974 to refine coca paste.[14] Rivera in turn was marketing cocaine supplied by one of the wealthiest families in Peru, the Paredes family, described by a DEA Centac analyst as "the biggest cocaine smuggling organization in Peru and possibly in the world."[15] Rivera and the Paredes family enjoyed the same influence in Peru as did Tascón and Ocampo in Colombia. They controlled a number of high officials of PIP, as well as two generals (General Mesias Sánchez Castillo and a General Miyana), and a comandante of State Security. The Paredes were part of an established oligarchy that "controlled not only the roots of the cocaine industry but, to a large extent, the country itself."[16]

A few years later another trafficker, Reynaldo Rodríguez Lopez, with drug links to Carlos Lehder and Jorge Ochoa of the Medellín cartel, was an adviser to the PIP director and maintained an office at PIP headquarters. According to Lee, "his drug ring allegedly included several PIP generals as well as the private secretary, Luis López Vergara, of Fernando Belaunde Terry's Minister of Interior, Luis Percovich Roca."[17] At this time, Belaunde and Percovich were among the foremost Latin American supporters of the Casey-Bush narcoguerrilla hypothesis, arguing that cocaine dealers provided the Peruvian Sendero Luminoso guerrillas with money and arms and Sendero protected drug shipments in return.

In fact, at the time, "the Peruvian military, which controlled the Upper Huallaga Valley during a 1984–1985 state of emergency, was enriching itself from the cocaine trade and collaborating with cocaine dealers in antiguerrilla operations. In addition, drug-related corruption had spread to the very top of the Peruvian government. . . . The narco-guerrilla, it can be hypothesized, was in part a projection of the Belaunde regime's own internal rot."[18]

As described by Mills's DEA sources, the Rivera-Ocampo-Matta-Mexico cocaine connection was so large as to admit of no sizable competitors. Moreover, its world market appears to have been established on the ruins of the French heroin connection of Auguste Ricord, a Latin American network favored by the intelligence services of Argentina and Paraguay until it was crushed by Nixon's anti-drug campaign in the early 1970s. Rivera, Tascón, and Sicilia all picked up pieces of the old Ricord network, and Tascón and Sicilia continued to distribute French heroin from Marseilles.[19] The intelligence connections, in PIP and elsewhere, apparently remained the same.

In short, the Matta-Ocampo-Rivera network had actually benefited from Nixon's War on Drugs and more specifically from the politically enforced extradition in 1972 of key members of the so-called French or Corsican Connection to the United States.[20] Sicilia, a young Cuban exile from Miami, took over elements of the Ricord organization in Mexico, shortly after Lucien Sarti, the local Ricord representative, was shot in Mexico City in April 1972, having been traced there by U.S. agents.[21] Two years later, in May 1974, Rivera's International Narcotics Organization was formed and took on the legal services of Peruvian lawyer Luis Cornejo, who had once represented "a close representative of Lucien Sarti."[22] Like the Ricord network before it, but with an emphasis on cocaine rather than heroin, the successor network continued the French

Connection's symbiotic relationship with the intelligence networks of right-wing dictatorships like Argentina, Chile, and Bolivia.

## Matta, Ocampo, and Right-Wing Governmental Narcoterrorism

Almost all recent American accounts of the Ricord network have noted that its principals, although mostly fugitives from French justice, enjoyed some degree of immunity as agents of French intelligence.[23] According to Mills,

> reports within the international intelligence community eventually listed Ricord associates—men with names like Christian David, Michel Nicoli, Lucien Sarti, Claude Pastou—as agents of French intelligence. A friend of Ricord's named Armand Charpentier was said to have participated in a plot in Brazil to assassinate Charles de Gaulle during a 1964 visit. Christian David was a reported accomplice in the 1965 Paris kidnapping and assassination of Moroccan leftist leader Mehdi Ben Barka, a crime in which French intelligence also participated. . . . As for Asia, French intelligence officials, assisted by expatriate Corsican criminals, were known to have participated in the opium traffic during the Indochina War.[24]

Thus American observers had enjoyed sufficient detachment and perspective to discern the narcopolitics of the French Connection. With comparable perspective, meanwhile, foreign sources have seen the CIA as exploiting the same narcopolitical resources that we have attributed to French intelligence. It is they, for example, who point out that it was American and Israeli intelligence, not the leaders of French intelligence, who had an interest in seeing Ben Barka killed.[25] It is foreign, not American sources, who have noted that Klaus Barbie, the war criminal once protected by American intelligence from discovery by the French, became associated with the Ricord network after exfiltration by American agents to a new home in Bolivia.[26]

This Ricord network (as noted in the Introduction) was a by-product of the CIA's mobilization of criminal elements in Europe against communism. Government agent Thomas C. Tripodi, in secret reports to CIA and DEA (as summarized by *New York Times* reporter Ralph Blumenthal) concluded: "Although the American authorities were instrumental in the revival of the Sicilian Mafia, they persuaded the Italian government to mount a successful crackdown on the heroin smugglers [into the United States]. This left the Corsicans, who had also been buttressed by the CIA as an anti-Communist force, as the major providers of illegal heroin to the United States."[27]

And when, in the 1970s, the United States mounted a successful crackdown on the Corsicans, it appears to have been CIA-trained Cubans like Frank Castro and José Medardo Alvero Cruz in Latin America who were the initial beneficiaries.

Like the Ricord network before it, the new International Connection performed arms-smuggling and assassination favors for right-wing dictatorships. In Mexico, for example, Sicilia began to negotiate a $250 million arms deal with the chief of the Portuguese secret service "for an anti-Communist coup d'état in Portugal," which ultimately failed to happen.[28] The deal was apparently sanctioned by the CIA and negotiated for Sicilia by a Cuban Bay of Pigs veteran (José Egozi Bejar) who maintained his CIA contacts while working for Sicilia (see Chapter 2).

Mexico in general offers an even better example than Peru of the systemic unity and continuity of the international drug traffic. In the 1950s and 1960s, long before either Sarti or Sicilia, Jorge Moreno Chauvet and Jorge Asaf y Bala, the latter known as "the Al Capone of the Mexican underworld," dominated the Mexican heroin trade, thanks to their governmental and intelligence connections, with the drugs they obtained from the Corsican connection in Marseilles via the Cotroni Mafia family in Montreal.[29]

The primitive unity of the global drug traffic, in those Cold War years of the intelligence-sanctioned Sicilian and Corsican channels, has today become obscured by the proliferation and articulation of trafficking groups and the involvement of new countries like Venezuela. But despite these developments, the drug trade retains signs of unity and continuity with its past.[30]

## The Intelligence-Drug Milieu, WACL-CAL, and the Origins of the Contras

The old Ricord connection, actually energized and rejuvenated by its decapitation during the strenuous Nixon war against it, was perhaps the best example in the 1970s of a milieu to be exploited, for a quid pro quo of toleration, by any national intelligence agency (American, French, Israeli, or Bulgarian) that needed a criminal job done. Thus it was easy for Frank Castro's Cuban CORU group (see Chapter 2) to pick up Ricord's right-wing intelligence connections in Latin America, such as Paraguay's intelligence chief Pastor Coronel.[31]

In the second half of the 1970s, especially after the Carter administration distanced itself from both right-wing Latin American dictatorships and ex-CIA Cuban terrorists, these rejected U.S. allies moved into closer association with each other. By 1980, as we saw in Chapter 2, they were meeting annually at the conferences of the Argentinian-backed Latin American Anti-communist Confederation (CAL), the regional section of the World Anti-Communist League (WACL). The Argentinians were mounting a continental WACL-CAL strategy of right-wing hegemony based on drug alliances. The most noted example was the 1980 Cocaine Coup of Luis García Meza in Bolivia; but WACL also supported the new ARENA party of Col. Roberto d'Aubuisson in El Salvador, and it is suspected that drug money did so as well.[32]

In 1980, as part of this continental strategy, WACL-CAL connections played a key role in forming the initial core Contra group, which later became the main FDN Contra faction of Enrique Bermúdez. In 1980 the Guatemala WACL chief, Mario Sandoval Alarcón, housed near his own home both Salvadorans and Nicaraguans, including d'Aubuisson and the core of Bermúdez's September 15 Legion, which was in 1981 enlarged into the FDN.[33] Bermúdez's original financer in early 1980 was Somoza's cousin Luis Pallais Debayle, a WACL activist.[34]

Sandoval also had strong connections to the U.S. government. As discussed in Chapter 2, his two original American backers were Nat Hamrick and John Carbaugh, two WACL-linked aides of Senator Helms who also arranged for delegates of the Argentine junta to attend the 1980 Republican Convention and subsequently to visit the Reagan White House.[35] Sandoval (an old CIA asset, and the so-called Godfather to all the death squads of Central America, including d'Aubuisson's) attended the 1981 Reagan inaugural and told U.S. journalists that he expected the new Reagan administration to honor "verbal agreements" that he had reached with campaign officials.[36]

In Costa Rica the Argentinian officer organizing the first Contra Southern Front had established contact with the head of the local chapter of WACL, which was also the political vehicle of the Argentine cocaine alliance in Latin America.[37] In 1980 another Argentinian, working with Contras under the protection of Sandoval, attacked a left-wing radio station in Costa Rica; the raiders had used a base camp on the ranch of the American John Hull. Hull and his neighbor, Bruce Jones, had connections to the local WACL Chapter, the Free Costa Rica Movement (MCRL), and the local CIA station.[38]

## The Political Immunity
## of the Cali Matta-Ocampo Connection

In Honduras the CIA-supported Contras and the drug-intelligence milieu provided mutual reinforcement and protection. Hence, ultimately, the flow of State Department funds to the Matta-linked drug-trafficking airline, Hondu Carib, even after (as we shall see in Chapter 6) the initial Reagan-Argentina-CAL collaboration had been broken.

The fact is that connections to powerful drug traffickers with local killers and political influence are assets to any international intelligence agency. Or, to turn the argument around, it is those who enjoy the best connections with the international intelligence milieu who gain the protection and power to emerge as the most powerful drug kingpins. Such was the case with all the principals of the Matta-Ocampo network channeling cocaine from Peru to Mexico.[39] It was true also of their lesser associates. Of one of these, José Franco, Mills notes that "the president of Honduras had even let him hide cocaine in government exports of tobacco to the United States"; also, that he obtained "intelligence directly from the chief of F-2, an elite Colombian police unit handling narcotics and sensitive internal security investigations."[40]

In the 1970s the Cali-based Ocampo and Gilberto Rodríguez had been the principal targets of a major DEA Centac investigation that resulted in indictments of Rodríguez in Los Angeles and New York in 1978.[41] But the political connections of the Ocampo-Matta network were so powerful that its extirpation (rather than the simple arrest of one or another leader) would have meant nothing less than a political upheaval in Latin America. John Allen, Matta's associate, accurately predicted to Mills that the United States would never arrest Ocampo, even though he had twice visited the United States: "They fuck it up on purpose. It's politics. They could have nailed him."[42]

Indeed, politics may have played a role in both the rise and the fall of the DEA's interest in the Ocampo-Matta connection under Jimmy Carter. Carter's "Human Rights" foreign policy in Latin America distanced the CIA under Stansfield Turner from the death-squad activities of former CIA assets like Frank Castro, now working for countries like Chile and Argentina. Thus the connection of Peruvian drug czar Alfonso Rivera with "a high-ranking Chilean army officer" under Pinochet[43] did not deter Carter officials who were actively pressuring Pinochet to cease his drug-financed death squad activities. But Mills strongly suggests that the Carter administration was ultimately reluctant to go after Ocampo and Tascón because of its determination in 1977 to sign a Panama Canal treaty with General Torrijos, even while Torrijos and his family were heavily involved at the highest levels of the world cocaine trade.[44] According to disgruntled DEA agents, some of whom suspected they were stumbling onto a CIA connection, the case against Ocampo was never pursued past the indictment level, and the Centac 21 task force was totally dismantled when Reagan and Bush came to office.[45]

Besides diplomatic reasons for America's failure to arrest Ocampo, considerations of internal politics may have been a factor. In Colombia, Ocampo was a principal organizer of the antiguerrilla death squad MAS, which from the outset collaborated with the Colombian military (who were among its founding members) to identify and kill left-wing targets. Such de facto collaboration between drug traffickers and government security forces, common in countries such as Mexico, Peru, Brazil, Chile, and Argentina, had been characteristic of Colombia through the 1970s, when high-level corruption pervaded the security police.[46] The drug cartel's death squads and the military were consolidated in 1981, when Colombian drug traffickers, in collaboration with the Colombian army, convened a "general assembly" to create their own counterterrorist network, Muerte a Sequestradores (Death to Kidnappers), or MAS.[47] Ocampo was elected president of this group, and his airline business associate Manuel Garces Gonzales was elected vice president. Jorge Ochoa of Medellín was elected treasurer.[48]

Rensselaer Lee has recorded how the MAS under Ocampo became a bridge between the cartels and the Colombian military in their common fight against leftists: "Designed originally to retaliate against guerrillas who kidnapped for money, MAS evolved into an instrument for the indiscriminate persecution of leftists, including labor organizers, peasants who collaborate with guerrillas, civil rights activists, and members of the Unión Patriótica (the civilian arm of the FARC). Some Colombian army officers have also been members of MAS; in fact, the organization seemingly served as a communication channel of sorts between the mafia and the military."[49]

The 1981 meeting of the traffickers appears to have resulted also in increased articulation, rationalization, and intensification of cocaine production in Colombia. The Cali traffickers apparently accepted a larger role for the rising Medellín syndicates of the Ochoas, Pablo Escobar, and Gonzalo Rodríguez Gacha, who (after the death of Torrijos in a 1981 plane crash) made the Colombians' first direct contacts with Manuel Noriega in Panama. Noriega was then still head of Panamanian army intelligence and on the CIA payroll.[50] From this time on the relations became more complex and obscure between the more traditional, less confrontational traffickers of Cali and their new, more violent counterparts in Medellín.[51]

The effect of this increased drug wealth and paramilitary clout was to shift Colombian politics to the right. MAS sabotaged the amnesty negotiated by newly elected, conservative President Belisario Betancur (over United States opposition) by its selective assassinations of amnestied guerrillas. Millions of dollars of drug profits helped elect Colombian politicians of both the right-wing establishment parties, even the courageous Justice Minister, Rodrigo Lara Bonilla, whose antidrug campaign ended with his assassination in 1984.[52]

Collaboration between Colombian security forces and the drug traffickers' death squads has significantly escalated since 1985, according to Amnesty International. In an October 1989 press release, Amnesty charged that in Colombia "sectors of the armed forces—often operating in alliance with alleged drug traffickers—and paramilitary groups acting on their orders had killed unarmed civilians on an unprecedented scale in the past 16 months. . . . The victims have included trade union leaders, human rights workers, teachers, priests, peasants, and more recently, members of the judiciary trying to investigate human rights abuses." The same document described the street murder of a 38-year-old woman judge who had confirmed warrants for the arrest of three armed forces members and two alleged drug traffickers in connection with the March 1988 massacre of twenty-one banana plantation workers in Urabá.[53]

In 1988 Rensselaer Lee reported that

> military factions in Colombia have been linked to cocaine traffickers through common membership in right-wing vigilante squads such as MAS. Colombian military units occasionally protect cocaine laboratories against [rebel] FARC extortion attempts. In a November 1983 incident, for example, a Colombian Special Forces team from Villavicencio helped a cocaine trafficker move an entire laboratory complex from an area controlled by the First FARC Front to a safer location near the Brazilian border. The operation, which involved 5 officers and 43 noncoms, required 26 days.[54]

Lee also corroborated the military-drug collaboration in the Urabá massacre, reporting that the hitmen had been paid by Pablo Escobar and Gonzalo Rodríguez Gacha on behalf of a local association of banana plantation owners, while "local military commanders in Urabá drew up lists of suspected subversives and led the killers to their targets."[55]

## The Cali Connection, U.S. Corporate Power, and Miami Narcobanking

The massacre in Urabá, where the banana plantations had been developed in a U.S.-Colombian joint venture, illustrates a convergence of interests between right-wing cocaine gray alliances and U.S. corporate power overseas. The Urabá banana industry was developed by the Colombian subsidiary of United Brands (Frutera de Sevilla), which minimized its own financial risks by encouraging investment by Colombian entrepreneurs. These latter, according to writer Jenny Pearce, "saw no need to change the backward, authoritarian pattern of labor relations that United Brands had established . . . in which there were no labor codes, social provisions or proper wages."[56] United Brands, formerly United Fruit, is no stranger to such alliances (see Chapters 3 and 4). The largest U.S. corporate employer in both Honduras and Panama, its encouragement of informers and strongmen has contributed to America's tolerance of drug corruption in the region.

Corruption can work in both directions. In the mid-1980s, when the Medellín cartel was still relying on street hoodlums and outlaw pilots, the Cali cartel had corrupted the middle-level local bureaucracy of Eastern Airlines and was, according to FBI and DEA informant Max Mermelstein, hiding cocaine "in the nose cones of Eastern Airlines jets."[57]

A former Eastern Airlines pilot, Gerald Loeb, testified to the Kerry subcommittee about drug-trafficking and money-laundering operations on Eastern aircraft from 1984 through 1988. He described how the discovery of a 15-kg shipment of cocaine, "underneath the pilot's seat in the forward electronics section," was part of "an ongoing scenario with drugs aboard the Eastern aircraft, particularly from Panama, the hub operation, and Colombia." He alleged that it was a usual situation, indeed a "standard joke," for the instruments in the cockpit to indicate that the plane was a lot heavier than the weight indicated on the manifest.[58]

Loeb told the Kerry subcommittee that the Eastern Airlines station manager in Panama was "absolutely" involved in the loading and offloading of drugs and drug money. His report to the FBI indicated corruption at an even higher level, involving the Eastern senior vice president for Latin American operations, the regional manager in Panama, and other senior managers.[59]

What was the FBI response to Loeb's report about smuggling on Eastern Airlines planes, a report confirmed by a 1985 report from a major FBI and DEA informant? Apparently the only person punished was Loeb himself. Loeb told the subcommittee he was fired from Eastern Airlines for "outrageous conduct, to wit turning over to the FBI a 19-page summary report involving details of drug trafficking, money laundering operations on Eastern aircraft over a period of approximately 4 years."[60] According to Loeb, Eastern Airlines, hearing from the FBI within hours of the memo, hired the InterContinental Detective Agency "to fabricate information" against himself and the other witnesses.[61]

Certain Miami banks, some of them with both mob and CIA connections, appear to have had a long-term involvement in laundering drug funds from the International Connection and others. Prominent among these institutions are the banks and companies associated with the lawyer and U.S. intelligence veteran Paul Helliwell. Helliwell was counsel for a number of Miami-based CIA proprietaries like Sea Supply, Inc., which shipped vast quantities of arms to the opium-growing Guomindang troops in Burma.[62] His Castle Bank in the Bahamas was identified by the *Wall Street Journal* as a laundry for both CIA and organized crime funds, while an investment firm for which he was counsel mingled CIA funds with hot money from Philippine dictator Ferdinand Marcos.[63] A certain percentage of the proceeds was siphoned off by Helliwell and others to pay off men close to party leaders in Washington.[64]

An arrangement good for the CIA was good for South Florida as well: "In the 1950s and 1960s Guomindang money from Thailand and Burma came via Hong Kong to be washed through [Meyer] Lansky-related property firms. The Trujillos, Somozas, and their confreres from South America bought up Miami mansions and filled up local banks. . . . One Florida real estate agent estimated, perhaps with considerable exaggeration, that of all foreign purchases in 1979, only 20% were the product of legitimate money."[65]

The closing of the scandal-ridden Castle Bank in 1977 was followed by the brief rise to prominence of the Nugan Hand Bank in Australia, staffed with many former CIA personnel. In its turn, the Nugan Hand Bank became involved both in the financing of major drug deals and with many of the principals (such as Richard Secord, Thomas Clines, and Rafael Quintero) allied with North in the Contra supply network.[66]

In 1979 the Nugan Hand Bank took as its president Donald Beazley, then president of the Great American Bank of Miami, which was indicted in 1982 for its cocaine money-laundering operations. In 1977 Beazley is also said to have negotiated for Nugan Hand the takeover of a Great American subsidiary, the Second National Bank of Homestead, allegedly once owned by Paul Helliwell.[67] When Nugan Hand collapsed in 1980, Beazley moved on. In 1982 he became president of the City National Bank of Miami. The bank's new owner, who hired Beazley, was Alberto Duque, a Colombian wheeler-dealer who also became involved with George Bush's son Jeb in the construction of a downtown Miami high rise.[68] According to reporter Jonathan Kwitny, "Duque's, and the bank's, lawyer happened to be Stephen W. Arky, son-in-law of Marvin Warner, Beazley's old boss and benefactor at Great American Banks."[69]

Scandals surrounded these banks at all points of the horizon. The collapse in 1985 of a small Fort Lauderdale dealer in government securities, ESM (for which Arky was attorney), led to the collapse of Warner's Home State Savings Bank in Ohio after violations for which Warner was convicted in Ohio state court in 1987 (this conviction was overturned in 1989).[70] Arky, who committed suicide in 1985, was also associated with a major bankruptcy scandal involving several Tennessee banks, which crashed with a loss of $700 million.[71] And in 1982 Duque's former New York partner, Eduardo Orozco, "was arrested, charged, and ultimately convicted of running the largest money laundry ever uncovered in the US." Most of the funds were apparently deposited with the CIA-linked exchange firm Deak Perera.[72] In 1986 Duque, then bankrupt, was found guilty on sixty counts of fraud and conspiracy.[73]

Through the years, the Miami narcobanking connection had enjoyed considerable political clout with both political parties. The drug-laundering World Finance Corporation that in the 1970s helped finance CORU (see Chapter 2) had high-level connections to both the Democratic party in Georgia and Washington (when Jimmy Carter was president) and also to the Miami circles of Bebe Rebozo and Richard Nixon.[74] Marvin Warner, the owner of the Great American Bank who hired Beazley, was a major Democratic fundraiser who was rewarded for his party work by being named Jimmy Carter's ambassador to Switzerland.

The Cali-Matta-Kattan connection described in the 1983 Customs report laundered its profits through Miami banks. Indeed, the exposure of the Great American Bank's laundering activities in 1982 derived from warrants issued after the arrest of Isaac Kattan, who was notorious for the scope of his money-laundering activity. In all, Kattan did business with four banks. One of the others, Northside Bank of Miami, was owned by Gilberto Rodríguez Orejuela of the Cali cartel. A third bank, the Popular Bank and Trust Company, was used by the State Department to transmit funds to the Contras. According to Jack Terrell, it had been owned by deposed Nicaraguan dictator Anastasio Somoza until his murder in 1980. It also allegedly employed a cousin (Barney Vaughan) of Federico Vaughan, who (as we shall soon see) was identified by the CIA through Barry Seal's photographs as a Sandinista drug trafficker.[75]

Warner's links to the Carter administration did not save him from conviction under Reagan. Kattan also went to jail. But for Matta, who is listed in the 1983 Customs report as Kattan's supplier, justice was delayed. In the meantime, Matta saw his airline become the Contras' air supplier in Honduras, while the DEA office was conveniently shut down.

The Reagan Administration had apparently found a new target for its War on Drugs: not the veterans of the old Matta-Ocampo-International Connection, but their junior colleagues, the Ochoas and Pablo Escobar from Medellín.

## The New Target under Reagan and Bush: Medellín and Narcoterrorism

In 1980, when Reagan was elected, the DEA considered the Cali traffickers more important than those in Medellín. In 1977–78, when Gilberto Rodríguez Orejuela of Cali owned his own airline, DEA had just missed arresting Jorge Ochoa in Miami for selling cocaine in the Dadeland Twin Theatres parking lot. As late as 1976, Pablo Escobar, a former car thief, was listed in Colombian drug files as a transporter, or "mule."[76] Nevertheless, in 1983 the DEA had begun to talk of a new enemy in Colombia, the Medellín trafficking cartel, with Ochoa and Escobar as kingpins.

This phrase was used in an internal DEA analysis of a 1,254-pound seizure of cocaine in Cleveland, Tennessee, whose principal source, Manuel Garces Gonzalez, was known to the DEA as an associate of Ocampo.[77] Other traffickers once linked to Cali were now associated with Medellín: one of the two cocaine shipments linked by the 1983 Customs report to Matta in Honduras (a 114-pound seizure of cocaine in Van Nuys, California) was linked in later DEA-inspired press charts to Jorge Ochoa of Medellín. Matta himself was now identified in the press as a "former hired gun closely allied with [the] Medellín cartel." Matta's money launderer Isaac Kattan, once known to the DEA as a Cali resident, now became "Isaac Kattan, Medellín" (at a time when he was in fact residing in a U.S. penitentiary).[78]

Some of this altered DEA consciousness must be attributed to changes in the traffic itself. After the MAS agreements among top-level Colombian traffickers in 1981, "an informal division of labor among the drug kingpins began to take shape," with Pablo Escobar specializing in security and the Ochoas of Medellín and Rodríguez Orejuela of Cali dividing the U.S. market geographically, Mafia-style.[79] The DEA does not appear to have allowed its own analysis to be politically distorted in these years. Even after its two major informants (Barry Seal and Max Mermelstein) pointed in 1985 to the "Ochoa cocaine cartel" and "the Medellín combine," DEA continued to give "equal weight to the Medellín group and the Cali group."[80]

This objectivity soon set DEA officials at odds with William Casey of the CIA, who came to office in 1981 with a vision of a left-wing narcoterrorist enemy, with U.S. Ambassador to Colombia Lewis Tambs, and officials in the Reagan White House, who fleshed out this vision with alleged links of the Medellín cartel to Colombian guerrillas and the Sandinista government.[81] The DEA analysis became subordinated to a White House propaganda blitz (or, to use the CIA's preferred term, psychological warfare campaign), especially after 1983, when Vice President Bush merged DEA and CIA resources in NNBIS (the National Narcotics Border Interdiction System), the Reagan administration's agency for coordinating the War on Drugs.

The first Medellín trafficker depicted in this blitz was Carlos Lehder. In 1981 Tampa U.S. Attorney Robert Merkle indicted and ultimately convicted Lehder, calling him a revolutionary whose motive was to use cocaine to destroy the United States.[82] Merkle's chief witness for this claim was a former prison cellmate of Lehder's, George Jung, who described Lehder as a self-professed Marxist and admirer of Che Guevara, who "talked constantly of revolution" and "wanted to tear down" America.[83] From the early 1980s the U.S. media printed leaked excerpts of Jung's charges that Lehder's smuggling partner was Robert Vesco, who (according to Jung's version of what Lehder told him in 1981) had introduced Lehder to Bahamas Prime Minister Lynden Pindling and to Cuban leader Fidel Castro. Lehder himself, according to Jung, "was supporting the M-19, a revolutionary group in Colombia."[84]

With such a helpful witness waiting to testify, one is not surprised that Carlos Lehder, although ranked "number twenty-two chronologically on a list of more than one hundred extraditions contemplated" from Colombia, became "number one" in U.S. Ambassador Tambs's efforts on behalf of U.S. law enforcement.[85] But Lehder's politics, although indeed passionately anti-American, were also racist and anti-communist; he claimed Adolf Hitler as one of his political mentors. In 1983, when he founded a new political party to oppose the U.S.-Colombian extradition treaty, its youth movement was urged to "defend the fatherland against the imperialists and the Communists."[86] Even after Lehder told a television crew in 1985 that "I am here to dialogue with . . . M-19," senior DEA officials discounted the statement as bluster unsupported by evidence. However "the pragmatic assessment of the DEA officials was not acceptable to Reagan's more ideological advisers [who] were absolutely convinced that M-19, the drug cartel, the Cubans, and the Sandinistas were all in bed together."[87]

Rensselaer Lee has written that "extant trafficker-guerrilla ties . . . are basically low-level, opportunistic, and intermittent; they do not constitute a pattern of strategic cooperation. . . . In general, the narco-guerrilla stereotype is a misleading one, obscuring a more fundamental and insidious reality: the increasing penetration by South American cocaine traffickers into established economic and political institutions."[88] Conceding that Lehder's "revolutionary politics set him apart from other Colombian capos," Lee nonetheless finds "no credible evidence that the M-19 received support from Lehder—or any outside support, for that matter—in staging the occupation of the [Colombian] Palace [of Justice]," as Reagan and Bush had charged (see below).[89]

The CIA and George Bush had their own reasons for targeting Lehder and the Medellín cartel in particular. In the early 1970s the Florida distribution of cocaine and money laundering had been largely in the hands of ex-CIA Cuban-Americans, not Colombians.[90] This arrangement broke down with the 1975 arrest of Alberto Sicilia Falcón and the murderous Miami cocaine wars of 1979–81, in which the CIA lost many of its informants. Matta replaced Sicilia as the major West Coast supplier, while representatives of the Medellín cartel replaced ex-CIA Cubans in Miami. Under the "informal division of labor" agreed upon at the time of the MAS drug traffickers' meeting in 1981, Medellín cocaine went to Florida, while Cali cocaine (and Matta's) went elsewhere. Soon afterwards, the CIA's Cuban informants became engaged in a shooting war with Lehder, the Ochoas, and Escobar in South Florida, in which Matta and the Cali cartel were not involved.[91]

Miami's bloody cocaine wars were a major factor in creating one of the most narrowly defined tasks ever assigned to a U.S. vice president. Bush was in charge of the South Florida Task Force of 1982, whose stated purpose was not to fight a national war on drugs but to keep drugs out of Florida. Such a regionally defined objective consolidated the alliance between ex-CIA director Bush and the ex-CIA Cubans of Miami, who had suffered great losses at the hands of the Medellín cartel. Bush's son Jeb, a Miami resident, became his father's personal representative in the Miami Cuban community.

The same regionally defined objective created a de facto common interest between the Bush Task Force and the Cali group and its representatives (such as Matta) whenever the market arrangements between the Medellín and Cali groups broke down, as they had in 1984–85, when Medellín representatives began to challenge the traditional Cali market in New York City. This conflict was followed by the 1988 War of the Cartels in Colombia between Escobar and the Cali group, motivated largely by Escobar's conviction that "Cali was cooperating with the [Colombian] government in a vendetta against the Medellín cartel."[92]

## Medellín, Tranquilandia, and Narcoguerrillas

Press interest in the Medellín cartel increased after the carefully planned Colombian-DEA raid in March 1984 on the Tranquilandia cocaine-processing lab in the Colombian jungle. In addition to fourteen tons of cocaine, the Colombian and DEA officials reported finding documents linking the lab to Fabio Ochoa and his son Jorge, Pablo Escobar, Carlos Lehder, and Gonzalo Rodríguez Gacha—all the principals of the Medellín cartel. U.S. accounts said nothing about Gilberto Rodríguez Orejuela of Cali, even after a top DEA informant, Max Mermelstein, reported that planning for the Tranquilandia lab, which he attended, had taken place in Cali.[93] One has to question why the Cali cartel had disappeared from the Reagan administration's sights.

The Tranquilandia raid was followed in rapid succession by the retaliatory assassination of Colombian Justice Minister Lara Bonilla on April 30, 1984, the declaration of a state of siege the next day, and the flight of cartel leaders into Panama. According to Mills, whose contacts worked at DEA during the Carter years and who gives the most detailed account of the Matta-Ocampo-Rodríguez Orejuela connection, the delegation to the "cocaine summit conference" in Panama City was led by Rodríguez Orejuela.[94] However, none of the more recent accounts, drawing on DEA sources from the Reagan years (Eddy, Shannon, and Gugliotta and Leen), mentions the presence of Rodríguez Orejuela at the Panama City meetings.[95]

From the outset, the Tranquilandia raid was used by Colombian police and the U.S. Embassy to link the labs to left-wing guerrillas and thus to Cuba. As we hear from one account,

> The Colombian police reported that they believed the snipers who fired at them [at the lab] were members of the Fuerzas Armadas Revolucionarias de Colombia (FARC), the Revolutionary Armed Forces of Colombia, the armed wing of the Colombian Communist Party. In the next weeks, Colombian forces . . . found . . . a camp that appeared to have been used by FARC guerrillas. [In] another large lab complex . . . they found three hundred empty ether barrels, an arsenal of weapons, and an FARC uniform. . . . For the Reagan right, all this was proof that the narcoterrorism marriage had been consummated. Lewis Tambs, the U.S. ambassador to Colombia, went so far as to suggest that the labs were somehow linked to Cuba. After the raid on Tranquilandia, Tambs flew to Washington and offered a background briefing to a few American reporters. He emphasized the presence of guerrillas.[96]

In short, the raid fulfilled a Reagan-Casey political goal. According to another account, "it appeared that the army's (and Ambassador Tambs's) long-held suspicions about a 'FARC-narc' connection were true."[97] The *New York Times* duly reported on its front page Tambs's story that Colombian police had attacked a cocaine processing plant guarded by communist guerrillas; an adjacent story added that, according to the Colombia military, smugglers were hauling cocaine out of the country and returning with Cuban arms for leftist insurgents.[98]

The notion of a narcoguerrilla alliance has since been derided by non-government experts like Bruce Bagley.[99] Indeed it was a notion for which Casey failed to get more than limited corroboration, even from the CIA's own analysis of the Tranquilandia evidence.[100] According to Rensselaer Lee, "recent journalistic accounts and the author's conversations with State Department officials suggest that the original reports of the FARC's involvement in Tranquilandia were incorrect."[101] There were six such labs in the Yari region, all probably known to the Colombian military. The FARC had in fact raided one of them in 1983, seized eighteen people and four planes, and demanded a ransom of $425,000. "Several days later, soldiers from the Colombian Army's Seventh Brigade rescued the hostages and recovered two of the planes. The entire operation was described in the Colombian media as a rescue of kidnapped cattlemen. . . . One informed U.S. source in Bogotá . . . claimed that the Army had long been aware of Yarí. Military leaders, he said, withheld the information from the antidrug police and even refused to let the police overfly the area. . . . [T]he sheer size of the Yarí complex suggests high-level complicity."[102]

However, the narcoguerrilla hypothesis was an important basis for the evolving Casey-Bush-Reagan strategy of militarizing the U.S. war on drugs. Thanks to the intervention of George Bush's office, the drug pilot Barry Seal provided timely photographic evidence of the narcoterrorist conspiracy that Casey was looking for. Seal later expanded the files on an Ochoa narcoterrorist network to include Nicaragua, rather than Seal's own supply line from Honduras.[103]

## The Seal Photos, North, the CIA, and Bush

We have seen that the Honduras DEA station was closed in June or July 1983, shortly after U.S. Customs had forwarded a request to it for information about Juan Ramón Matta Ballesteros and his airline SETCO (and after George Bush, as head of the newly created drug task force NNBIS, had integrated the CIA more directly into Reagan's War on

Drugs).[104] This closure did more than protect the Matta-SETCO-Contra connection: it also helped protect Barry Seal, the man whose farm was reported in the 1983 Customs report as the destination for drugs dropped from Hondu Carib's DC-4, and ultimately (by inference) from Matta's SETCO.[105]

Barry Seal was a major cocaine importer in the Southeastern United States. He was also rumored to be part of the CIA's anti-Sandinista campaign; one account dates Seal's CIA collaboration back to 1982.[106] Although much remains controversial about the Seal story, it is clear that at some point Seal, Bush, and the CIA became allies in the propaganda war to secure Contra funds from Congress. This section examines the disputed story of the photographs that Seal claimed to have taken of Sandinistas loading cocaine at a Nicaraguan airport.[107] Chapter 11 will return to the possibility that these photos were part of Reagan's "public diplomacy" program, a propaganda operation that has been described as "a covert domestic operation designed to manipulate the Congress and the American public."[108]

In March 1983, after a DEA investigation, Barry Seal was indicted in Fort Lauderdale for a shipment of 200,000 Quaaludes. Through 1983 and 1984 Seal attempted to beat the indictment by offering to become an informant for the DEA's Miami Field Division. His offers were refused.[109] Then, after his conviction in February 1984, Seal found a more sympathetic audience for his problem (perhaps aided by his knowledge of Hondu Carib and SETCO), who arranged for Seal to stay out of jail and in the cocaine business: in March 1984, while out of jail on an appeal bond, "Seal flew his Lear jet to Washington and telephoned Vice President Bush's office"; and he spoke on the street to staff members of the vice president's South Florida Task Force.[110]

Since Bush had overlapping responsibilities under Reagan for crisis management, counterterrorism (which in the Reagan administration came to include Contra support), and narcotics policies, Seal's decision to contact Bush's staff was well informed. And because of the informal arrangement that gave the Medellín cartel the south Florida market, the decision to send Barry Seal to Miami as an informant virtually guaranteed that he would be targeted against Medellín, rather than against those named with him (such as Matta and Ocampo) in the 1983 Customs report.

The Task Force's DEA liaison sent Seal to DEA's Washington headquarters, which then found a supervisor, newly posted to the Miami Field Division, who reversed previous DEA policy and agreed to handle

Seal as an informant. Less than a month later, on April 6, 1984, Seal flew to Colombia for a drug shipment that soon led to one of the White House's bigger propaganda efforts against the Sandinistas: photographs allegedly linking them to the Medellín cocaine trafficker Pablo Escobar.[111]

The DEA's use of its new informant is an instructive story in both the achievements and the limitations of our current strategies of law enforcement. There is no doubt that DEA was able to use Seal to prosecute drug cases successfully:

> On January 24, 1985, Seal engineered the seizure of ninety kilos of cocaine and the arrests of nine Colombians in Las Vegas. It was the biggest cocaine bust in the history of Nevada. Less than a month later, Seal scored another amazing coup at a meeting in Miami. He paid a $20,000 bribe to the chief minister of the Turks and Caicos Islands, a British colony south of the Bahamas. . . . [The chief minister] and two other government officials were arrested immediately after a second meeting with Seal in Miami. It marked the first time a foreign head of government had been arrested on drug charges in the United States.[112]

However precedent-setting these arrests may have been, they involved much pettier targets than Matta and Ocampo. Not surprisingly, the Reagan-Bush War on Drugs failed to pursue Seal's connections to Hondu Carib, SETCO, Matta, Honduras, and Cali.

Instead, after the Bush Task Force had signed him up with the DEA, Seal flew to Colombia to meet with the Ochoas of the Medellín cartel. He told DEA on his return that "the cartel had struck a deal with some ministers in Nicaragua's Sandinista government," and that Seal had been ordered to fly to Nicaragua to pick up cocaine.[113] Thus Seal allegedly flew to Nicaragua on June 24, 1984, and took the controversial photographs, which were soon leaked as evidence that Sandinistas were involved in the drug traffic.[114]

The Kerry report treats the Seal mission as an example of a bona fide DEA investigation that was disclosed prematurely "in an effort to influence a pending Congressional vote on Contra aid."[115] The truth of what happened still cannot be ascertained. There is some evidence that Seal did fly into Nicaragua with a planeload of cocaine and was shot at and forced down. His claim that he flew back with a C-123 to retrieve the cargo depends primarily on the evidence of the photographs. (One veteran of the Contra scene, who has proved reliable on other matters, has told us that these photographs were not taken in Nicaragua at all, but at a small Caribbean airstrip on Corn Island.)

Skeptical accounts have pointed to other problems in the Seal story. There is for example the little-noticed revelation in a congressional hearing that the Managua telephone number of Seal's alleged Sandinista contact, Federico Vaughan, which Seal called to set up his Nicaraguan rendezvous, "was a phone number controlled by the U.S. Embassy since 1985, and by the U.S. or other foreign missions continuously since 1981."[116] Moreover, those involved in the exploitation of the photos, at first in a vain effort to prevent the Boland II Amendment cutting off CIA aid to the Contras, have never agreed which of the Medellín leaders are shown: Ochoa, Rodríguez Gacha, or Escobar. Gen. Paul Gorman of U.S. Southern Command, who interrogated Seal directly, later testified under oath that Seal's film "showed Ochoa personally."[117] Richard Gregorie, the federal prosecutor who used Seal as a witness, and who indicted the leaders of the Medellín cartel, said under oath that the photographs "caught Jorge Ochoa and Gonzalo Rodríguez Gacha loading cocaine onto an airplane."[118] Like most published accounts, Oliver North's detailed notes on the photos at the time mention only Pablo Escobar and Federico Vaughan.[119]

The CIA was certainly involved in the preparations for Seal's trip to Nicaragua: it was CIA that provided the cameras for Seal's C-123K cargo plane in 1984.[120] It was the CIA that provided the disputed description of Seal's Nicaraguan contact, Federico Vaughan, as "an aide to [Nicaraguan Interior Minister] Borge."[121] It was almost certainly Duane Clarridge, the CIA's Latin American Division Chief in charge of the Contras, who was responsible for Oliver North's learning, the very day of Seal's return with the film, that the "Photos show Vaughan and Nic[araguan] Int[erior] Troops."[122] General Gorman claimed three days later that the U.S. now had "firm proof" of Sandinista drug trafficking; and DEA officials soon learned to their dismay that Clarridge and North had somehow obtained the Seal photos. Within weeks both the story and the photos had been made public, and DEA had to break off the Seal flights to Nicaragua.

North's diaries show a number of references to Seal during this period, such as a call from Clarridge on July 6 saying that "DEA thinks CIA leaked info to Gorman."[123] On July 17, the day that the Seal story was broken by the right-wing *Washington Times*, his diary suggests that behind the interest of the CIA in the Seal story lay that of the man first responsible for Seal's recruitment as an informant: Vice President George Bush.

> Call from [NSC staffer] Bob Sims. Washington Times story on cocaine. Call from Johnstone [possibly Craig Johnstone, director of the State Department Central America Affairs office]. [Doyle] McManus, L.A. Times says NSC resource claims W[hite] H[ouse] has pictures of Borge loading cocaine in Nic[aragua] [Redaction] Call from Phillip Hughes [a Bush aide on Contra matters] Re. Mtg w[ith] V[ice] P[resident]. Drugs. . . . Call to Frank M—Bud Mullins [DEA Administrator Francis Mullen] Re—leak on DEA piece—Carlton Turner [NSC narcotics adviser].[124]

By 1985 DEA officials were pointedly dissociating themselves from the government claims, based on the Seal photos, of a high-level Sandinista drug connection. DEA skepticism did not stop Bush, Poindexter, and North from expanding this story; they claimed, for example, that the November 1985 attack by M-19 guerrillas on the Colombian Palace of Justice had been coordinated by Nicaragua and the Medellín cartel. This unlikely charge against Nicaragua (discounted by the DEA chief) led Reagan to sign a secret National Security Decision Directive on "Narcotics and National Security" in April 1986—the original authorization for the present Bush drug strategy. This NSDD was intended to supply

> a philosophical basis for insisting the U.S. military and the intelligence community play a bigger role in countering drug trafficking. In disclosing the NSDD, Bush told a Houston press conference, "The demonstrable role drug trafficking played in the [Colombia Palace of Justice] massacre is anything but an isolated event." Ten days after Bush made this statement, a special investigative tribunal appointed by the surviving members of the [Colombian] Supreme Court announced its conclusions: the guerrillas had attacked the Palace of Justice to further their own interests, not at the instigation of the traffickers or of Nicaragua.[125]

The Reagan-Bush bluster against Nicaragua was, in short, a classic example of the Big Lie. Whatever Nicaragua's true relationship to the international drug traffic (not one country in the region has managed to escape involvement), it is surely small compared to the historical involvement of the CIA. Before the 1989 Cuban drug trials, the judicious Rensselaer Lee, who does not discuss the CIA role at all, examined the circumstantial evidence linking Cuban and Nicaraguan officials to the drug traffic and concludes: "The role played by Cuba and Nicaragua in

really t
accoun
Fernar
it adds
in San
brothe
claime
ber of
full of
mitted
had ov
U.S. g

On
subcon
Menes
source:
investi
he was
subcon

a 1
Ca
he
kil
ad
Dl
wh
co

in the h
largely b
a month
2. T
gro" Ch
ex-Moss:
nick, and
connecti
member
1982 an
Duane (
to Edén
flight of
vember
3. A
of the N
aides Oc
Adolfo
U.S. go
Clarridg
manager
amanian
associate
at Flori
and Car
story ha
supply
hands o
4. T
ex-CIA
ñez, and
dated b
forces
Vidal re
faction.
closely
North's
this con
belatedl
been dr

drug smuggling is minuscule compared to the role played by countries that are friends and allies of the United States."[126] Even today it seems relatively small.

Was the CIA in the 1980s still in alliance with the right-wing political elements of the International Connection's politics of cocaine in Central America? This impression is certainly corroborated by the evidence of CIA involvement in the Contra drug connections that eventually prevailed in Costa Rica.

on Contra drug allegations; that report focused instead on a source it called "a major Colombian cocaine smuggler, Alvaro Carvajal Minota," suppressing the fact that Carvajal was merely a regional distributor based in San Francisco. The State Department suppressed the names of the suppliers in Colombia, who according to the FBI teletype were "Humberto Ortiz, and Fernando Ortiz from Cali, Colombia."[10]

The Kerry subcommittee reprinted the misleading State Department report and followed it with its own finding:

> The Subcommittee found that the Frogman arrest involved cocaine from a Colombian source, Carvajal-Minota. In addition, Zavala and Cabezas [the arrested men] had a second source of supply, Nicaraguans living in Costa Rica associated with the Contras. FBI documents from the Frogman case identify the Nicaraguans as Horacio Pereira, Troilo Sanchez and Fernando Sanchez. Pereira was convicted on cocaine charges in Costa Rica in 1985 and sentenced to 12 years in prison. An important member of the Pereira organization was Sebastian "Huachan" Gonzalez, who also was associated with ARDE in Southern Front Contra operations. Robert Owen advised North in February 1985, that Gonzalez was trafficking in cocaine. . . . During the Pereira trial, evidence was also presented by the Costa Rica prosecutor showing that drug traffickers had asked leader Ermundo Chamorro, the brother of UDN-FARN leader Fernando "El Negro" Chamorro, for assistance with vehicles to transport cocaine and for help with a Costa Rica police official. Troilo and Fernando Sanchez were marginal participants in the Contra movement and relatives of a member of the FDN Directorate.[11]

Thus the Kerry report indicated a high-level Contra drug connection centered on the families of two Contra leaders (Sánchez and "El Negro" Chamorro) which dated back to 1981–82. This connection appears to have undergone modifications as the Argentine management was replaced in 1982 by the CIA, and the CIA in 1984 (with the Boland Amendment prohibiting CIA aid) by Oliver North.

Aristides Sánchez was the sole hold-over from the original three-man FDN directorate in 1981–82, when the Reagan administration used the Argentine military junta as a go-between in the day-to-day management of the Contras. In 1982, after the Falkland War and the fall of the junta, the CIA, having failed to persuade Israel to stand in for Argentina, assumed that management role itself. The new CIA men, who "had no use for Sánchez," moved to diminish his importance and that of the Argentines, backing instead the other two FDN leaders (José Francisco Cardenal and Mariano Mendoza). But after some persuasive threats (said to have been orchestrated by Bermúdez and his death-squad specialist, Ricardo Lau), Cardenal and Mendoza left Honduras in panic. Only Sánchez and the local Argentines remained.[12]

The CIA's disenchantment with Sánchez was part of a disengagement by the Reagan administration in 1982–83 from its embarrassing collaboration with the Argentinian-backed CAL, the regional section of the World Anti-Communist League, and the continental WACL-CAL strategy of right-wing hegemony based on drug alliances (see Chapter 5). After the Falkland Islands fiasco, the spell of the Reagan-WACL-CAL romance was broken. García Meza in Bolivia and d'Aubuisson in El Salvador both lost power. In Guatemala, a briefly successful coup in 1982 by WACL-leader Sandoval and his lieutenant, Leonel Sisniega, was quickly frustrated by a U.S.-backed military countercoup.[13] U.S. narcotics law enforcement helped to dismantle these remnants of the old Argentine connection. D'Aubuisson's decline from favor with the Reagan administration was followed by the temporary seizure of a plane in Texas belonging to one of his financial backers, which carried a cargo of $5.9 million in cash.[14] Following García Meza's ouster (under U.S. pressure) in 1982, his former Minister of the Interior and cocaine connection, Luis Arce Gomez (a cousin of Bolivian drug kingpin Roberto Suarez Gomez) was indicted on drug charges in Miami in 1983 and subsequently arrested in Argentina.[15]

In Honduras, Aristides Sánchez survived (and as of November 1989 was the lone civilian survivor in the latest Contra military junta).[16] But a spate of drug arrests in the United States between December 1982 and February 1983 wound up the Sánchez family Frogman connection.[17]

## The "El Negro" Chamorro Family Connection to Noriega

The effect of these arrests was not to abolish but rather to realign the Contra drug connection and apparently to increase the importance of Contras in Costa Rica associated with Fernando "El Negro" Chamorro, such as his brother Ermundo and Contra leader Sebastián "Guachan" González. "Guachan" González was part of the old international Tercerista (noncommunist left) coalition that had backed Edén Pastora against Somoza and again against the Contras. The Terceristas had been supported by Panamanian leaders Omar Torrijos and Manuel Noriega and led by the Panamanian Hugo Spadafora. Also a member of the older Horacio Pereira drug trafficking network, "Guachan" González, was arrested on cocaine charges in Costa Rica in 1984 and then mysteriously released. He soon escaped to Panama, where he worked for Panamanian President Eric Arturo del Valle and for Noriega, an old personal friend.[18]

Between the arrest of Pereira in 1982 and that of "Guachan" González in 1984, cocaine was flown to Costa Rica from Panama by a number of Panamanian pilots, such as César Rodríguez, Floyd Carlton (who was Noriega's personal pilot), and Teofilo Watson, all of whom as in 1979 flew support for Edén Pastora. José Blandón confirmed to Senator Kerry that "where drugs were used, the money, the proceeds, was used to support the Contras through Mr. ['Guachan'] Gonzalez."[19]

Blandón described the César Rodríguez-Floyd Carlton gunrunning operation as being much closer to Noriega than to Torrijos; he testified that Noriega's support for the two pilots led to an investigation of Noriega by Torrijos shortly before the latter was killed in a plane crash.[20] Blandón also testified that a network under Mike Harari, an adviser first to Torrijos and then to Noriega, supplied arms via "Israeli citizens, Panamanians, and United States citizens" to the Contras from 1982 to 1986. The Kerry report apparently identifies the Harari network with the Rodríguez network, but other accounts suggest that Rodríguez worked with two Panamanian financiers, Jorge Krupnick and Ricardo Bilonick, both now wanted in the U.S. on drug charges.[21]

The Kerry subcommittee was able to demonstrate the same kind of U.S. protection and subsidy for the Floyd Carlton drug group as for the Frigorificos and Frogman connections. In 1986, the U.S. State Department again chose to provide "humanitarian assistance" through a company owned and operated by drug traffickers. In this case the company was DIACSA, "a Miami-based air company operated as the headquarters of a drug trafficker enterprise for convicted drug traffickers Floyd Carlton and Alfredo Caballero."[22] After one of their planes was forced down in Florida on September 23, 1985, with nine hundred pounds of cocaine, Floyd Carlton and Alfredo Caballero (a Cuban veteran of the Bay of Pigs) were indicted, and eventually arrested and convicted. Caballero got probation; Carlton got nine years. This case led to the 1988 indictment in Miami of Manuel Noriega for drug trafficking.[23]

According to Blandón, who should know, Carlton flew drugs in 1985 for the Cali cartel in Colombia. This connection would represent a continuation of the supply line of the late 1970s, when the cocaine for Torrijos's cocaine-financed arms deliveries to guerrillas came from Santiago Ocampo and Eduardo Tascón in Cali.[24] But after 1984 the leadership of the "Guachan" González-Ermundo Chamorro connection was effectively broken up. "Guachan" González was indicted in Costa Rica in November 1984.[25] A Miami DEA case was opened in early 1985 against Caballero and other members of the firm DIACSA, which until then had been supplying ARDE (see the discussion of Morales below). The pilot Teofilo Watson was murdered in May 1985, as was César Rodríguez in March 1986. In April 1984, "El Negro" Chamorro defected to the ranks of the FDN Contras and their Costa Rica ally John Hull.

By accident or design, this termination of what we may call the first Panamanian supply line to the Contras in Costa Rica followed the April 1984 termination of U.S. support for Edén Pastora (who had been the main beneficiary of this Panamanian connection) and the increase of support for Pastora's arch-enemy John Hull under North. Hull's influence with the ARDE Contras was enhanced by the collapse of the Noriega-Carlton supply line, beginning with the Costa Rican drug-smuggling indictment of "Guachan" González. González's place in the terrorist group M-3 was taken over by a CIA-trained Cuban-American from Miami, Felipe Vidal, who throughout 1983 and 1984 had been working with Hull to undercut Pastora's influence.[26]

The CIA appears to have been behind the infiltration of Vidal into the Contra front in 1983, for which the arrangements were made by the American rancher Bruce Jones and the Costa Rican Civil Guard Col. Rodrigo Paniagua.[27] There is no reason to think that the CIA meant to encourage Vidal to develop a drug connection in 1983. On the contrary, Bruce Jones has since told investigators that at the time he was told to "stay away from Frank Castro," Vidal's most notorious drug associate. But with the unexpected Boland Amendment cutting off all CIA funding in 1984, it became more difficult to be fastidious.

By 1985 the conflict between Pastora and Hull had taken on the coloring of a local cocaine war. José Blandón and Floyd Carlton, a close friend of Spadafora, told the Kerry subcommittee how Teofilo Watson's murder was part of a larger deal in which Watson's drug plane was hijacked and diverted from its intended destination to John Hull's ranch.[28] The end of the "Guachan" González network cleared the way for the emergence of two new drug-linked supply networks based in Miami: that of the Colombian trafficker Jorge Morales, who flew arms and drugs for the Pastora faction from 1984 to 1986, and that of the Miami Cubans Francisco Chanes, Moisés Nuñez, and Felipe Vidal (who worked with Hull, Owen, North, and the anti-Pastora faction).[29] Both of these connections, as we shall see, were contacted by John Hull during his visits to Miami from as early as 1983.

Thus it is possible to see crude correspondences between shifts in overall responsibility for the Contra support effort and the main sources or connections in the local drug traffic. Just as the Frogman connection, broken up in 1983, corresponded to the Argentine era, so the "Guachan" González connection corresponded chiefly to the era of Duane Clarridge and the CIA from the fall of 1982 until May 1984.

The Miami-based Morales and Cuban-exile connections to John Hull, which we examine next, had their ascendancy from May 1984 (when Duane Clarridge introduced his successor Oliver North to Contra leaders in Central America) to 1986. "April or May" 1984, as it happens, is when Morales claims to have first spoken directly to the Contra leaders Adolfo "Popo" Chamorro, Octaviano César, and Marcos Aguado, who introduced himself as the chief of the air force of the Southern group from Nicaragua.[30]

## John Hull Brings in Jorge Morales and the Miami Cubans (1983–84)

The years 1983–84 saw two concomitant changes in the political status of the Southern Front Contras, which were reflected in further modifications of the "El Negro" Chamorro drug connection. The first was the curtailment of congressional funding by the successive Boland Amendments of December 1982 and September 1984. (The first of these, by prohibiting CIA use of funds "for the purpose of overthrowing the Government of Nicaragua," amounted to cutting off aid to the Southern Front, since it held the CIA to its stated purpose of stopping Nicaraguan arms flows to insurgents in El Salvador, on Nicaragua's opposite border.) The second was the ending, by May 1984, of all CIA support for ARDE forces loyal to Edén Pastora.

These changes shifted CIA responsibility for the Southern Front away from the CIA embassy station in Costa Rica and towards the CIA's operational asset on the border, the American rancher John Hull. In mid-1983 Hull made trips to Miami and Washington that put him in touch with Miami-based drug trafficking organizations of Jorge Morales and former CIA Cubans like Frank Castro. And in mid-1983 both Morales and his pilot Gary Betzner first began using Fort Lauderdale Executive Airport and Ilopango Air Force Base in El Salvador.[31] Both of these networks began trafficking through Costa Rica in 1983; both made flights to airfields owned or controlled by John Hull; and both appear to have benefited from the developments that eliminated the César Rodríguez supply line from Panama in 1984–86.

The Hull-Miami connection appears to have been initiated by the ex-CIA narcoterrorist Frank Castro and his close colleague Porfirio Bonet. Both men had been arrested and then released in the Miami drug bust "Operation Tick-Talks" of 1981 (see Chapter 2).[32] The two men visited

Hull and his neighbor Bill Crone in Costa Rica and arranged for the introduction of Miami Cubans into the Southern Front. Soon afterwards, in June 1983, Hull came to Miami with the Morales-trained drug pilot Gerardo Duran and went to the office of Jorge Morales.[33] At the same time, Crone also came to Miami and visited a training camp near Naples, Florida, which was financed by Tick-Talks suspects Frank Castro and Jose Marcos. In August 1983 Morales's pilots began flying arms to the Contras and drugs on the return flights.[34]

On both trips to Miami, Hull and Crone discussed the transfer of a DC-3, apparently the one eventually delivered to the ARDE "air force" by Morales.[35] Robert Owen later reported to North that it was "former 'Bay of Pigs' veteran Frank Castro, who is heavily into drugs . . . who gave Pastora the new DC-3" delivered by Morales.[36] This DC-3 has often been used to link Edén Pastora to drug traffickers, but it was actually given to Marcos Aguado, his air force chief, and to Octaviano César.

According to Morales's sworn testimony, Aguado and César represented themselves as CIA agents. Leslie Cockburn, checking on Morales's claim, found "no less than eight separate sources, ranging from senior contras to high-level administration officials in Washington [who] attested to the fact that Cesar was an operative of the Central Intelligence Agency."[37] Aguado had connections to Hull as well as Pastora; and on the June 1983 flight to Miami he served as Hull's pilot.[38] In the break-up of ARDE at the time of the La Penca bombing, the DC-3 followed the anti-Pastora faction of Alfonso Robelo into service for the FDN, and was based at the Ilopango air base in El Salvador.

John Hull's trip to Miami appears to have been a search for a financial and recruiting base from which to displace his enemy Edén Pastora. On July 21, 1983, Hull, Crone, and an alternative Contra leader called "Wycho" (Luis Rivas) came to Washington to lobby against Pastora as well. As American citizens from Indiana, Hull and Crone went to the Washington office of Indiana Sen. Dan Quayle, where they met Quayle's young legislative assistant Robert Owen. Owen took Hull to meet Oliver North, whom he then knew by reputation only.[39] In September 1983 Hull and Crone flew Owen to Costa Rica, where they introduced him to Alfonso Robelo, a Nicaraguan millionaire based in Costa Rica.

To judge by Owen's subsequent close collaboration with Hull, Hull sought not just to bring the Southern Front Contras more closely into line with Calero and the FDN in Honduras, but also to give them a more secure base in Washington. In late 1983 Owen left Quayle's office to join the powerful Washington public relations firm of Gray and Co. and later to do public relations work for the Contras.[40] This involved creating a new umbrella organization, the United Nicaraguan Opposition (UNO), in which the Calero-Bermúdez FDN link was disguised by the presence of more liberal Contra political leaders (and ex-Sandinista allies), like Robelo, who could be used to garner votes for Contra assistance from congressional Democrats.

In 1984–86, at least on the UNO masthead, Calero shared leadership with two such liberals. One of these was Robelo, who endeared himself to Hull when, on May 29, 1984, he led a majority of ARDE's governing council into alliance with the Honduras-based FDN. (The next day, a bomb exploded at the La Penca press conference that Pastora had called to disavow the Robelo faction.) Afterwards the wavering "El Negro" Chamorro, no longer the force he had been in the Pastora-"Guachan" González days, appears to have allied himself, at least tentatively, with the Rivas-Robelo faction.[41]

## The Jorge Morales Cocaine Connection, 1984–86

After the Robelo defections at the time of La Penca, Pastora, according to his colleague Karol Prado, appointed a new second-in-command, Adolfo "Popo" Chamorro. Soon afterwards, Pastora was approached by "Popo's" cousins, Octaviano and Alfredo César, as new political allies.[42] In the fall of 1984, two or three weeks after Pastora's return from a July 1984 visit to Washington, Octaviano César and "Popo" Chamorro went back to Morales in Miami. Morales claimed that the three men worked out a deal in which he would provide financial and material support for the Contras of the Southern Front, and César, in exchange, would intercede with his CIA friends to help Morales in the matter of a March 1984 drug indictment in Miami.[43] The Kerry subcommittee obtained U.S. government records of an October 1984 plane trip into the U.S. from the Bahamas showing that César had signed a declaration for $400,000 in drug money that Morales was donating to the Contras.[44]

In 1984 Betzner also started flying for Morales and the Contras again, this time from Fort Lauderdale to John Hull's ranch.[45] Betzner told the Kerry subcommittee that after two separate flights in 1984 to Costa Rica, he and Hull watched together while arms were unloaded and cocaine loaded for the return flight to Florida.[46] Betzner's co-pilot, Fabio "Tito" Carrasco, testified in 1990 that he too saw workers at John Hull's ranch load their plane with cocaine.[47]

To summarize: after the CIA cutoff, Pastora had accepted a CIA agent (César) as his new fundraiser; César then, according to Morales, developed the Morales drug connection to which Pastora was later linked by U.S.

government sources. For a little over a year, Morales arranged for arms flights to John Hull's ranch and other airports, which were paid for by returning cargoes of cocaine. Both Betzner and his co-pilot, Carrasco, testified under oath that they saw the loading of smuggled arms and the unloading of cocaine take place in broad daylight at Florida airports controlled by U.S. Customs, who (as Morales had promised them) did not interfere.[48] Morales even heard through one of his sources that Miami law enforcement knew about, but did not act on, one of his 1985 flights; this "led me to believe that I was very well protected."[49] Morales's impression was corroborated by his extraordinary freedom of movement to other countries after his 1984 indictment, despite DEA objections.[50]

Morales understood that Octaviano César's protection for him derived not just from the CIA, but also from César's connections to " 'high-level Washington people'. . . . Specifically, Morales remembers Cesar telling him that 'he had spoken with Vice President Bush about my situation,' that is, about clearing up his indictment on drug charges."[51] Morales later told another author that "this was no rogue operation . . . : the CIA, the State Department and the White House knew all about it, and, indeed, in May 1986 Morales was due to meet Vice-President Bush to discuss the 'secret operation,' but the meeting was abruptly canceled at the last moment."[52]

Such a meeting is not hard to imagine, given George Bush's habit of frequenting Republican fundraisers in Miami, which were sometimes hosted by his son Jeb. Morales himself testified that he had given away about $600,000 for political protection in other countries. But in response to questions from Senator Kerry, Morales testified publicly that he had not given political contributions in the United States, and specifically not in Miami.[53]

Morales's claim to have flown arms and drugs for the Contras in a CIA-approved arrangement was dismissed as "not credible" by Miami U.S. Attorney Leon Kellner and his assistant Richard Gregorie, and the two men discouraged the Kerry subcommittee staff from meeting with Morales. The State Department acknowledged only one drug flight for the Contras, in which Morales's pilot, Gerardo Duran, was arrested in January 1986.

However, Fabio Carrasco, the government's own witness in a 1990 drug-smuggling case (against José Abello in Oklahoma) testified that on thirty or forty occasions he had delivered millions of dollars from cocaine earnings, on orders from Morales, to Contra leaders Octaviano César and "Popo" Chamorro. He also said he had personally supervised flights of arms to Costa Rica that had returned with cocaine. Carrasco said "he believed the operation, including bringing several planeloads of 300–400 kilograms to the United States, was known and approved by the CIA."[54] He also testified that none of the five to seven loads brought to Florida (including one he flew personally) was ever seized, perhaps because they came aboard Contra-related aircraft that operated under an aura of official protection.[55]

This witness, unlike Morales, had no clear motive for this testimony, which was elicited from him under cross-examination. Moreover, he corroborated earlier testimony to the Kerry subcommittee from another drug pilot: that the Morales-Duran operation overlapped with that of Floyd Carlton, flying cocaine from Panama via the facilities and personnel of DIACSA and the Guerra family in Costa Rica.[56] Thus we may talk of the Morales connection as the second Panamanian supply line to the Contras. Noriega's 1984 contribution of $100,000 to "Popo" Chamorro and Octaviano César may have been motivated by the desire to buy protection for his trafficking through Carlton, for which Noriega was ultimately indicted.

Despite the revelations about Adolfo "Popo" Chamorro in the Kerry subcommittee, and his April 1986 arrest in Costa Rica, Chamorro was named in June 1990 by his aunt, President Violeta Barrios de Chamorro, to be her government's consul in Miami. Also in 1990, Carrasco was interviewed by Jonathan Winer of Senator Kerry's staff. Winer told us as this book was going to press that the witness supplied details about the personal involvement of Octaviano César and "Popo" Chamorro in drug deals.[57]

In December 1985, when the Contra-drug story finally reached the American mainstream press, Morales, a Colombian, was made the scapegoat. Before the story was broken by Associated Press reporters Brian Barger and Robert Parry, their superiors had removed their references to John Hull and "virtually all" Contra factions and replaced them with a CIA report attributing drug-financed arms purchases to one of Pastora's top commanders (see Chapter 11).[58] Three weeks later, on January 16, 1986, Morales's magical protection vanished. Bahamian police authorities, advised by DEA, seized an 80-kg shipment of cocaine that had been flown in from a Costa Rican airport, Liberia, close to Hull's ranch.[59] In the same month, Duran, Carlton, and DIACSA were indicted. In 1987, summoned before the Iran-Contra Committee, CIA Central American Task Force chief Alan Fiers again pointed away from Hull and towards Pastora: "there was a lot of cocaine trafficking around Eden Pastora. . . . None around FDN, none around UNO."[60]

We have already noted that Mario Calero of the FDN had a part interest in Hondu Carib, the airline operated by suspected drug trafficker Frank Moss. For two years, Robert Owen had been reporting to North about FDN and UNO drug problems. On April 1, 1985, for example, Owen registered "concern" to North about "El Negro" Chamorro (now affiliated with the FDN) because his military commander, José "Chepon" Robelo, had "past indiscrestions [sic]" including "potential involvement with drug running and the sales of goods provided by USG."[61] Alfonso Robelo of UNO had a nephew, Araldo Lacayo Robelo, who was later named in connection with a 50-kg shipment of cocaine for arms.[62]

But the heart of the new drug connection to the Southern Front seems at first to have been the new connection between Pastora's aide Octaviano César and Miami-based Morales. And by 1987, after the political retirement of Alfonso Robelo, the most powerful Contra survivor from Costa Rica was Octaviano's brother, Alfredo César.

It is hard to trace the politics of shifts in the Contra-drug connection with any certainty after 1984. After defections from Pastora to the FDN, the political and military significance of the Southern Front declined; and some observers speculate that, as for some CIA Cubans a decade or so earlier, for some Contra leaders drug smuggling became no longer a means but an end in itself.[63]

From 1984 to 1986, Morales, even though under indictment, was free to travel abroad, while his planes (according to Morales, Betzner, and Carrasco) made at least two arms flights to Hull's airstrips that were paid for with Contra cocaine.[64] This situation, interrupted by the arrest of Betzner in November 1984, ended with the arrests of Duran and Morales in January 1986 and the separate indictment of Carlton one week later, which led to his arrest.[65]

By 1986, thanks to Oliver North and Robert Owen, Richard Secord had displaced most of the competitive arms suppliers for the Contras.[66] Most of the military equipment for the Southern Front was coming via Ilopango in El Salvador rather than from Noriega in Panama. With the end of the Morales operation, and with all of his Panamanian allies and pilots arrested or murdered, Pastora in 1986 announced his retirement from the fight.

## Eliminating the Foreigners: The John Hull–Miami Cuban Connection

The winding up of the Morales smuggling operation in 1986 left untouched the other drug-linked network contacted by Hull in Miami: that of Frank Castro, Rene Corvo, and Corvo's friend Moisés Nuñez, who had installed himself in Costa Rica as the head of the seafood company Frigorificos de Puntarenas. In fact, as the Kerry report noted, Frigorificos de Puntarenas was a "cover for the laundering of drug money."[67]

The function of Frigorificos was not to facilitate arms-for-drugs deals, as the Morales network did, but rather to serve as a CIA operational asset using Cubans who were also CIA agents. Robert Owen's memos and other sources clearly document the close collaboration between Moisés Nuñez, John Hull, Robert Owen, and CIA Costa Rica station chief Joe Fernandez. This evidence explains why a frozen shrimp company was among the drug-linked companies chosen to receive State Department funds ($261,937) in 1986.[68] At the time, Frigorificos was being used by Hull, North, and the CIA as a front for a covert maritime operation against Nicaragua. The arrangement is summarized in one of Owen's memos to North:

> Moises Nunez, a Cuban who has a shrimping business in
> Punteranous [*sic*] is fronting the [maritime] operation . . . I have
> met with him on a number of occasions and he seems up front
> and willing to keep his mouth shut. Joe [Fernandez] has agreed
> to have him used. . . . If we can get two shrimp boats, Nunez is
> willing to front a shrimping operation on the Atlantic coast.
> These boats can be used as motherships. I brought this up awhile
> ago and you agreed and gave me the name of a DEA person who
> might help with the boats.[69]

Although a version of this memo was released in the Iran-Contra hearings, the relevant section was censored. Thus the public did not then learn that Owen was plotting with North to use the DEA in support of known drug traffickers. It is not clear whether the document was censored in the interests of national security or of Owen himself. At the time, Owen was a defendant in a suit brought by the Washington-based Christic Institute alleging that Owen's involvement with Secord, Hull, Vidal, Corvo, Chanes, and Nuñez constituted a criminal conspiracy.[70] Secord's investigator in the Christic matter, Glenn Robinette, turned for help, via Robert Owen, to the same Moisés Nuñez.[71] But Nuñez was no outside investigator; like Owen, he was a codefendant and coconspirator actively interested in stopping the Christic lawsuit. Once again, profits from a U.S. covert operation (the Iran arms sales from which Secord paid Robinette) may have been used to protect, rather than prosecute, the drug traffic.

FBI documents appended to the Kerry report confirm that the Miami-based Cuban network of Corvo and Nuñez in Costa Rica was involved in a number of conspiratorial illegalities, as originally alleged in 1986 and denied by government representatives. Rene Corvo himself admitted to the FBI that on March 6, 1985, he had smuggled arms out of the United States in a plane flying to Hull's ranch in Costa Rica. These arms, he told them, included a 20-millimeter cannon, a 60-millimeter mortar launcher, and a .308 sniper rifle from Tom Posey, leader of the American Contra support group CMA.[72] Yet CIA representatives assured members of Kerry's staff in a secret meeting of May 6, 1986 that "no weapons were aboard" this flight.[73]

According to a Costa Rica prosecutor's report in January 1990, Moisés Nuñez was running a drug front through which "monies coming from narcotrafficking were delivered to the Nicaraguan contras."[74] An informant told the FBI that Nuñez's partner Francisco Chanes, another Cuban-American associate of John Hull and an official of Frigorificos, was giving money "from narcotics transactions" to "the Nicaraguan Contra guerrillas."[75] The same informant called Chanes a "close associate" of Frank Castro (see Chapter 2).[76]

In yet another FBI report, Castro admitted working with Chanes to supply Corvo with food and ammunition and also to meeting Hull.[77] In one interview, Corvo told the FBI he had trained Moisés Nuñez, who was "assisting the anti-Communist cause in Central America," as a paratrooper. Nuñez and Chanes were identified by company records as officers of Frigorificos de Puntarenas.[78] In a later interview, Corvo readily confessed to his conspiratorial violation of antineutrality laws as part of a network involving John Hull, Frank Chanes, and Felipe Vidal: "CORVO stated that the only crimes he had committed are United States neutrality violations for shipping weapons from South Florida to Central America. . . . The non-lethal equipment and para-military supplies were stored at the residence of FRANK CHANES in Southwest Miami. . . . STEVEN CARR and ROBERT THOMPSON were also on the cargo plane. . . . CORVO stated JOHN HULL and FELIPE VIDAL, aka MORGAN, drove CARR and THOMPSON to the new training camp . . . in Pocosol."[79]

In short, the Kerry report exhibits corroborate the initial allegations explored by Kerry's personal staff in 1986 that linked Hull, Vidal, Corvo, Chanes, Nuñez, and Frank Castro to a conspiratorial network involved in both drug trafficking and gunrunning.[80] The same allegations were at the core of the Christic Institute suit filed in May 1986. In 1988 the Justice Department itself, after prodding from Senator Kerry, belatedly indicted individuals both for gunrunning (Rene Corvo), and for drug trafficking and money laundering through a complex of shrimp companies, including Frigorificos de Puntarenas.[81] (The indictments have since been dismissed or dropped.)

Of the Cubans inserted into the Southern Front in 1983, the most important, and the most controversial, was Felipe Vidal. North's notebooks show him as one of three men working in 1984 with John Hull, and Owen wrote to North later in 1985 that both he and Joe Fernandez "would suggest using Felipe Vidal" as a liaison with the "Costa Rican Situation."[82] A 1986 Owen memo on the Frigorificos operation talks of putting an American Special Forces veteran on to the project, "in the hands of Max (Felipe Vidal) and Nunez."[83] Joe Fernandez reportedly testified to the Iran-Contra committees that "Vidal and Corvo were 'our people' (CIA) and had a 'problem with drugs,' but that the agency had had to 'protect' them."[84] Journalists went further, calling Vidal a CIA contract agent and overt advocate of terrorism who "has been arrested at least seven times in Miami on narcotics and weapons charges."[85]

The FBI documents reprinted in the Kerry report contain relatively little information on Vidal, but they roughly outline the "Corvo" or "Costa" investigation that was rendered inactive in 1986 after the Justice Department in Washington became aware of it.[86] The Corvo gunrunning incident was sensitive not just because it might have deterred Congress from restoring military aid to the Contras (as they did in June 1986) but also because the smuggling was protected. The arms, including the cannon, had, according to witnesses, been loaded on to the plane in broad daylight, even though the export declarations given to Customs described the shipments as "clothing" and "medical supplies" for "the refugees of San Salvador."[87] The same documents prove that the plane flew to Ilopango, a military air base (at which both Contra representatives and U.S. military personnel were stationed) where planes required special prior permission to land. Moreover, at least one of the Kerry staff witnesses had seen the weapons stored in the presence of cocaine. Thus the March 1985 Corvo shipment represented a guns-for-drugs operation protected by the U.S. government in which those protected included suspected major drug smugglers and CIA-trained terrorists.

This U.S. government protection appears to have been ongoing. We see from the FBI documents that it was extended to individuals with previous narcotics indictments, which were always thrown out. Frank Castro, for example, had been indicted under both Operation Tick-Talks and Operation Grouper, two notorious DEA cases that went nowhere: Operation Grouper had been handled by a corrupt member of Vice President Bush's Task Force on Drugs, who skipped town after being indicted on corruption and smuggling charges.[88]

Those protected in the Corvo investigation were not only drug traffickers, but also notorious terrorists. The FBI investigation involved Frank Castro, the former organizer of CORU, and many others with records of terrorism. The FBI documents confirm that, as FBI agent Currier suggested to the Iran-Contra committees, Corvo, Francisco Chanes, Frank Castro, Armando López Estrada, and others were at the time of the flight already under investigation for their alleged role in the May 1983 bombing of the Continental National Bank of Miami.[89] The list of Rene Corvo and Frank Castro associates in the FBI documents is a litany of terrorists associated with previous incidents in the United States and Canada, from Omega 7 (Luis Crespo) back to the *pragmatista* terrorists of the Watergate era (Eduardo Paz and Rafael Perez, alias Torpedo).[90] One (Ramon Sánchez) had even been part of a 1963 attempt by Frank Sturgis (later a Watergate burglar) to sink a Soviet tanker and thus frustrate the entente established between Kennedy and Khrushchev after the Cuban missile crisis.[91] The documents from the Iran-Contra and Christic depositions offer strong evidence that the illegalities of this Corvo-Castro-Vidal connection were more extensive, more high-level, and more murderous than the FBI documents alone indicate.

The protected terrorism of this group in the 1980s (when George Bush was in charge of the War on Drugs and counterterrorist activities) was a prolongation of the protected terrorism of the Frank Castro-Armando López Estrada-Luis Posada Carriles connection in 1976 (when Bush was director of the CIA). Indeed, these connections are only the most recent antiterrorist manifestations of a thirty-year pattern of drug-financed covert operations.

The scale of both protected trafficking and protected terrorism ensured that when Senator Kerry and his staff began to look into it, there would be the most strenuous efforts to discredit them and their witnesses. In the next chapter, we shall see that the Justice Department itself contrived to obstruct Senator Kerry's efforts to investigate the Contra-drug connections in Costa Rica and to discredit his witness Jack Terrell.

# Part II

# EXPOSURE AND COVER-UP

# 7 Jack Terrell Reveals the Contra-Drug Connection

Between 1985 and 1989, the story of Contra drug involvement was gradually revealed in the U.S. press and ultimately in the Kerry report. That revelation did not come easily; North, the FBI, and the Justice Depart ment mobilized to prevent it. Unusual things happened to the journalists and Congressmen who were brave enough to investigate the story.

Perhaps the strangest story of all is what happened to a whistle-blower, Jack Terrell, who was a prime source for many journalists and for Senator Kerry's staff. Terrell's problems became acute after he told the FBI about the drug-trafficking operation, Frigorificos de Puntarenas, which was part of the North-Owen-Hull Contra support apparatus in Costa Rica. The story is not yet over, but enough has already happened to Terrell to discourage others from following his example.

## How Released Documents Confirm
## Jack Terrell's Credibility

Terrell was an important source in bringing Contra drug involvement to the attention of the United States government. Although Justice Department officials tried to destroy Terrell's credibility at the time, many of his claims are now corroborated by the revelations of the Kerry report. In May 1986, National Public Radio ran a story on the Kerry investigation, featuring an interview with Jack Terrell in which he spoke of Corvo's gun-running "out of Fort Lauderdale, Florida . . . to Ilopango Air Base in El Salvador," and of his conversation with Contra supporters in Miami, who asked him to participate in a "seafood" front operation in which he could make a million dollars.[1] At the time of Terrell's broadcast, an anonymous Justice Department spokesman (later identified as Patrick Korten) was quoted as saying, "The U.S. Attorney in South Florida and the FBI have conducted an inquiry into all of these charges and none of them have any substance. . . . All leads were completely exhausted and interviews in Florida, Louisiana and Central America turned up absolutely nothing."[2]

Yet the FBI in Miami had already heard these allegations from Terrell; and they had already obtained independent corroboration of both the gunrunning and the alleged narcotics involvement of Francisco Chanes, said by Terrell's source (Steven Carr, who was on the flight) to have supplied the weapons.[3] And, as we have seen, the Justice Department finally indicted individuals both for the gunrunning (Rene Corvo), and for drug trafficking and money laundering through the seafood front (Luis Rodríguez).[4]

Terrell also charged that there was both drug smuggling and gunrunning through the ranch of Contra supporter John Hull in Costa Rica. The Kerry subcommittee heard from five witnesses, including one eyewitness, who testified that "Hull was involved in cocaine trafficking." In January 1989, as noted in Chapter 1, Hull was arrested by Costa Rican law enforcement authorities and charged with drug trafficking and violating Costa Rica's neutrality. These charges were set aside in July 1989, and Hull returned to the United States. But in January 1990, after the U.S. invasion of Panama, Costa Rican authorities sought to have John Hull and Felipe Vidal prosecuted on murder charges in connection with the La Penca bombing.[5]

These developments tend to corroborate Terrell's testimony on these disputed points and refute the Justice Department spokesman. This does not mean that all of Terrell's sensational charges, such as allegations of plots to assassinate Edén Pastora and Ambassador Tambs, have now been proved. And there is one specific area where many journalists suspect Terrell may have dissembled: his own account of how he came to be involved with the Contras. (Although he first presented himself to journalists as a self-trained mercenary, many have come to suspect that he was trained and directed by others.) But in a number of specific and serious drug charges, which in 1986 seemed hardly credible, Terrell has been corroborated beyond question. Indeed the credibility now called into question on the drug issues is that of the U.S. judicial system and indeed the U.S. political process.

In the next two chapters, we shall see how Oliver North used secret counterterrorism powers, conferred on him by Vice President Bush's Task Force on Combating Terrorism, to have the FBI place Terrell under continuous surveillance as a "terrorist threat" who might kill the president. We shall see also how elements of the FBI collaborated with North against one of their own witnesses. We shall see how in 1988, long after North had left his position, the Justice Department indicted Terrell for the very crimes which, as a whistle-blower, Terrell had brought to its attention. Finally, we shall see how the U.S. Congress, although controlled by Democrats, declined to investigate this abuse of power. In 1988, in the face of accurate threats and predictions that Terrell would soon be indicted, he refused, on the advice of counsel, to repeat under oath the story that the Christic Institute had counted on to help bring John Hull and others to account for the 1984 attempt at La Penca to kill Edén Pastora.

## How North and Terrell Came to Be Enemies

Although they became enemies, North and Terrell had initially been part of the same secret effort to keep the Contras' "body and soul together" after Congress voted in October 1984 to cut off all CIA support. Of the ragtag crew of American mercenaries and volunteers who emerged to help the Contras in the wake of the Boland Amendment, Terrell was probably the most experienced. Intelligent and well-spoken, he had been denied a conventional career by a youthful crime (driving in a stolen car over a state line) that had earned him a felony conviction and time in an adult prison. By his own account, his brief business career had been followed by experience with the white mercenaries fighting in Ian Smith's Rhodesia.[6]

With this experience, and with the help of some $20,000 whose source has never been explained, Terrell was accepted as an officer by a group of U.S. volunteers helping the Contras, who called themselves CMA, or Civilian Military Assistance.[7] He was given the nom de guerre of "Colonel Flaco" (The Thin One). In November 1984 CMA leader Tom Posey delegated Terrell to lead a CMA mission to the chief Contra bases in Honduras, where Terrell met the FDN leaders.

Further research has indicated that neither Posey's CMA nor Terrell's joining of it was the amateurish matter that it appeared. CMA had attracted journalistic and even Congressional attention in September 1984, when a Hughes 500MD helicopter was downed inside Nicaragua and two CMA "private volunteers," Dana Parker and Jim Powell, were killed. North promptly told McFarlane in a memo that he and a CIA official had urged Calero to postpone the raid; nevertheless he requested authorization to solicit funds from a private donor to replace the helicopter. McFarlane turned North down: "I don't think this is legal."[8] At the time, according to reporter Steven Emerson, "the CIA denied any responsibility for the crash to Congressional Committees and no connection was ever disclosed—but Army officials have revealed that the CIA 'borrowed' the helicopter from the Army and did not inform them ahead of time how the machine would be used."[9]

This incident occurred at the time of Operation Elephant Herd, under which the CIA stockpiled for the Contras weapons and material provided by the Defense Department at the lowest possible cost under the Economy Act.[10] The helicopter was clearly part of Duane Clarridge's CIA support operation, in which, as we shall see, Clarridge worked closely with some Pentagon personnel but reported directly to CIA Director Casey, cutting out his superiors in the CIA Operations Directorate.

These superiors included so-called moderates like John McMahon, who were quite at odds with North because of their unwillingness to revive the hostility that had divided CIA from Congress in the Watergate era. Two weeks after the helicopter fiasco, someone leaked to the *Washington Post* the existence of Elephant Herd and information that the CIA had also delivered to the Contras three light aircraft declared "excess" from the inventory of the New York Air National Guard.[11] In other words, the CMA helicopter raid had provoked a bureaucratic leaking battle in September 1984, just when Terrell presented himself to CMA.

Was Terrell positioning himself inside CMA to be a future part of this battle? Terrell himself told reporter William Thomas in April 1986 that his mysterious cash contribution to the CMA came to him after he was asked by a CIA employee (possibly one of those suspicious of Clarridge and North) "to probe CMA's Contra efforts."[12] Terrell in fact had managed to implant himself not only inside CMA, but also inside a more professional commando unit, code-named Pegasus, that was using CMA as a cover.

Pegasus, the brainchild of U.S. special operations veteran Frank Camper, planned under CMA's aegis to train Contras for future deep-penetration raids against Sandinista military targets in Nicaragua and (in Camper's words) "to eliminate Sandinist leadership personnel in 'secured' or rear areas."[13] In other words, Pegasus involved training for assassinations, an activity which the CIA had publicly renounced in the 1970s, and which after much debate had been renounced again in Reagan's 1981 Executive Order 12333 on intelligence.

In April 1984 North had drafted a National Security Decision Directive "for CIA-backed and -trained teams of foreign nationals to 'neutralize' terrorists," but after a stormy confrontation McMahon and others had blocked this effort, or so they thought.[14] Then in October, Associated Press and the *New York Times* broke the story of the CIA's assassination manual for the Contras with the front-page *Times* headline, "CIA Primer Tells Nicaraguan Rebels How to Kill."[15]

It was in this context that, in early December 1984, someone leaked the existence of the FDN-sanctioned Operation Pegasus to William Thomas of the *Memphis Commercial Appeal*. The story was widely reported in the U.S. press. As a result, the Government of Honduras ordered the twelve-man CMA/Pegasus mission deported. On December 12, 1984, Frank Camper (the originator of the Pegasus unit) reported to U.S. military intelligence that a CMA member known to him only as "Colonel Flaco" (i.e., Terrell) was the unit member who had been the leaker.[16] Whether Terrell acted alone or as the agent of a concerted operation (as North later saw him), this allegation initiated his reputation as a whistleblower.

On his return from that trip, apparently at the request of Adolfo Calero, Terrell met John Hull and Robert Owen, the two principal Americans in North's Costa Rica Contra support operation. According to Terrell, Hull appeared to be interested in using Terrell's commando skills against his personal enemy Edén Pastora.

In Terrell's words,

> It was Hull who first brought up Pastora. He asked if I knew Pastora. I didn't know who the hell he was. Then he said Pastora was a communist who flew the Sandinista flag in his camp. . . .
> He went on and on about how terrible this Pastora was. Then he said, "We gotta get rid of the sonuvabitch." I said, "What do you mean?" He said, "Kill him." I was told to draw up a scenario how it was gonna be done, and be ready to present it in Miami a week later at a meeting in [Adolfo] Calero's house.[17]

Owen later denied under oath Terrell's allegation that he was present during discussion of the killing of Pastora. But his own account of his actions in this period suggests that his services for the FDN were intended to complement those of Operation Pegasus. It was Owen who had introduced Hull to Calero in Honduras in late October 1984. Shortly thereafter Owen conveyed from North to Calero CIA maps of the Sandino Airport in Managua, where the Sandinistas' HIND-D helicopters, recently received from the Soviet Union, were stored.[18] And Camper, in his December 12, 1984, report on Operation Pegasus, had specified that, according to Posey, "The Soviet HIND-D helicopters were a priority target of the new unit."[19]

Owen has testified to his presence at the second meeting with Terrell and denied Terrell's account of it. Terrell told *Boston Globe* reporter Ben Bradlee, Jr., that at this meeting he himself "raised the Pastora issue by way of preparing to lay out the plan that Hull had instructed him to draw up. 'Calero went into a tirade about Pastora,' Terrell remembers. . . . He said 'That sonuvabitch has got to go.' Terrell then presented his plan to kill Pastora, which was designed to make it appear as if the Sandinistas were responsible."[20] According to Terrell, at this meeting Cuban exile Felipe Vidal allegedly commented, "We put a bomb under him the first time, but it didn't work because of bad timing."[21]

Terrell's account of two of these meetings may help explain why North and Owen were so alarmed when Terrell spoke later to Senator Kerry's staff, the Christic Institute, and the U.S. media. Had Terrell not been deterred from testifying, his statements would have been important pieces of evidence in the Christic Institute suit. Robert Owen later denied under oath that at the meeting in Calero's house there was "discussion of assassinating Eden Pastora again."[22] But in March 1985 Owen wrote to Adolfo Calero that (according to Tom Posey and Joe Adams, both present at the second meeting) Terrell himself "had volunteered to hit Pastora or anyone else provided the money is right." Owen advised Calero that Terrell was "a crazy" and should be avoided.[23]

North's first diary entry on Terrell is not a hostile one; it merely talks of his training mission to Honduras the next day.[24] After the leak, however, Owen and North treated Terrell much as Camper came to: as an enemy with financial backing who might penetrate, discredit, and ultimately expose their operation. As Owen wrote to North in January 1985,

> Would seem a good idea to deal with Flacko as soon as possible. . . . Best bet might be to dry up his funds, have someone talk to him about National Security and put the word out that he is not to be touched. But, if possible it might be wise to do this in some way that doesn't ruin whatever potential CMA has for the good of the cause. Posey has been doing the best he can to either sit on Flacko or deal him out, but that is not possible because right now Flacko knows too much and it would do no one any good if he went to the press. He has got to be finessed out.[25]

Although their campaign to oust Terrell had begun after the meeting in Calero's home, it was a month or more before Terrell was separated from CMA and its Miami Cuban contacts. According to Terrell, one of the things he learned in that month was that the Miami Cubans working with CMA hoped to use the Contra support operation as a cover for drugs. As we noted earlier, he later said in a radio interview that someone in Miami offered him a million dollars to move some of their seafood into the United States; he explained to his interviewer that he "learned later they were speaking of a cocaine operation disguised by imports of frozen fish from Costa Rica."[26] In a memo prepared for the Kerry subcommittee, Terrell identified Francisco Chanes of Frigorificos de Puntarenas as "the centerpiece of a drug operation smuggling cocaine from Colombia through northern Costa Rica into the United States." (Owen confirmed to the Iran-Contra committees that Chanes had been present at his Miami meetings with Posey, Terrell, Hull, and Calero and that he had been introduced to Chanes's partner Moisés Nuñez in Costa Rica by John Hull.)[27]

A key role in maneuvering Terrell out of CMA was played by a mysterious former free-lance narcotics agent called Larry Spivey (a man whose sources of intelligence baffled Posey and whose motives Owen mistrusted).[28] On December 21, 1984, probably the day after the Houston meeting, Spivey alerted the State Department to the plans of CMA, referring to "a man known only to him as Colonel Flaco."[29] Spivey had introduced himself to Terrell and Posey as an independent film producer who hoped to produce a documentary about American citizen military involvement in Nicaragua. One week later, the State Department forwarded Spivey's report to the FBI, which was then authorized by the Justice Department to open a Neutrality Act investigation.[30]

North's own notebooks confirm that he had been alerted to Terrell's mercenary activities by January 5, 1985, only a fortnight after the meetings with Owen.[31] According to FBI Executive Assistant Director Oliver Revell, North phoned FBI Agent Michael Boone the same night and left the impression that he "wanted to be certain that the FBI was investigating this [Terrell] matter in an effort to interdict the group's activities." On January 8, according to Revell, an agent from the Miami FBI anti-terrorist squad, George Kiszynski, interviewed Spivey and had FBI Headquarters in Washington relay the substance of his report to North at the National Security Council.[32] Although there is much confusion as to how and when Spivey stimulated the FBI's curiosity in Terrell, it is clear that Kiszynski played a key role. Kiszynski received Posey and Spivey together in his FBI office and quizzed them about Terrell. Spivey then placed a call on Kiszynski's phone to North at the NSC.[33] Kiszynski, like Owen and North, appears to have helped to separate Terrell from the Miami Cubans in CMA, some of whom may have acted as Kiszynski's informants. Because of his position in the counterintelligence and counterterrorism sections of the local FBI, Kiszynski, like Posey, was no stranger to the Miami Cuban milieu.[34]

Thanks to two FBI counterterrorism agents, Kiszynski and Revell, North thereafter received the FBI cable traffic on Terrell. North swiftly found a use for this information. Terrell, now separated from CMA, went back to Honduras in February 1985; North, by his own admission, had Terrell expelled from that country in mid-March.[35]

## Terrell and the Miami Investigation of Rene Corvo

North's first move against Terrell was to contribute to his own undoing. In his few short weeks with CMA and the Contra support operation, Terrell had acquired considerable knowledge in Miami, some of it first-hand, of illegal gunrunning and drug trafficking. For almost a year Terrell, living in New Orleans, did little to share what he had been told. At first he had still some hopes of finding employment or business opportunities through his old mercenary contacts. He later offered his information to the DEA but was unwilling to become a DEA informant. He also gave his information to a newspaper contact, Brian Barger, who used it in an Associated Press story on Contras and drug trafficking in December 1985 (see below and Chapter 11).[36]

However, the interest of the FBI in Rene Corvo (or Corbo) had been stimulated by an article about gunrunning in the *Miami Herald* for July 21, 1985. Based on the allegations of the mercenary Steve Carr about the John Hull ranch, the article led to the opening of a new FBI investigation of Corvo and others, in which Terrell's information soon became important evidence.[37] FBI Agent Kevin Currier's zeal to pursue the Corvo investigation (in contrast to the Justice Department's later measures to slow it down) seems to have derived from the fact that many of the people important in it were extremists allegedly involved in earlier terrorist actions, notably the bombing of a Miami bank in 1983.[38] The statements of Currier's informant Joe Coutin, as transmitted to the Kerry staff by Terrell, again suggested that the Miami Cuban network in the Contra supply operation included key members of the so-called CORU network of Orlando Bosch that in 1976 took credit for the bombing of a Cuban civilian airliner.[39]

Joe Coutin told the FBI in mid-January 1986 that they should interview his acquaintance Jack Terrell.[40] Terrell was interviewed in New Orleans on March 5 and 25, 1986. At the second interview were an Assistant U.S. Attorney from Miami, Jeffrey Feldman, and the Miami FBI antiterrorist agent, George Kiszynski. Terrell says that he told the two men all he knew about three topics: gunrunning, drug trafficking, and an alleged plot to assassinate Lewis Tambs, U.S. ambassador-designate to Costa Rica.

A subsequent Justice Department memo makes it clear that the Corvo investigation rested primarily on the information provided by two witnesses, Jesus Garcia and Jack Terrell. The information that particularly concerned North came from Terrell, since it was Terrell who "had mentioned Hull's name" and also Robert Owen's.[41]

Recently released depositions of Justice Department officials about the Miami investigation have provided a fresh and generally more credible account of the confused and controversial way in which the investigation was subsequently handled. In particular, they confirm that the matter was being followed by Attorney General Edwin Meese and other senior Justice Department officials in Washington, particularly Meese's Deputy, Lowell Jensen, and Deputy Assistant Attorney General Mark Richard.

These officials later all presented the investigation as restricted to gunrunning and assassination plots and explicitly or implicitly denied that it had to do with narcotics.[42] The Select Committees in their Report also called it a "gunrunning investigation," suppressing all reference to drug trafficking.[43] But from an FBI memo on Terrell we learn that "the investigation concerned alleged activities of the Civilian Military Assistance (CMA) including smuggling weapons from south Florida into Central America on behalf of the 'Contra' guerrillas, *smuggling narcotics*, plotting the assassination of the U.S. Ambassador to Costa Rica and discussing bombing the U.S. Embassy in Costa Rica."[44] It is clear from an FBI teletype released belatedly by the Select Committees that Terrell had been interviewed by them about "alleged . . . smuggling of weapons *and narcotics*."[45] FBI Agent Kevin Currier confirmed that he had questioned Garcia about "narcotics trafficking with the Cubans."[46] FBI Executive Assistant Director Oliver Revell also testified later that the investigation focused on "allegations of drug smuggling and gun smuggling and so forth."[47] In short, the Iran-Contra committees misled the U.S. public by tacitly backing the administration's denials that there was a *drug* investigation in Miami.

One man who perceived that the Miami investigation did involve narcotics allegations was Oliver North. In a memo he drafted for the president about Terrell (whom he called "an active participant in the disinformation/active measures campaign" against the Contras), he also described Terrell as "a cooperating witness in a neutrality investigation concerning alleged activities of the Civilian Military Assistance (CMA) group—involving weapons and narcotics smuggling, plotting the assassination of . . . Tambs, and bombing his embassy."[48]

## The Administration Moves to Silence the Terrell Story

By this time the Corvo investigation, mired in conspiratorial subplots, had attracted the hostile interest of North and Poindexter at the NSC and of Attorney General Meese and his deputy Lowell Jensen at the Justice Department. One witness, Jesus Garcia, was now a convicted prisoner, having allegedly been set up for arrest by another witness, a mysterious Major Alan Saum.[49] Convinced that Garcia had been railroaded, imprisoned, and then put in solitary confinement because of what he knew, Garcia's public defender, John Mattes, had raised with the staff of Senator John Kerry the issue that the Justice Department was putting Garcia away to cover up Contra support illegalities. Mattes had intended to discuss these illegalities at Garcia's sentencing, but he never had the chance: the sentencing expected for March 18 was suddenly postponed by Jeffrey Feldman after his boss, U.S. Attorney Leon Kellner, received a phone call from either Lowell Jensen or his subordinate Mark Richard in Washington.[50]

This was only the first of such interventions from Washington. On March 19, North's colleague Richard Secord met in his Virginia office with retired CIA agent Glenn Robinette and engaged him to conduct investigations that rapidly became an effort to silence Terrell. Present at this meeting were two of Secord's associates in the Contra supply operation, Thomas Clines and Rafael Quintero. Both Clines and Quintero (who had earlier done business with the famous rogue ex-CIA agent Ed Wilson) had close connections to some of the Miami Cubans whom Terrell had linked to the Rene Corvo investigation. Robinette later reportedly told two DEA agents "that he was retained by Clines to investigate a civil suit against Clines and others alleging assassination plots and drug dealing in Central America."[51]

Robinette told the Iran-Contra committees that he was engaged to work on two civil suits, presumably the opposing suits in Costa Rica and the United States (the latter the as yet unfiled Christic suit) between John Hull on the one hand and journalists Tony Avirgan and Martha Honey on the other. Clines and Corvo were also later named, along with Richard Secord, John Hull, Rene Corvo, and Felipe Vidal, as codefendants in the May 1986 Christic Institute suit.[52]

On March 20, a thirty-eight-page memorandum on the Corvo case was submitted to Oliver Revell at FBI headquarters.[53] Lowell Jensen discussed a summary of the memo, by Revell, with Meese and also showed it to John Poindexter at the NSC.[54] Jensen later testified that he briefed Poindexter because of the "high drama" of the case, including possible "disclosures" by Garcia at his sentencing, as well as "references to the whole Nicaraguan situation."[55] Apparently on Jensen's orders, Mark Richard phoned Leon Kellner in Miami to advise him that decisions on the investigation "should be run by" Richard in Washington.[56]

North too appears to have interfered with the developing Corvo investigation. At the end of March, Feldman, Kiszynski, and Currier went to Costa Rica to get depositions from sources named by Terrell, including Steve Carr (the original source of the gunrunning story) and John Hull.[57] Hull "initially agreed and then declined" to talk with them.[58] An embassy employee later told Feldman that Hull (who has since identified himself as a one-time CIA contract agent) "had been to the embassy, had spoken to Ambassador Tambs, and that he had been in contact with National Security Council officials in Washington regarding our inquiries."[59] Feldman has since complained publicly that "individuals in the U.S. Embassy overtly interfered in my attempts to interview witnesses."[60]

Hull had good reason to contact the NSC; and the NSC had good reason to advise him not to talk. Robert Owen later sent North a memo from Costa Rica saying that Feldman had shown "[deleted: probably CIA Station Chief Joe Fernandez, alias "Tómas Castillo"] and the Ambassador a diagram with your name on the top, mine underneath and John's [Hull's] underneath mine."[61] This relationship between the three men was one that Terrell would later repeat on the CBS show "West 57th."[62] But a fourth name was also on the chart, underneath Hull's: that of the self-admitted arms smuggler Rene Corvo.[63]

North's own notebook makes it clear that someone in Costa Rica, probably Joe Fernandez, alerted him immediately to Feldman's investigation, which included North among its suspects. In the words of the Select Committees' Report, "North's notes suggest that he was advised of the investigation by Castillo. In an entry dated '31 Mar 86,' North wrote: '1700—call from [Thomas [Castillo?]]***–Asst. U.S. Attorney [Feldman]/2 FBI + Resident Agent–Rene Corbo–*Terrell (Flaco)*–CMA–Guns to [a Central American location—probably Ilopango].[64] At this time Terrell was only a source for the Corvo investigation, although much later the grand jury investigation he had helped launch would be turned against him. Thus this North notebook entry (reprinted in a footnote to the report) helps explain North's later motivation: North knew Terrell had been talking to the FBI about Contra support illegalities when he took steps to launch a "counterterrorism operations plan" against Terrell.

## The Justice Department Response when Terrell Talked to Senator Kerry's Staff and the Press

On March 27, 1986, two days after the Terrell-FBI interview, Senator John Kerry and his staff, having assessed the importance of John Mattes's story of a Contra gun-running cover-up in Miami, met with Lindsay Mattison of the nonprofit, public interest International Center for Development Policy in Washington. Mattison agreed to finance and help conduct a full-scale investigation for Kerry of the allegations coming out of Miami. The next day Kerry's chief of staff Ron Rosenblith, Mattes, and Mattes's investigator Ralph Maestri interviewed Terrell in New Orleans. Kerry's aides decided that Terrell should come to Washington.

Terrell arrived on about April 5, 1986, and was soon engaged by Mattison as a consultant to the International Center. In this capacity Terrell talked to Jack Blum, then the counsel for the International Center and later the counsel for the Kerry subcommittee. Terrell subsequently spoke to several print and TV journalists, including Leslie Cockburn of "West 57th," the show that so upset North. Two other such journalists were Brian Barger and Bob Parry, whose Associated Press story on Contra support gunrunning and drug trafficking on April 11 named Terrell as a source for the federal investigation being carried on in Miami. On the same day, John Poindexter convened an NSC Senior Staff meeting on the "FBI story on drugs and gunrunning by Contras."[65] One day later, Attorney General Meese, in Miami on other business, asked Kellner about the status of the Corvo investigation.[66]

Despite the roadblocks put in his way by the U.S. Embassy during his investigation in Costa Rica, Assistant U.S. Attorney Feldman continued to look into the allegations assembled by the FBI against Corvo et al. On May 14, 1986, Feldman wrote a memo to his superior Leon Kellner advising that "we have sufficient evidence to begin a grand jury investigation." This recommendation was later reversed, without Feldman's knowledge, by higher authority: "At present it would be premature to present this matter to a grand jury."[67] The rewritten memo (of which Feldman was unaware) was then leaked to the press.

This reversal was not initiated by Kellner, who initially agreed with Feldman. The Iran-Contra committees' report fails to address the allegation that this change came after Edwin Meese and Lowell Jensen "turned on the heavy pressure on Kellner."[68] Kellner and others in the U.S. Attorney's office initially told the Iran-Contra committees that there had not been any such pressure; and one attorney's eyewitness account of an earlier order from Washington by telephone to "go slow" was denied by all others present in the room.[69] But more recently Kellner has said publicly that he now believes there were "improprieties" in the way the investigation was handled.[70] The Kerry report presents a strong case that the reversal of the decision to investigate Terrell's charges was made, and then leaked improperly to the press, to prevent Senator Kerry's investigation of the drug charges from proceeding. Feldman himself raised with

Senator Kerry the question, "Was my memo revised for disinformation purposes? Was it revised so that it could be used against you?"[71]

Justice Department hostility to Terrell increased on May 23, 1986, the day that a Costa Rica court ruled against John Hull in his libel suit against Avirgan and Honey, and the day after Terrell had testified in the same suit. On May 23 Ken Bergquist of the Justice Department requested from the Criminal Division information about the arrest and polygraph records of Jack Terrell, Steven Carr, and Jesus Garcia. Although Bergquist requested these records because of statements the three men had made "to Senator Kerry's staff," the information of the three men had just formed the successful defense of Martha Honey and Tony Avirgan against John Hull's charge that they had libeled him in the matter of the La Penca bombing.[72]

The Christic Institute filed the suit of Tony Avirgan and Martha Honey on May 29, 1986, using Terrell's charges to accuse Hull and Owen of being part of a terrorist conspiracy. North's concerned response is well documented. For example on June 2, 1986, North's notebook linked the names of Terrell and Kerry's staff aide Jonathan Winer; it then added that the "FBI cannot find Terrell," and is "looking at what can be done to expand surveillance of Av[irgan]/Honey."[73]

On June 1, a story in the *Miami Herald* by Alfonso Chardy revealed that the House Judiciary Committee planned to set up a special investigative unit to consider the allegations of Contra support illegalities such as gun running, assassination plots, and drug smuggling. The article named Garcia and Terrell as sources for the allegations. The next day Feldman's revised "May 14" memo was still further toned down by his superiors (without his knowledge or approval) to read that a grand jury investigation would constitute nothing more than a "fishing expedition." This falsified version of Feldman's memo, still dated May 14, was then sent by Kellner to Washington, where it was leaked by Justice Department officials to Republicans at the Senate Foreign Relations Committee seeking to block Senator Kerry's proposed investigation. Soon after, it was also leaked to the *Washington Times*.[74] Kellner confirmed that this was the only instance in his tenure as U.S. Attorney when he sent an unsolicited status report on a pending investigation to the Justice Department in Washington.[75]

At some point in the summer, FBI headquarters in Washington was alerted to the concern of Feldman and the FBI case agents (particularly Kevin Currier) that the case "was not being brought before the grand jury on a timely basis." Asked by House Iran-Contra committee counsel "why they felt it was being so slow," Revell gave as the first reason, "It seems to me there was a civil suit"—the Christic Institute suit.[76]

On June 3, North asked the FBI to have its Intelligence Division investigate the Christic Institute, along with other aspects of what he and the FBI called a "Nicaraguan Active Measures Program" directed against North. In the words of the Iran-Contra report, North "complained that the FBI . . . had not investigated Daniel Sheehan of the Christic Institute . . . [and] had not examined allegations made by Senator Kerry against North." Specifically North complained that the FBI had not learned from Daniel Sheehan of the Christic Institute "the source [i.e., Terrell] of the allegations he provided against North," and had not obtained "the information presently at the Department of Justice [which would include the rewritten Feldman memo] involving Senator Kerry's allegations."[77]

In June 1986 North apparently tried, and failed, to have the FBI's Intelligence Division investigate both the Christic suit and the Kerry investigation. The FBI had already concluded that "there is a definite association between the dates of the Congressional votes on Contra aide [*sic*] to the Nicaraguan rebels and the 'active measures' being directed against Lieutenant Colonel North," but trying to stay out of a sensitive political fight between the White House and Congress, they declined to pursue the matter.[78] (One month later North succeeded in using counterterrorism powers to invoke a different part of the FBI to the same end.)

On June 25, 1986, Terrell aired his charges about the relationship of North and Owen to the John Hull ranch in Costa Rica on the CBS show "West 57th." By then Richard Secord, who (unlike North) was a defendant in the Christic suit, was paying Glenn Robinette to interview Terrell, using funds from the Secord-Hakim Enterprise. On July 15 Robinette submitted a report on Terrell's unpaid relationship to the Christic Institute. In it, he noted that Hull's airstrips, according to Terrell, "were used for landings and transfer of military equipment but also drugs."[79] Robinette also transmitted to North excerpts that Terrell had given him from a book proposal he had written, in which Terrell claimed to have heard discussions at Calero's home of past and future attempts to assassinate Edén Pastora. In the words of this proposal, which Robinette on North's instructions gave to the FBI,

> The next day, at Adolfo Calero's home in Miami, Jack was
> present while Calero, a young CIA agent named Rob Owens, and
> John Hull, an American farmer living in Costa Rica, plotted the
> assassination of Eden Pastora, the Costa Rican Contra leader.
> Also present were Felipe Vidal Santiago. . . . Jack listened while

the other men discussed a previous attempt to kill Pastora during a May 1984 press conference in La Penca, Nicaragua. . . . No one had been arrested for that outrage, but there in Miami Jack learned the name of the assassin: Amac Galil, a Libyan terrorist.[80]

North and Secord now knew that Terrell would be the star witness in the Christic Institute suit against Hull, Owen, Vidal, Secord, Clines, and Amac Galil concerning the May 1984 La Penca bombing, in which Tony Avirgan had been injured.[81]

At this point North turned to the counterterrorism powers conferred on him by Bush to investigate not Hull or the La Penca bombing, but Terrell the whistle-blower.

# 8　North Moves to Silence Terrell

To silence Jack Terrell, Oliver North and the FBI turned to North's secret network of counterterrorism units in the administration: the Operations Sub-Group (OSG) of the Terrorist Incident Working Group (TIWG). Later, they tried to use the same resources to undermine Senator Kerry's efforts to launch a Congressional inquiry into Contra drug trafficking.

North described Terrell's revelations as a threat, part "of a much larger operation being conducted against our support for the Nicaraguan [Contra] resistance." By defining Terrell's political threat as a "terrorist threat," he was able to use the extraordinary law-enforcement powers invested in him through his central position in OSG. What makes this story much more than a personal feud is that both the FBI and the Justice Department, under Ed Meese, supported North. In short, the FBI and Justice Department were collaborating with North in a documented effort to silence an FBI witness who threatened to expose Contra-related drug trafficking.

## North's Citadel of Secret Power: The OSG

The OSG, with concomitant powers conferred on North, had been created by National Security Decision Directive NSDD-207 of January 1986, as a result of the report of then Vice President Bush's Task Force on Combating Terrorism. It was an operational strengthening of an earlier group, the TIWG, which had been created by a National Security Decision Directive NSDD-138, drafted by North in April 1984.

The stated purpose of both groups was to centralize the counterterrorism powers of the military and the intelligence agencies to capture international terrorists. OSG-TIWG was authorized to bypass normal communications channels and deal with counterterrorists directly; it was even given its own secure "FLASH" communication network to do so.

This ability to dispense with red tape was the key to North's operational successes at the NSC, above all when he was able to coordinate the capture of the terrorists who murdered Leon Klinghofer aboard the Italian liner *Achille Lauro*.[1]

But these stated objectives of OSG-TIWG were not its only ones. From its creation, TIWG was the core of a counter-bureaucracy, separating the administration's hard-liners from the CIA's moderates (or, in North's terms, the Men from the Mice). Operations that the CIA moderates opposed (like the Iran arms negotiations with the suspected arms dealer Manucher Ghorbanifar) were simply handled by Casey through North and his network of counterterrorists. Strengthened with powers and personnel from Bush's Task Force, the OSG-TIWG became the network that North used both to supply the Contras and to negotiate the controversial arms sales to Iran.[2]

On the domestic side, North's counterterrorism liaison responsibilities authorized him to receive from the FBI all relevant cables, including those that implicated him. In early 1985 George Kiszynski in Miami had begun forwarding all FBI memos on Terrell to North at the NSC. NSDD-207 was issued on January 20, 1986, just four days after the Miami FBI's interest in Terrell had been reactivated by their interview with Joe Coutin. Thus, probably by coincidence, NSDD-207 was just in time to sanction this practice. As Oliver Revell told the Iran-Contra Committees, copies of the FBI memos on the Garcia and Terrell revelations in the Rene Corvo investigation were forwarded continuously to North's office "because it was an international terrorist matter."[3]

## North Calls Terrell a "Terrorist Threat"

On July 15, 1986, Glenn Robinette confirmed that Terrell was the witness linking Secord, Clines, Hull, and Owen to drug activities and the La Penca bombing of 1984.[4] On the same day, the FBI heard from "a classified source that pro-Sandinista individuals might have been contemplating an assassination of President Reagan." The source apparently knew of "a mercenary who would avail himself to conduct assassinations."[5] This "classified source" has never been identified, although subsequent FBI behavior suggests that the information came in part from NSA intercepts of two individuals in the Nicaraguan Embassy.[6]

On July 17, the FBI Washington Field Office decided they believed "the information pertained to a mercenary by the name of Terrell."[7] Once again, the grounds for this belief are not given, but circumstantial evidence corroborates the sworn testimony of Robert Owen that it conveniently came to the FBI "through Glenn Robinette."[8] As we shall see, the FBI's decision that Terrell might constitute an assassination threat empowered North, and the Terrorism Section of the FBI, to bring against Terrell the full panoply of counterterrorism powers conferred on them by the Task Force on Combating Terrorism.

Later on July 17, Revell told North of this identification of Terrell as a suspect. North met with Robinette at 7:00 the same evening and told him to take Robinette's July 15 memo, along with Terrell's book excerpts about Contra-drug collaboration and the alleged plots against Pastora, to Revell at the FBI. North then phoned Revell, who arranged for an FBI car to bring Robinette from North's office to his own.[9]

### The Real Terrell Threat: "Enough Information . . . to Be Dangerous"

By this time Robinette had prepared a second memo on Terrell, dated July 17, assessing that what Terrell knew "could be embarrassing to R[ichard] S[ecord]," and "could be dangerous to our objectives." Robinette saw Terrell as a possible "serious threat to us based on the foregoing."[10]

Robinette's July 17 memo corroborates Terrell's own story that Robinette tried to silence Terrell by offering funds for a proposed helicopter service business in Costa Rica. It recommends that Robinette's "interest" in this project be increased: "The 'investors' would require that he reduce or stop his 'political talking' as it would 'affect our investment.' " The memo concludes that by this means "the chopper or air freight service in Costa Rica" could be "connected to some future non-commercial work"; and that "we would have him [Terrell] in hand and somewhat in our control."[11]

On the basis of Robinette's second memo, North prepared a memo for Admiral Poindexter, calling Terrell a "terrorist threat" and focusing at the outset on Terrell's role in the Christic Institute suit, in media stories on Contra drug running, and in providing information to Senator Kerry's staff. The text is given below.

> SUBJECT: Terrorist Threat: Terrel [*sic*]
>
> Several months ago, a U.S. citizen named Jack Terrel became an active participant in the disinformation/active measures campaign against the Nicaraguan Democratic Resistance. Terrel's testimony was used in the Avirgan/Honey suit in Costa Rica and has been entered in the Florida [Christic] law suit against Richard Secord, *et al.* Terrel has appeared on various television "documentaries" alleging corruption, human rights abuses, drug running, arms smuggling, and assassination attempts by the

resistance and their supporters. Terrel has also been working closely with various Congressional staffs in preparing for hearings and inquiries regarding the role of U.S. Government officials in illegally supporting the Nicaraguan resistance.

After the "West 57th" piece by CBS two weeks ago, Project Democracy officials [i.e., Richard Secord] decided to use its security apparatus to attempt to determine how much Terrel actually knows about their operations. One of the security officers for Project Democracy [i.e., Robinette] met several times with Terrel and evaluated him as "extremely dangerous" and possibly working for the security services of another country.

This afternoon, Associate FBI Director, Oliver Revell, called and asked for any information which we might have regarding Terrel in order to assist them in investigating his offer to assassinate the President of the United States [deletion] The FBI now believes that Terrel may well be a paid asset of the Nicaraguan Intelligence Service (DGSE) or another hostile security service.

Mr. Revell has asked to meet with the Project Democracy security officer who has been meeting with Terrel. A meeting has been arranged for this evening. The FBI has notified the Secret Service and is preparing a counterintelligence/counter-terrorism operations plan for review by OSG-TIWG tomorrow.

It is interesting to note that Terrel has been a part of what appears to be a much larger operation being conducted against our support for the Nicaraguan resistance. We have not pursued this investigation—which includes threatening phone calls to the managing editor of the *Washington Post*—because of its political implications. It would now appear that [deleted] of Terrel's activities, this may well be much more than a political campaign.[12]

In his own memo, North reported Robinette's evaluation of Terrell as "dangerous" but also went further. Where Robinette had called Terrell an "Operational Threat"—a possible "serious threat to us based on . . . his previously spoken statements"—North called him a "Terrorist Threat." Robinette had said Terrell "may possess enough information . . . to be dangerous to our objectives"; North wrote that "one of the security officers for Project Democracy" (Robinette) had evaluated Terrell as " 'extremely dangerous' and possibly working for the security services of another country."[13] (In his first Terrell memo of July 15, Robinette had actually reported that Terrell "does not want to align himself with any political group or cause," except insofar as he wanted to end the skimming by the Nicaraguan Contras of the CIA monies intended for the Miskito Indians.)[14]

The flamboyant style of North's memo was, understandably, something for which the staid Admiral Poindexter was unwilling to accept responsibility. He turned down North's recommendation that the memo be discussed with the president and attorney general and returned the memo with a handwritten request for "another memo," addressed this time to the president himself, and including "the results of OSG."

Poindexter's caution induced North to write a remarkably different memo, dated July 28, in which the president was told of Terrell's "anti-contra and anti-U.S. activities" as a "principal witness" for the Christic suit and for Senator Kerry, but which said nothing about the alleged assassination plot or about the FBI's alleged belief that Terrell was a foreign agent.

This second memo was accompanied by an FBI memo on Terrell dated July 18. In its declassified portions, the FBI memo says nothing about Terrell as a paid asset of Nicaraguan intelligence. Instead it confirms that the FBI had interviewed Terrell because he was "knowledgeable" in such possible crimes by CMA as "smuggling weapons from south Florida into Central America on behalf of the 'Contra' guerrillas, smuggling narcotics, plotting the assassination of the U.S. Ambassador to Costa Rica and discussing bombing the U.S. Embassy in Costa Rica."[15]

North forwarded the FBI memo to Poindexter with his own memo for President Reagan. In his covering memo to Poindexter, North wrote, "At Tab III is the March report of Terrell's debrief by FBI New Orleans. It is important to note that shortly after Terrell offered this information, reports began to circulate regarding Contra drug running and a plot to kill Ambassador Tambs. Much of this information was eventually reported in the media."[16] In his memo for the president (which is initialled "RR"), North spelled out the real nature of Terrell's threat more explicitly: "It is important to note that Terrell has been a principal witness against supporters of the Nicaraguan resistance both in and outside the U.S. Government. Terrell's accusations have formed the basis of a civil law suit in the U.S. District Court in Miami [the Honey-Avirgan Christic suit] and his charges are at the center of Senator Kerry's investigation in the Foreign Relations Committee."[17]

This memo makes it clear that North's obsession with Terrell had nothing to do with terrorism or counterterrorism, but rather centered on the danger that Terrell posed as a witness.

North's memos did not mention what had chiefly concerned his aide Robert Owen: that Terrell's reports to the FBI about Hull, Owen, and North had launched an investigation in Costa Rica by Assistant U.S. Attorney Jeffrey Feldman in Miami. Since Terrell had volunteered his information to the FBI, the Justice Department, and a congressional committee, Robinette's actions and recommendations might appear to constitute improper interference with a witness.

## The OSG and FBI Investigate Terrell and His Allies

Terrell was placed under FBI surveillance by July 24, although not without misgivings from Revell and the FBI about the political implications of the decision. North by this time was a controversial figure, with enemies even inside the higher levels of the Reagan administration.[18] The FBI had to remain on good terms with North's competitors as well; and the FBI liaison on the NSC had already told one of these competitors, Vince Cannistraro from the CIA, "that North was trying to interfere with a Bureau investigation into allegations that the Contras were involved in running drugs."[19] Revell later told the *Wall Street Journal* that he and other FBI agents were concerned that North might be using Secord and Robinette to run a "plumber's unit" from the White House aimed at gathering intelligence to discredit political opponents.[20]

The Bush Task Force, however, had determined that the OSG was the lead agency on counterterrorism matters. Despite the unambiguously political nature of North and Robinette's concerns, Revell convened the FBI Terrorism Unit personnel to deal with Terrell and his possible coconspirators. The Select Committees, in their evaluation of the Terrell case, explicitly exonerated U.S. law enforcement agencies, concluding that "the fault lies with members [like North] of the NSC staff."[21] But it is hard to come up with an innocent explanation why the FBI, in convening their Terrorism Unit to deal with "a threat to President Reagan," should also decide that the Washington FBI Field Office "would open this matter as a Neutrality Act Case."[22]

By this bureaucratic sleight of hand, the FBI Field Office proceeded to investigate Terrell's political contacts in Washington, such as his hosts at the International Center for Development Policy, for links to foreign governments. These groups were indeed opposed to North's Contra support activities, but to treat them as potential assassins was ridiculous. Yet in the following months they were subjected to surveillance, interrogations, and even an unexplained break-in.

We know from North's later memos on Terrell that by July 25, "the Operations Sub-Group (OSG) of the Terrorist Incident Working Group (TIWG) ha[d] made available to the FBI all information on Mr. Terrell from other U.S. Government agencies. Various government agencies—Customs, Secret Service, the Bureau of Alcohol, Tobacco and Firearms—

have information of some of Terrell's activities and the FBI is currently consolidating this information for their investigation."[23]

The FBI seems to have been subsequently embarrassed by its actions. Indeed, some FBI officials appear to have taken steps to lie about them. In a report of its July 17 interview with Robinette, the date is twice given falsely as July 16, with the effect of concealing North's role that same evening in initiating the matter. The original teletype's reference to "NSC officials" (i.e., North) is suppressed, as is the presence of the book excerpts about the Pastora plots among the documents on Terrell supplied by Robinette to the FBI.[24] A call the next day from Robinette to Ellen Glasser, the Terrell case agent in the Washington Field Office, is also wrongly given as July 17.[25] (Glasser herself initiated and initialled both wrongly dated memos. Later the FBI detached Glasser to assist Independent Counsel Walsh in his investigation of the Iran-Contra affair, which in the event did not bring charges concerning the FBI-North campaign against Terrell.)

Revell in particular went out of his way to assure the Iran-Contra Committees that North had concealed the fact that Robinette was with him the night of the July 17 phone call, and that he had been disturbed to learn later of Robinette's presence, to the point of sending Glasser to interview North:

> I found out later from [Deputy Assistant Director] Schreiber that when North called me, Robinette was in the office with North. I did not know that. . . . When we found out Robinette had been in North's office, that disturbed me. I wanted to know exactly what he knew about these people, so I sent agents [Glasser and David Binney] over to interview him formally. [Q: Why did that disturb you?] Because he didn't tell me. It would indicate a closer association than he had indicated on the phone, so I wanted to get to the bottom of it.[26]

Revell said all this under oath. But an FBI document of July 18 states succinctly that "When EAD [Executive Assistant Director] Revell called North, it was apparent that Robinette was there."[27] (One would think it must have been apparent, since North was telling Revell where the FBI should come—to North's office—to pick Robinette up and take him to Revell's office.)[28]

Revell and the FBI clearly faced a delicate political situation, but they do not appear to have earned the clean bill of health given them by the Iran-Contra Committees.[29] It is hardly reassuring to learn that, as of November 1989, the chief of the FBI's "drug section" is now David

Binney, who investigated Terrell and North and (as we shall see) spoke to Robinette in 1986.[30]

More importantly, the dangerous concentration of counterterrorism powers first invested in North has not been diminished. As of 1989, his successor in the Bush National Security Council, Jon Wiant, was charged with both counterterrorism and counternarcotics matters. G. Phillip Hughes, the former Bush aide with whom North dealt concerning the Barry Seal photographs, and later concerning Noriega, works with him. The days of the North secret power network may not be over.

# 9 How the Justice Department Tried to Block the Drug Inquiry

We have seen how North and Owen's collaboration with drug-tainted covert agents in Central America drew them into schemes to cover up drug operations by interfering with Jack Terrell.[1] Next we shall see how the Contra-drug cover-up was taken up by the FBI and the Justice Department and how it effectively silenced Terrell as a witness.

On July 18, 1986, the day after North and Revell each met with Robinette, the FBI arranged to place Terrell under full-time Special Operations Group surveillance.[2] This surveillance also included two members of the Nicaraguan Embassy, and a little later it was extended to include David MacMichael, an ex-CIA anti-Contra activist who, like Terrell, worked at the ICDP and was another source for the Christic suit. Robinette had told the FBI on July 17 that he had reached Terrell at the International Center for Development Policy, the group that had brought Terrell to Washington to be interviewed by the staff of Senator Kerry's subcommittee. The FBI now also began, apparently through its Terrorism Unit, to include the ICDP in the purported Neutrality Act investigation that it had opened against Terrell, and it soon reported evidence that the Center was giving Terrell money.[3]

When Terrell flew to Miami in late July, the Justice Department secured a court-ordered "PEN register" to learn whom Terrell was calling from his hotel room; the FBI established that he had placed calls to both the ICDP and the office of Senator Kerry.[4] Soon afterwards, as we shall see, the FBI's counterterrorist staff joined in the Justice Department efforts to contain the Kerry investigation of the Contra-drug connection.

U.S. Attorney Kellner later told the Kerry subcommittee that, having been "asked to do things" about Terrell's alleged threat against the president, he had woken up a judge one night to obtain an order for the PEN

148

register. Obviously embarrassed at this revelation of his personal involvement in the Terrell affair (normally handled at a much lower level), Kellner added, "That went away within a couple of hours, really, and that was the end of the issue. . . . It was determined that the threat was not real, and a very short period of time, and that was the end of the issue. I never heard about it again, because it was felt it was wrong and that was the end of the issue. . . . the information just was not as strong as to signify doing anything else."[5]

But that was not the end of the issue. In early August 1986, Robinette's diaries show three telephone calls with David Binney, the number-two man in the FBI Washington Field Office and the man coordinating the FBI's surveillance of Terrell in Washington. In October, Jim Egbers, the Unit Chief who watched the Terrell case from FBI headquarters, was still apparently involved in efforts to contain the Kerry investigation.

On July 29 and 30, the FBI and the Secret Service interrogated Terrell with polygraph equipment, after which the FBI "eliminated him as being a threat to the President. . . . That particular portion of our involvement vis-à-vis him ceased at that point."[6] Revell reported this to the OSG, adding however that the FBI was still "pursuing other possible areas of investigation."[7]

The FBI's investigation of the ICDP continued for some weeks, and at least three employees were interviewed by the FBI about their foreign contacts.[8] This interest appears to have been sustained by a letter to U.S. Attorney Kellner from John Hull on August 27, 1986, "making serious allegations of impropriety by members of Senator Kerry's staff," which Kellner had brought with him to Mark Richard in Washington on August 29. Terrell's activities at the International Center were central to Hull's allegations.[9] Although Kellner testified that Hull's affidavits were "amateurish" and that he did not believe them, his own deposition confirms that the allegations were investigated.[10]

Meanwhile the controversial Corvo investigation had been languishing since mid-August on the desk of Feldman's superior, Chief Assistant U.S. Attorney Richard Gregorie. However, when a Contra supply plane was shot down and Eugene Hasenfus was captured, the case was rapidly reactivated. "On October 6, the day after the Hasenfus crash, [Chief Assistant U.S. Attorney] Gregorie responded to [U.S. Attorney] Kellner that he felt the case was ready to go to the grand jury. The prosecution memorandum then rested again with Kellner, who forwarded his own approval to Feldman in the first week in November—six months after Feldman had first suggested the need for a grand jury."[11]

Sending the case to the grand jury had two political consequences.

One was that the Rene Corvo investigation, being *sub judice,* was now closed to the Iran-Contra Select Committees. The other was that Jesus Garcia and Jack Terrell, the two men whose volunteered information had led to Feldman's grand jury recommendation, were told repeatedly that they would themselves be indicted.

Nor did the pressure on Terrell cease with North's departure from the White House staff on November 25, 1986. A break-in at Terrell's office in the International Center for Development Policy occurred on November 29, shortly after Terrell, having examined the Southern Air Transport logs on the downed Hasenfus plane, became one of the first to talk of Secord's unified Iran-Contra operation. In 1987, under recurring threats that the U.S. Attorney in Miami was expected to indict him, Terrell was successfully "encouraged" to seek employment overseas.

The efforts of North and others to bring pressure on Terrell were also sufficient to prevent him from giving formal evidence in the Christic Institute suit. When Terrell returned to the United States in 1988, he was again warned of his impending indictment by Feldman's grand jury in Miami. Subsequently, when subpoenaed as a witness by the Christic Institute, Terrell declined, on his lawyer's advice, to answer questions.

## The FBI, the Justice Department, and the Kerry Investigation

Late in 1987, Assistant U.S. Attorney Jeffrey Feldman began to be concerned that the Corvo case was being delayed because of its relevance to Senator Kerry's proposed Contra-drug investigation in Washington.[12] Feldman informed the Kerry subcommittee in 1988 that a Justice official had told him of an October 14, 1986, meeting in the office of Deputy Assistant Attorney General Mark Richard "to discuss how Senator Kerry's efforts to get [Republican Committee Chairman Senator Richard] Lugar to hold hearings in this case could be undermined."[13]

The Justice official, Thomas Marum, confirmed to the Kerry subcommittee staff that the meeting "was in fact about the continuing . . . Foreign Relations Committee interest in the . . . Posey-CMA case."[14] Yet all but one of the six FBI agents at the meeting were from the counterterrorism staff of Oliver Revell, who had placed Terrell under surveillance. Four agents were from the headquarters Terrorism Unit; the fifth was the unit chief, Jim Egbers, who first interviewed Glenn Robinette on July 17 in Revell's office and in May 1986 had figured in the FBI meetings about "an active measures program being directed against Lieutenant Colonel Oliver North."[15]

It is hard to justify the convening of members of the FBI's Headquarters Terrorism Unit to a discussion about the Senate Foreign Relations Committee, except on the pretext of the alleged threat by Terrell
against the president. There are other indications that both North and
the Justice Department were especially concerned to keep Senator Kerry
away from Terrell's allegations.

The Justice Department did not turn over any of its rich documentation on the Corvo-Vidal-Frank Castro connection despite the subcommittee's requests for information. The Kerry report contains significant
FBI memos only because they were supplied to the subcommittee in late
1988 by Miami attorney John Mattes, to whom they had been released
under the legal procedure of discovery in the Southern District of Florida
prosecution of Jack Terrell and Rene Corvo.

The Kerry Report's Appendix also proves that in the spring of 1986
the Justice Department had transmitted a stolen document from Senator
Kerry's personal staff to the U.S. Attorney's office in Miami, presumably
as part of the compaign to scale back the Corvo judicial investigation for
political reasons. The stolen document was an April 1986 staff memorandum to Senator Kerry, based on Terrell's revelations, that strongly
recommended investigation of a number of charges that collectively constituted "Violations of the Racketeering Influenced Corrupt Organizations (RICO) Act, and ongoing criminal enterprises by the contras." The
list of allegations included the assassination plots against Pastora and
Tambs, and

> an on-going drug smuggling operation connecting Columbia
> [*sic*], Costa Rica, Nicaragua, and the United States, in which
> contras and American supporters, with the apparent knowledge
> of the contra leadership, handled the transport of cocaine
> produced in Columbia, shipped to Costa Rica, processed in the
> region, transported to airstrips controlled by American supporters
> of the contras and contras [*sic*], and distributed in the U.S.
> Allegations have also surfaced regarding other operations
> involving shrimp boats operating out of Texas, Louisiana, and
> Florida.[16]

These are allegations which, thanks to Terrell, had begun to appear in the
press and which the informed public expected the Kerry subcommittee
to investigate.

The Justice Department copy of the Kerry staff memo was returned
to Senator Kerry by U.S. Attorney Feldman from his files. He also provided a copy of minutes from a 1986 meeting in which CIA represen-

tatives falsely assured Senator Kerry that the May 1985 Corvo flight "carried no lethal arms."[17] After resigning his post as Assistant U.S. Attorney in Miami, Feldman decided on his own to tell the Kerry subcommittee in October 1988 (when the investigation was essentially complete) about Justice Department efforts to prevent the Kerry investigation from taking place.[18] Thus the internal Kerry staff agenda, an important document, found its way into the Kerry report via a pilfered copy that had been given, quite improperly, to the Justice Department (and to the CIA), and then given back to the Kerry subcommittee by Feldman.

Of the charges in this agenda, the subcommittee report corroborated the specific allegations about the Chanes shrimp operation and the abuse of the State Department humanitarian aid program.[19] But many of the allegations, and particularly the allegations against the Contra leadership, are not addressed in the final report. According to the subcommittee record, none of the key witnesses who had talked to Kerry's personal staff of these matters in 1986 ever testified to the bipartisan Kerry subcommittee. Sealed depositions were taken by committee staff from Jack Terrell and his colleague Joe Adams, but they are not cited or used in the report.[20] While the Kerry report's retreat from the CIA origins of the Contra-drug connection may be attributed partly to the difficulty in engineering a bipartisan consensus to investigate this area, it is also clear that the administration, North, and Secord jointly tried to resist the committee investigation and even to sabotage it.

## The Silencing of the Kerry Subcommittee's Witnesses

On April 17, 1986, Senator Kerry transmitted one memo summarizing the allegations to Senate Foreign Relations Committee Chair Lugar, a Republican, requesting a formal investigation.[21] On April 18, North's personal diary revealed that he was being kept abreast, however inaccurately, of developments both at the Christic Institute (which had not yet filed its suit) and the Foreign Relations Committee: "Sheehan [the Christic Institute Attorney] investigating La Penca in consort with Sen. Kerry trying to get evidence linking RR [Ronald Reagan] to La Penca."[22] In the next seven months North's notebooks contain no less than seven separate references to the secret Kerry investigation, and one of these makes it clear that material was being leaked to him, and to the State Department, the Justice Department, and the CIA, by Lugar's aide Richard Messick: "13 May [1986] 19:30—Call from Rick Messick—Terrell told not to talk to FBI, Jonathan Winer [a Kerry staff aide]."[23] Telling Terrell not to talk to Winer is understandable politics. But telling Terrell not to talk to the

FBI, as he indisputably was told not to do, could constitute criminal interference with a federal witness.

Former Assistant U.S. Attorney Jeffrey Feldman revealed to the Kerry subcommittee his discovery, after the fact, that "there were people from the Foreign Relations Committee speaking with people at the Department of Justice . . . about your investigation. . . . Specifically, an individual named Ken Bergquist," from the Justice Department's Office of Legislative Affairs, was talking with Richard Messick.[24] Committee-restricted documents reached not just the Justice Department's files in Washington, but also Feldman's files on the Corvo investigation in Miami, along with memos that "concerned liaison between Ken Bergquist and Richard Messick on how they could coordinate their efforts to basically show that what you were saying wasn't necessarily correct."[25] Feldman gave Senator Kerry a routing slip showing that Messick had forwarded committee-sensitive documents to Ken Bergquist at the Justice Department, John Russo (or Rizzo) at the CIA, and William Walker at the State Department (who later became Bush's Ambassador to El Salvador).[26]

North's diary for June 2, 1986, again mentions Winer and Terrell, and then (after a deletion) the words "FBI cannot find Terrell—looking at what can be done to expand surveillance of Av[irgan]/Honey."[27] The next day North complained to FBI officials, who were operating under guidance from Jim Egbers, that the FBI had made "no review of any charges placed by Senator Kerry against North, nor any attempt to obtain the information presently at the Department of Justice (DOJ) involving Senator Kerry's allegations."[28] By June 3 this information included not only that passed by Messick to Bergquist, but also Feldman's rewritten memo, which had arrived that day from Miami.[29]

Messick in this period was speaking not only to Oliver North and to Bergquist, but also to Vice President Bush's Deputy National Security Adviser, Sam Watson.[30] Messick spoke to Watson on Monday, April 21, 1986, the first working day after he received Senator Kerry's letter of April 17. The next day, April 22, William Perry of the Republican committee staff was in touch with North, whose diary reads "Bill Perry—Kerry investigation—violations."[31] Soon afterwards, Bill Perry shifted from the Committee's staff to the NSC, where he became a direct pipeline for leaks from the Committee to Oliver North.[32] This move indicates the importance of North in the coordinated campaign to contain the Kerry and Feldman investigations and suggests that Vice President Bush's office may also have been involved.

The Messick-Bergquist channel also allowed for the rewritten Feldman memo (altered without Feldman's knowledge) to be leaked to the Committee and the press. This charge, originally made by *Village Voice* reporter Murray Waas in July 1987, is now corroborated by Feldman's testimony and by the Justice Department itself. Without naming names, the 1988 Annual Report from the Office of Public Responsibility to the Attorney General describes Feldman's memorandum and adds that "the Office obtained evidence indicating that a senior Departmental official may have disclosed the memorandum to a staff member of a Senate committee who in turn leaked the memorandum to the press. . . . In addition, a routine FBI computer check disclosed that the Senate staff member had previously been convicted for a federal felony narcotics violation."[33]

Thus the Justice Department and Vice President Bush's office appear to have participated, along with North, in the cover-up of arms and drug-smuggling activities. Some of these dirty tricks may also have been crimes. As the Kerry report notes,

> The North notebook entries raise the further question of whether North and others took steps to interfere with the Committee investigation. In August North's courier, Robert Owen, was asked by John Hull to transmit copies of falsified affidavits charging the Kerry staff with bribing witnesses to both the U.S. Attorney's office in Miami and to the Senate Ethics Committee. The U.S. Attorney then provided a copy of these affidavits to the Justice Department in Washington. Shortly thereafter, these false charges against Kerry staff appeared in press accounts, while the Committee investigation was pending. Taken together, these facts raise the question of whether North, Owen, and Justice Department officials may have sought to discredit the Kerry investigation.[34]

The falsified affidavits concerned two witnesses to the alleged Tambs assassination plot, Steven Carr and Peter Glibbery, who were also key witnesses in the Christic Institute suit. In all, Hull asked Owen to pass documents (presumably these affidavits) "to Rich Messick and W. Rudman (Senate Ethics) & the US attorney in Miami."[35] Hull's efforts from Costa Rica to have Senator Kerry investigated by the Senate Ethics Committee were reinforced by concomitant efforts inside the United States; and there was in fact a disconcerting delay before the Ethics Committee declined to pursue Hull's trumped-up charges.

The falsified affidavits had been forwarded to U.S. Attorney Kellner in "a letter from John Hull making serious allegations of impropriety by member of Senator Kerry's staff," and Kellner brought it with him to Justice Department official Mark Richard in Washington on August 29. Hull's letter enclosed affidavits from Carr and Glibbery "retracting some of their prior statements regarding gun-running and Contra support."[36]

This powerful campaign was a clear attempt to discredit the Kerry investigation. The coalition behind it may indeed have succeeded in its primary objective of deflecting the Kerry investigation away from the list of topics in the April staff memorandum (which were closely related to the Christic charges). In particular, the report does not deal with the assassination plots or the links between drug trafficking and Contra leaders (as opposed to Contra members and supporters). The report's account of interference with its investigation cites two Kerry personal staff interviews with Peter Glibbery in 1986, but these were never followed up by the committee.[37]

The chief blame for this does not lie with the Kerry subcommittee. There were at least five witnesses to the Tambs assassination plot and related crimes, some of whom had never met each other, but by 1987 none was in a position to testify. Terrell and his friend Joe Adams had been silenced by threats of indictment. John Mattes's client Jesus Garcia had been intimidated by a bomb in front of his family's house, while his credibility had been falsely impugned by the unauthorized rewriting and leaking of U.S. Assistant Attorney Feldman's account of Garcia's lie-detector test. Glibbery had been silenced by the sudden death in December 1986 of his friend and fellow witness Steven Carr. (Garcia and Carr, unlike the other witnesses, claimed to have seen three kg of cocaine at the Miami home of Francisco Chanes when they picked up the arms for the Corvo flight of March 1985.)[38] In April 1987 Glibbery told John Mattes that Hull had again pressured him to sign a retraction; when he refused, "Hull issued a threat, shouting, 'The CIA killed Steven Carr, and they can do the same to you.' "[39]

Carr's sudden death in Van Nuys, CA, on December 12, 1986, is surrounded by mysteries and false press accounts of death from ingested cocaine. Three separate autopsies, although mutually contradictory, "were unanimous in reporting that there was no sign that Carr had swallowed three bags of cocaine, as press reports quoting police sources had indicated."[40] In his last year Carr told a number of friends and associates he feared for his life.[41] He also wrote to his mother of the risks he faced:

> Dear Ma
>
> Just found out today. I'm supposed to be shot on my return to Fla. It seems a guy names [*sic*] Morgan/Felipe [Vidal] who worked for the FDN and John Hull has been given orders to shot [*sic*] me and Pete [Glibbery] because we spoke out against John Hull.

And in a second letter: "I'm supposed to be eliminated very soon. One of John Hull's hired guns is in Miami awaiting my return."[42]

Under such circumstances, any retrenchment from the original Kerry agenda cannot be attributed to weakness on the part of the senator or his staff. On the contrary, they persevered and reported forcefully about Hull, Corvo, and Chanes, men who were clearly formidable targets. But it would be wrong to assume from the Kerry report's silence on such allegations as the Tambs assassination plot that these allegations were unfounded.

The Kerry subcommittee investigation did succeed in documenting, through its exhibits, the ongoing, symbiotic relationship between U.S. Contra support activities and drug smuggling to which its original staff memo referred. But things happened along the way to divert the subcommittee from areas that the CIA, as well as North, clearly regarded as sensitive.

In conclusion, the U.S. Government in the midst of its self-proclaimed War on Drugs, was using its own powers of law enforcement and justice to protect known drug traffickers. The successful silencing of Terrell was only part of a larger Reagan administration campaign, lodged chiefly in the Justice Department, to prevent exposure of the Contra-drug connection and more specifically to prevent the Kerry staff investigation from being taken up by a Senate foreign relations subcommittee. This larger cover-up led the administration to engage in illegal acts with the suspected drug traffickers: for example, Steven Carr had been illegally smuggled out of Costa Rica in a conspiracy involving U.S. embassy officials and John Hull.[43]

It would be reassuring to think that the cover-up of the Contra-drug connection was a passing anomaly that could be explained by Reagan's obsession with the ill-fated Contra project or by the abuse of the extraordinary powers that North accumulated as a consequence. Unfortunately, the Kerry subcommittee found such official U.S. collaboration with corrupt governments, and official U.S. cover-ups of drug trafficking, to be more the rule than the exception.

As the Kerry report points out in its introduction, the governments that the United States works with in the area, from Mexico and the Bahamas to Paraguay, have been corrupted or co-opted by the drug traffickers. Yet the "international drug trade, historically, has been relegated to the backwaters of U.S. foreign policy concerns." For example, U.S. Ambassador Lev Dobriansky, in his relations with the corrupt government of the Bahamas, "focused on base rights negotiations, and the drug issue was relegated to a much lower priority." The United States has continued to certify the Bahamas as providing "full cooperation" in fighting the war on drugs. When Sen. Claiborne Pell, chair of the Senate Foreign Relations

Committee, sought the declassification of eleven U.S. Government documents that would corroborate the role of the Bahamas in the narcotics trade, the State Department notified Senator Pell that the request had been denied.[44]

This paradigm of local corruption, U.S. collaboration, and ultimately U.S. cover-up has repeated itself in Mexico, Honduras, and elsewhere. Today the public is most aware of it in Panama, where the U.S. Government turned against the corrupt dictator it had once protected. The U.S. cover-up of Noriega's drug involvement is particularly relevant to the U.S. cover-up of the Contra drug connection because of Noriega's participation (admitted by the U.S. government in the Oliver North trial) in North's Contra support operation.[45]

The Reagan administration covered up for Noriega not just because he was the leader of a friendly state, but because he was a coconspirator. Noriega did more than pass money to the Contras; he also controlled the air operations of César Rodríguez and Floyd Carlton, who supplied arms to the Contras at the same time that they were flying cocaine.

Referring to such operations, General Gorman told the Kerry subcommittee, "If you want to move arms or munitions in Latin America, the established networks are owned by the cartels. It [*sic*] has lent itself to the purposes of terrorists, of saboteurs, of spies, of insurgents, and of subversives."[46] Yet because of Noriega's dominance of these networks in Central America and their work for the Contras, the Reagan administration covered up for them rather than suppressed them.

## The Campaign to Block the Christic Suit

In view of the Kerry subcommittee's forced retreat from some items on its agenda, the Christic Institute's suit becomes especially significant. Many of its allegations are corroborated in the Kerry report exhibits.[47]

Much of the material in the April 1986 Kerry staff memo was also included in the May 1986 Christic Institute suit on behalf of Martha Honey and Tony Avirgan, in which a number of North-Secord associates (including Richard Secord himself, Robert Owen, John Hull, and Alfred Hakim) were accused of drug-financed criminal and covert operations. Miami Judge James Lawrence King granted the defendants' motion for summary judgment against Avirgan and Honey in June of 1988. Since then, the defendants and some journalists have talked as if the judge's ruling proves that the original Christic suit was groundless.

In fact the judge's opinion was much more specific and deserves attention. He pointed out that the Christic suit's main charge against the defendants had been brought under the Racketeering Influence and Corrupt Organizations Act ("RICO"), which concerns direct participants in any "enterprise" which is engaged in or affects interstate or foreign commerce, by "a pattern of racketeering activity."[48] The plaintiffs, in consequence, had to prove three essential elements: "The first element is a violation of 18 U.S.C. § 1962 [the RICO statute concerning such an enterprise]. The second requirement is causation, that is, a direct injury of the plaintiffs from such violation. The third requirement is damages sustained by the plaintiffs."[49] The defendants had moved for summary dismissal on the basis that the plaintiffs had failed to connect them to the La Penca assassination ("causation") or that they caused any loss or injury to the plaintiffs ("damages").

Judge King granted the motions for summary judgments on the basis that the plaintiffs had failed to prove causation. He did not rule that the plaintiffs had failed to establish that the defendants were associated with a RICO enterprise (one generating income from "a pattern of racketeering activity"), nor did the defendants make such a claim. The Iran-Contra revelations, supplemented by the Kerry report revelations about gunrunning and drug trafficking, corroborate a "pattern of racketeering activity" by several of the defendants.

Judge King's opinion rejected the various evidences of causation: the ways in which the plaintiffs had linked the defendants to the La Penca bombing. Here the judge, unlike nearly all other investigators into the case, ruled that there was no admissible evidence to prove that a mysterious journalist, using a stolen passport and the false name of "Per Anker Hansen," had left the bomb at La Penca in his camera equipment case. He hence ruled as immaterial the deposition of a former Costa Rican security official, Alberto Guevara Bonilla, who claimed to have seen both Hansen and his equipment case in the presence of John Hull.[50]

The Christic Institute had planned to present Jack Terrell and his colleague Joe Adams as "causation" witnesses. As we saw, Terrell once swore he had heard La Penca discussed knowledgeably in Miami at a meeting that included Christic suit defendants Hull and Owen, Galil [the supposed assassin, Per Anker Hansen], Adams, and Adolfo Calero. But under the threat of a grand jury indictment, Terrell and Adams took the Fifth Amendment when deposed by the Christic Institute for the suit. In the absence of their own deposition from Terrell, the Christic Institute presented to the judge earlier sworn testimony by Terrell, given in the May 1986 libel suit brought by John Hull in Costa Rica against Honey and Avirgan.

In his opinion Judge King noted Terrell's testimony "that in this meeting 'Felipe [Vidal] stated that we put a bomb under him [Pastora] and it didn't work because of bad timing. But no one used the name La Penca.' "[51] Whereas he had ruled other overheard statements inadmissible as hearsay, he made no such ruling here, for Vidal's statement constituted an admission "against interest" and hence was admissible. Instead, Judge King ruled that none of Terrell's testimony was admissible on other grounds, because it was transmitted in a publication entitled *La Penca: On Trial in Costa Rica: The CIA vs. the Press,* edited by plaintiffs Tony Avirgan and Martha Honey. "The testimony contained in plaintiffs' publication cannot be considered as admissible evidence," King wrote.[52] The judge neglected to state that the publication in question was a translation of sworn videotaped testimony, including Terrell's, in the Costa Rica libel trial, Hull vs. Avirgan and Honey, and that parts of the same testimony were used in Feldman's indictment of Terrell.[53]

In his February 1989 order granting costs and attorneys' fees to the defendants, King further wrote:

> The plaintiffs were unable to produce a single witness who could state that the defendants exploded the bomb or were responsible for the assassination attempt. . . . The attorneys for the plaintiffs, the Christic Institute, must have known prior to suing that they had no competent evidence to substantiate the theories alleged in their complaint. . . . The Christic Institute's allegations . . . were based on unsubstantiated rumor and speculation from unidentified sources with no first-hand knowledge. These actions establish that plaintiffs "had every reason to know they stood no chance of proving" that the defendants were responsible for the injuries to Tony Avirgan.[54]

The absence of witnesses was hardly the result of the malice or sloppiness that King seems to imply. When the suit was filed in May 1986, the Christic Institute could not possibly have known that Jack Terrell and Joe Adams would be prevented from testifying. The threats against Terrell had not yet been made; the grand jury that indicted him had not yet even been convened. The FBI's collusion in interference against Terrell, one of its own witnesses, had not yet begun. The evidence we have examined suggests that all these events took place in large part because of the launching of the Kerry and Christic investigations.

## Other Domestic Victims of Counterterrorism

The surveillance and harassment of Jack Terrell by the device of labeling him a terrorist is by no means the worst instance of political repression in the Reagan era. It is, however, the most amply documented in the official memoranda released by the Iran-Contra committees.

According to one of North's former Contra supply collaborators, Phil Mabry from Texas, North was targeting other Americans who opposed his activities in Central America. According to Ben Bradlee, Jr., Mabry said he

> took photographs of demonstrators and collected their literature, then sent the material to North at the White House. Mabry says North also asked him to write the FBI to urge it to investigate these opposition groups. Mabry did so, in November 1984, naming such groups as the National Network in Solidarity with the Nicaraguan People and the Inter-Religious Task Force on Central America—as well as such individuals as former U.S. Ambassador to El Salvador Robert White, actress Jane Fonda, singer Jackson Browne and Raymond Bonner, a former New York *Times* reporter. Mabry received a letter in reply from Revell saying, "Your concerns and comments will be carefully reviewed."[55]

After being fired by Reagan for exposing the right-wing murderers of El Salvador Archbishop Romero, Robert White became the president of the International Center for Development Policy, the public interest group that brought Terrell to Washington. White was indeed investigated as a terrorist by Frank Vareli, a controversial El Salvadoran informant on the payroll of the Dallas FBI office. When his counterterrorist activities for the FBI were investigated by a House Judiciary Subcommittee, Vareli proved to be a confusing and often less than credible witness. Yet there is no doubt that, having visited the national Counterterrorism Center at Fort Meade, Vareli compiled on FBI stationery a photo album of such "terrorists" as Robert White and Congresswoman Pat Schroeder.

The Bush Task Force's counterterrorism program and one of its offshoots, the Alien Border Control Committee, were used extensively to justify the surveillance and infiltration of groups such as CISPES (Committee in Support of the People of El Salvador) and the Los Angeles Arab-American Club, in which significant numbers of aliens participate. In January 1988 the Center for Constitutional Rights revealed that under the Freedom of Information Act, it had obtained 1,200 pages of files showing that from 1981 to 1985 the FBI had conducted surveillance of hundreds of individuals and organizations who opposed the administration's policies in Central America.

The procedures contemplated in the contingency plans of the Alien Border Control Committee appear to have been tested provocatively in January 1987, when six Palestinians and a Kenyan in Southern California were imprisoned as a step towards deportation, allegedly for their "terrorist" connections.[56] For three weeks, the seven were held without bond, one of them as a "national security threat," as the contingency plan envisaged.[57] A Reagan-appointed judge later commented that to deport people "because of a viewpoint—and that's all it is, a viewpoint—seems to be bordering on the outrageous."[58]

Another instance of such harassment was that of the decorated Vietnam war veteran Brian Willson, now a dedicated practitioner of nonviolent resistance, less than a year after he, and the three other members of the Veterans' Fast for Life on the Capitol steps in Washington, had been named as part of an organized nationwide terrorist conspiracy by the FBI's Chicago Terrorist Task Force.[59] One striking similarity between the case of Terrell and that of the Fast for Life is that, in both instances, after they were declared "terrorists," their offices were broken into. In September 1987 Willson was run over by a train at a naval weapons station.

As we have seen, the bureaucratic device of using counterterrorist procedures to investigate political opponents of the administration's Central America policies appears to go back to the revised FBI guidelines of 1981. The practice also confers a much broader and more sinister significance to the recommendation of the Vice President's Task Force that "terrorists" should be denied access to their FBI files under the Freedom of Information Act, a recommendation enacted into law in October 1986 by amendments to the Anti-Drug Abuse Act.[60]

The question of domestic repression and harassment should remain a matter of public and congressional concern. The forms of harassment used in so-called counterterrorist cases appear to have gone beyond surveillance and investigation to include infiltration by informants and a wave of break-ins at the offices of those opposing Reagan's foreign policies.

## The Failure of Congress

It is hardly surprising that North used the powers conferred on him to conceal his support operation's illegalities, and particularly the stories about drugs and assassination plots. What is more surprising is that Congress, despite its professed concern about drugs, acquiesced in this cover-up. It is clear from FBI teletypes that Terrell had been interviewed by them about "alleged . . . smuggling of weapons and narcotics."[61] Yet the report of the Iran-Contra Commitees suppressed every reference to Terrell's drug allegations as well as to the plot against Pastora. It falsely presented Terrell as a self-admitted CIA assassin and let it appear that Terrell had been interviewed as a suspect in alleged assassination plots, rather than as a witness. Because Congress afforded this whistle-blower no relief, it was easier for the Justice Department to silence him as a witness.[62]

By their studied refusal to pursue the Enterprise's and OSG's harassment of Terrell, the Committees increased the likelihood that such harassment could and would be repeated. One would like to think that the Committees avoided the subject because they knew that Robinette might face criminal prosecution for his surveillance activities, and they did not wish to contaminate a criminal investigation by the independent counsel. Unfortunately the report suggests that the Committees were overlooking not just Robinette's activities but all the so-called counterterrorist activities of North and the Enterprise.

If this view is correct, Congress was implicated in covering up the domestic scandal and the crimes of counterterrorism. The Committees have never had to account for their suppression, until long after Robinette's televised testimony, of the documents relating to Terrell as a terrorist threat. One of these documents, North's copy of Robinette's July 17 memo on Terrell ("Terrell may actually possess enough information . . . to be dangerous"), gave the lie to North's statement that Robinette had evaluated Terrell as "extremely dangerous." Although they released other documents that gratuitously labeled Terrell as an assassin, the Committees never released this exculpatory document at all.[63]

Indeed there appears to have been a three-way consensus (involving the independent counsel as well as Congress and the administration) to avoid exposing the harassment of Terrell. This "fix" may have been arranged at the beginning of the Iran-Contra investigation. Committee Counsel Barbadoro is reported to have told another Hill staff member that the Committees avoided the Terrell topic in open session at the request of the independent counsel, who intended to grant Robinette immunity and use him as a credible witness in order to prosecute North on another matter (surely trifling by comparison): the security fence that Robinette had constructed at North's residence, using funds supplied by Secord's Enterprise. Much later, Independent Counsel Walsh did successfully convict North on the matter of the fence, using Robinette as a witness. No charges against Robinette have been forthcoming.

Why have the Select Committees participated in a cover-up of domestic repression of one of North's critics by the institutional components of the counterterror apparatus? The Committees' overall performance is difficult to assess. The case of Jack Terrell is only one of many in which institutional excesses were covered up or actively misrepresented, while important documents (like the unclassified Robinette memo) were suppressed. And yet much important new information has been revealed and made generally accessible in a reasonably short time by the Committees' report.

Both the Committees' own performances and the narrowly drawn Congressional resolutions under which the Committees were established show a reluctance to expose present or even former CIA assets (especially the drug-trafficking ex-CIA Cubans in Miami, some of them with connections to Watergate) and a general concern to sidestep the larger issues of secret powers and secret wars. Where the Iran-Contra Committees' report suppressed or misrepresented the truth (as happened too often), it usually did so to prevent disclosure of past or current covert operations already authorized by Congress.[64]

Congress's demonstrated reluctance to raise the larger issues of covert operations was understandable. The track record of those isolated members of Congress who have challenged covert operations or foreign interventions in the past is not encouraging. After Congressman Otis Pike's House Select Committee in 1975 produced a report critical of the CIA, he was defeated at the next election; the Pike report, after a House vote without precedent or parallel in two centuries of U.S. Congressional history, could not even be presented directly to Congress.[65]

When Congressman Michael Barnes, "a vocal opponent of military assistance to the Contras," was defeated in his 1986 Senate primary bid, North's domestic political fundraiser "Spitz" Channell boasted in a telegram to North, "We, at the Anti-Terrorism American Committee (ATAC), feel proud to have participated in a campaign to ensure Congressman Barnes' defeat."[66] One of the related Channell documents stressed the effect this defeat would have on other Congressmen: "If we get rid of Barnes we get rid of the ring leader and rid of the problem. Special PAC to do 1 thing only: to RID Congress of Congressmen that are trying to undermine President in his anti-terrorist policies. . . . Destroy Barnes—use him as object lesson to others."[67]

The average Congressman was not likely to ignore a lesson so richly subsidized by public and private resources. As Peter Kornbluh has written, "The administration's tenacious public diplomacy campaign so intimidated Congress that not even a succession of scandals in the spring and summer of 1986 could prevent the president from eventually achieving his goals. Even as the contra program became mired in charges of misappropriated funds, rampant corruption, drug trafficking, and gross mismanagement, Congress approved a quantum escalation in U.S. intervention."[68]

The example of the Vietnam War reminds us that if Congress will not lead a resistance to covert power, it may respond to popular pressure. Before that happens, the press must give the people a much better picture of the extent to which counterterrorist campaigns have been misused against critics of the Administration's covert drug alliances in Central America.

# 10 Covert Operations and the Perversion of Drug Enforcement

The sheer scale of the Contra-drug connection through Central America in the 1980s raises the troubling question: Where was the DEA all that time? Either through incredible incompetence or willful blindness, the organization still maintained as late as 1987 that its agents had found no evidence to support any of the Kerry subcommittee's findings linking the Contras to drugs.[1] A DEA spokesman insisted that "this story about drug smuggling and the Contras was placed into the ears of congressional investigators by convicted traffickers" who "concocted" it "to have their cases dismissed."[2]

Three factors may have converged to make the drug agency see, hear, and speak no evil about the Contras. One was the alleged, if unproven, corruption of some DEA agents in Central America. Another was the systemic tendency of drug enforcement agents to protect their sources—who by necessity are usually implicated in crimes themselves. Finally, the agency's mission was blocked by administration officials who pushed the DEA to serve their broader political agenda in Central America.

Whatever the pressures, however, the DEA could hardly plead ignorance about the criminal intersection of the Contras and drugs. It directly employed as an informant—and protected from prosecution—one drug pilot who was under contract to the State Department to deliver humanitarian supplies to the Contras. The pilot, Michael Palmer, smuggled enormous amounts of Colombian marijuana into the United States from 1977 to 1986. Yet the DEA managed to have his 1986 indictment dropped as "not being in the interest of the United States." The Kerry subcommittee noted that "other agencies suspected that he was continuing his own drug business using his work for the DEA as a cover, a charge Palmer denied."[3] Several of Palmer's associates believed that he enjoyed protection from

165

connections within the U.S. Coast Guard and Customs.[4] One of his fellow smugglers swore in an affidavit that Palmer "stated that he had been smuggling weapons and ammunition in cargo vessels from Argentina to Honduras for the Nicaraguan Contras and that he was given a code or password which was changed every week and would ensure a safe and undisturbed passage."[5] In subsequent court testimony, the same associate linked Palmer to a "one-time operative for the Central Intelligence Agency" who was involved in "international weapons smuggling" and narcotics trafficking.[6]

But the cover-up of the Contra case started much earlier. As we saw in Chapter 3, the DEA closed its key Honduran office in 1983, just as the leading Central American cocaine trafficker Juan Ramón Matta Ballesteros and his allies in the Honduran military were lending their services to the Contra supply network. For several critical years, the DEA had only indirect intelligence from its overworked Guatemalan station as to the growing significance of Honduras in the drug trade.

The Guatemalan DEA office also had responsibility for El Salvador. Here, too, the agency short-circuited investigations when they ran into the NSC's Contra logistics operation, run out of Ilopango Air Force Base. In a little-noticed dispatch, the *New York Times* reported in January 1987:

> Officials from several agencies said that by early last fall the Drug Enforcement Administration office in Guatemala had compiled convincing evidence that the contra military supply operation was smuggling cocaine and marijuana. The Guatemala office is responsible for El Salvador. After dropping arms in El Salvador, rather than returning to the United States in empty cargo planes, the pilots stopped on occasion in Panama, a major drug transshipment center, to pick up cocaine or marijuana. . . .
> Although the drug investigation was not officially closed, it was no longer actively pursued. "It was not one of the big smuggling rings anyway," a drug enforcement official said.[7]

In keeping with this relaxed attitude toward drugs, the DEA in 1987 put on its payroll the former top security aide to the Salvadoran death squad leader Roberto d'Aubuisson. D'Aubuisson was financed by an Argentine-linked businessman suspected by the U.S. government of involvement in the drug trade. D'Aubuisson's aide, Hector Regalado, known as "Dr. Death" for his infamous technique as a torturer, taught marksmanship to American drug agents in El Salvador.[8]

The DEA's conduct in Costa Rica was even more negligent. One of the most signal failures of the DEA's Costa Rica station was its blindness toward the drug-trafficking front Frigorificos de Puntarenas. The shrimping firm's principals had been reliably implicated in high-level smuggling and money laundering as early as 1983. When two free-lance investigators offered to bust the Miami subsidiary of Frigorificos for allegedly bringing multi-ton loads of cocaine shipped to the United States, high-level DEA officials in Washington indicated that they were well aware of the firm's activities. "We got the impression that they had a lot of information but were sitting on it," one of the private investigators later recalled. "In fact, while we were sitting there, there was a big map behind them of Central America. And there's a pin on the map at Puntarenas, a little pin on the map."[9]

Yet as late as 1987 the DEA still denied any knowledge of an investigation of the firm. The agency left it to Customs to pursue the case. Only in late September 1987 was one of the principals in Frigorificos, Luis Rodríguez, indicted on drug charges—for an old marijuana shipment into Massachusetts, not for cocaine.[10]

One explanation for DEA's reluctance to act, and for the apparent immunity of another Frigorificos principal, Moisés Nuñez, was suggested by the CIA's former Costa Rica station chief Joseph Fernandez. He testified that Nuñez "was involved in a very sensitive operation" for North and the Enterprise.[11] Some details of that operation were supplied in the Owen memo to North cited in Chapter 9, outlining a plan for covert maritime activities against Nicaragua using Frigorificos ships and referring to North's offer of "the name of a DEA person who might help with the boats."[12] If Owen's first-hand account can be believed, not only did the DEA ignore a major cocaine smuggling ring for four years, but one or more DEA agents may even have helped one of the ring's leaders run covert operations against the Sandinista regime at a time when Congress had banned military assistance to the Contras.

The administration's commitment to the Contras alone may not account for the Kerry subcommittee's finding that not "a single case against a drug trafficker operating in [the war zone of northern Costa Rica] . . . was made on the basis of a tip or report by an official of a U.S. intelligence agency."[13] That remarkable record might also be explained by the allegation that Colombian drug trafficker and Contra backer George Morales had three DEA agents on his payroll to protect drug flights through Costa Rica.[14]

The U.S. Customs Service developed specific information pointing to possible corruption among DEA agents. In the spring of 1986, Joseph Kelso, an investigator and free-lance agent for U.S. Customs, went to Costa Rica to infiltrate and expose a counterfeiting ring. Soon, through a high-level source in the country's narcotics authority, he stumbled onto

# 11 The Media and the Contra Drug Issue

One symptom of something deeply wrong with U.S. drug enforcement is that since World War II it has been promoted with the aid of blatant lies. In the 1950s Harry Anslinger, the head of the U.S. Federal Bureau of Narcotics, wrung his annual appropriations from Congress with the accusation, which he knew to be groundless, that the U.S. was being flooded with a tide of "Yunnan opium" from Communist China, "the uncontrolled reservoir supplying the worldwide narcotics traffic." Only in the 1970s, as the United States moved towards normalization of relations with Beijing, did a U.S. narcotics agent admit that "there was no evidence for Anslinger's accusations."[1] Thus the U.S. media have faced a special problem when reporting on the international drug trade. They are accustomed to drawing their stories from government sources; what should they do when they suspect these sources are lying?

In the 1980s the Eisenhower-Anslinger propaganda about Red Chinese heroin was replaced by the Reagan-North propaganda about Red Sandinista cocaine. The climax of this campaign was Reagan's charge in a nationally televised broadcast "that top Nicaraguan government officials are deeply involved in drug trafficking." Reagan made this charge on March 16, 1986, only a few hours after the *San Francisco Examiner*, in a front-page story, had revealed the involvement of Contra leaders and supporters in the Frogman cocaine bust three years earlier. Reagan's charges reached a national audience; the *Examiner*'s story remained a local one.

It was a sign of improvement in U.S. narcotics enforcement that Reagan's charge was almost immediately undercut by the Drug Enforcement Administration:

> Reporters who called the DEA public affairs office after Reagan's speech were read a brief statement, which said: "DEA receives

sporadic allegations concerning drug trafficking by Nicaraguan nationals. One DEA investigation resulted in the indictment of the Nicaraguan aide to the minister of the interior [i.e., Federico Vaughan]; no evidence was developed to implicate the minister of the interior or other Nicaraguan officials." The statement earned the DEA an unwelcome headline in *The New York Times:* "Drug Agency Rebuts Reagan Charge." DEA's stock sank at the White House. *The Washington Times* attacked [DEA Administrator] Lawn's senior spokesman, a respected former journalist, Robert Feldkamp, for failing to support the president.[2]

At the same time, Vice President Bush was helping spread the administration story, also discounted by DEA Chief Lawn, that Nicaragua, as well as the Medellín cartel, had inspired the 1985 attack by M-19 guerrillas against the Colombian Supreme Court.[3]

Despite the lessons of Watergate, the methods and protocol of United States journalism are not well equipped to handle government spokesmen who are out to peddle lies. It is true that establishment media, which have longer-lived reputations to worry about than do politicians, do not connive willingly at these lies; but as the government is the usual source for political journalism in Washington, the establishment media are reluctant to find themselves at odds with it.

In this episode the nonestablishment *Washington Times* reinforced a right-wing propaganda line. As we have seen, it was the *Washington Times* which, on July 17, 1984, had sabotaged a promising DEA investigation by publishing a front-page story (almost certainly fed to it by either Oliver North or the CIA) about the Barry Seal plane trip to Federico Vaughan in Nicaragua.[4] But one cannot treat the *Washington Times* as representative of the American press, inasmuch as it is owned by the Sun Myung Moon Unification Church, financed from abroad, and not a commercially viable entity.[5] In the intrigues of the Iran-Contra affair, it was the *Washington Times* that implemented Oliver North's plan for a "Nicaraguan Freedom Fund" to obscure the fact that funds were actually reaching the Contras from other, illegal sources.[6] In contrast, the *New York Times,* by reporting the DEA's factual rebuttal of Reagan's claim, was performing the critical investigative role that we are taught to expect from the U.S. press.[7]

The Sandinista drug-trafficking story is illustrative of the U.S. establishment press at its worst and best. Eventually the U.S. media, on the authority of disaffected senior DEA officials, collectively rebutted this charge, which at first they had uncritically aired. From this journalistic anecdote we can easily see the pressures on the establishment media, whose status depends on continued access to the highest levels of the administration. Neither journalists nor their employers are likely to incur the displeasure of the White House, except in unusual circumstances (such as Watergate) where they are backed in doing so by other powerful segments of the Washington political establishment.

To acknowledge this relationship is to recognize an important proposition: the media do not set their own investigative agendas independently, but operate as part (some politicians would say the most important part) of the political establishment. This is particularly true in matters of intelligence, where government agencies regularly ask for media forbearance and occasionally invoke a 1950 law providing for criminal penalties for anyone publishing classified information about communications intelligence, and in narcotics enforcement, in which a war mentality now prevails against dissenters from the establishment.[8]

The administration holds very real powers over the press: in addition to its influence over such lucrative matters as the allocation of TV channels, it is by far the largest provider of information. Nearly all that is published about government comes from named or unnamed officials, either as releases or as leaks. As a journalist with a good Iran-Contra reporting record told us, "I had the Oliver North story for two years before it broke, but never ran it. Ollie was my best Washington source."

The result is what the establishment media itself recognizes as "pack journalism," competition to maintain access to top sources in the administration by repeating their claims. More than once, we have heard reporters say that they could not afford to touch a controversial story until some other journal had run with it first. Paradoxically, it is the journals with the highest national reputations, such as the *New York Times* and the *Washington Post,* that find it hardest to undermine their government sources, at least when the story concerns drugs and the U.S. intelligence community.[9]

These self-imposed restrictions by the leading newspapers are mimed by their competitors. Robert Parry, who broke both the Oliver North story and the Contra drug story, has observed, "The real effect of *The New York Times* and *The Washington Post* is not only that they can sanctify something, but if they're *not* covering it on anything like a regular basis, if they've decided it's not news, it's very hard to convince your editors at AP and even at *Newsweek* that it *is* news. . . . So they think, is this a guy who is off on his own tangent, following something that really isn't a story that's going to get us in trouble?"[10]

Both the *Times* and the *Post* have had top-flight investigative journalists, such as Seymour Hersh and Bob Woodward, who from time to time have broken major stories critical of U.S. intelligence excesses. Their ability to do this depends, however, on access, the price of which has been discretion.[11] Their infrequent stories about CIA assets who are involved with drug activities are usually (as in the case of Hersh's Noriega story in June 1986) published in the wake of high-level dissension about the wisdom of maintaining such assets.[12]

Behind the phenomenon of pack journalism, we might add, is the reinforcing phenomenon of pack publishing. With the recent spate of court decisions stiffening the nation's libel laws, publishers are less willing to print books that say something substantially new on controversial subjects. The costs of vetting a book to minimize the risks of future lawsuits can become so prohibitive as to prevent publication of startling new charges. Even the reporting of a potentially libelous claim made by a congressional committee can be regarded as too controversial. And one of New York's leading agents has told us that if the legal department of one major New York publisher has raised problems with a book, no other major publisher will want to take it on.

These constraints do not amount to a total blackout. In 1987 CBS journalist Leslie Cockburn aired Jack Terrell's Contra-drug story on "West 57th" and then published it in her important book *Out of Control*. For this courageous act she and her publishers were promptly rewarded by a multimillion-dollar lawsuit. And even her book's title page ("A Morgan Entrekin Book/Atlantic Monthly Press") proclaims that it was an unusual publishing arrangement that bypassed the major Madison Avenue houses.

Other American journalists have also done excellent work on the international drug story, and only because of their efforts could the Kerry report and this book have been written. But where reporters themselves have broken ground on the drug story by their investigations, it has usually been for regional American newspapers, like the *Boston Globe,* the *Miami Herald, Newsday,* or the *Philadelphia Inquirer*. For example, Steve Kurkjian of the *Boston Globe,* one of the few reporters to do justice to the Jack Terrell story, quoted customs officials to the effect that "between 50 and 100 flights that had been arranged by the CIA took off from or landed at U.S. airports during the past two years without undergoing inspection. . . . The system provided for the CIA to notify the Customs Service that a certain flight was about to leave from or land at a U.S. airport. As one customs official put it, 'our inspectors took that to mean hands off everything.' "[13]

The insights offered to Boston readers on the nation's drug problems were not afforded readers of the congressional *Iran-Contra Report,* or the *Washington Post,* or the *New York Times*.

The result is precisely what the Bush administration likes to denounce as an uneven playing field. Reagan's charges about Sandinista drug trafficking on March 16, 1986, were broadcast to the entire nation. There was no such attention in the national media for a *San Francisco Examiner* story the same day that revealed the U.S. government had returned funds seized in a 430-pound cocaine bust after a defendant submitted letters from Contra leaders claiming the funds were theirs.[14] Even in the midst of the Iran-Contra hearings, the national media were silent about testimony in a Wisconsin trial from a DEA agent attesting that a fugitive dealer in a local cocaine ring had told him that "75 percent of the profits from the drug operation went to the . . . Contras."[15]

By ignoring these controversial drug stories about the Contras, the *New York Times* and *Washington Post* were conforming to their role as "responsible" newspapers publishing only what was "fit to print." Only under exceptional circumstances have they deviated from that role. For example, on December 27, 1985, the *Washington Post* ran a story by Associated Press reporters Brian Barger and Robert Parry revealing that Contras in northern Costa Rica had "engaged in cocaine trafficking . . . according to U.S. investigators and American volunteers who work with the rebels."[16]

Stories such as this one can be cited to contest the allegation that there is high-level manipulation of public opinion on the drug issue in the national media establishment. But except for the mistake of a Spanish-language Associated Press night editor, the Barger-Parry story, although based on reliable sources and largely confirmed since, might not have run in the United States. According to a carefully researched report on the story in the *Columbia Journalism Review,* on December 16, 1985,

> an editor working overnight at La Prensa Asociada, the AP's
> Spanish-language wire, called up the Parry-Barger story on his
> computer and, without checking to see if it had been cleared for
> publication, translated the latest draft and sent it out over the
> wire. The next morning the story appeared in Spanish-language
> papers in New York, Miami, and throughout Latin America.
> Included in the story was a quote from a U.S. official linking
> "virtually all" contra factions to drug smuggling, as well as a
> reference to John Hull, from whose farm drug shipments were
> allegedly flown. (The story also included a denial from Hull, who
> said that the charges amounted to "communist
> disinformation.")[17]

For weeks Barger and Parry were at loggerheads with their AP superiors in Washington and New York, especially after "a senior White House ington. The role of opium in financing the Afghan resistance had been reported by the Canadian journal *MacLeans* in April 1979, the same month that President Carter's National Security Advisor, Zbigniew Brzezinski, pushed through a decision to support the Afghan rebels.[22] In May 1980 two concerned members of President Carter's White House Strategy Council on Drug Abuse, cut off from the classified information that the law entitled them to receive, warned *New York Times* readers in a dissident Op-Ed piece: "We worry about the growing of opium poppies in Afghanistan and Pakistan by rebel tribesmen who apparently are the chief adversaries of the Soviet troops in Afghanistan."[23] Yet to judge from the *New York Times* index, the first *Times* news story referring to the Afghan rebel drug connection was in June 1986, even though by 1983 the *Times* could report that the Afghan-Pakistani border was supplying 85 to 90 percent of all heroin sold in New York City.[24]

The flow of cocaine through Honduras, under the protection of traffickers allied to the Honduran military and the Contra support operation, also went unnoticed by the *Times* in the mid-1980s, despite the DEA's early warnings (see Chapter 4).[25] Not till after the record four-ton seizure of Honduran cocaine in November 1987 did the *Times* run a story on the involvement of Matta and Honduran military officers in the drug traffic, and even this story was silent about Matta's role in the Contra support effort. (Instead it mentioned a claim by U.S. and Honduran officials that Matta's military ally, Col. Torres Arias, "dealt in guns for Salvadoran leftist guerrillas and the Sandinistas in Nicaragua.")[26]

In retrospect it would appear that the flows of drugs through the Afghan rebels and the Honduran military (with both of which the U.S. was deeply involved) dwarfed any from the Sandinistas. Yet in the key years 1984–86 the *Times* ran four stories linking the drug traffic to Afghanistan, three about Honduras, and no fewer than fourteen about Nicaragua; nine of these reported on the Reagan administration's controversial charges against the Sandinistas, and a tenth was the government's whitewash (through Justice Department spokesman Korten) of the Contras.

This media astigmatism extends to other aspects of Latin American affairs. In their book *Manufacturing Consent,* Edward Herman and Noam Chomsky note that the political murder of one pro-Solidarity priest by agents of the Polish government attracted three times as many articles in the *New York Times* (to say nothing of far greater candor) than, for example, the political rape and murder of four American nuns by members of the El Salvador National Guard.[27] From such recurrent discrepancies and biases, they conclude that the U.S. mass media function not as an official called" and asked that references to John Hull in the story deleted.[18] Long after the story, which one AP staffer called "the π heavily edited in the history of the bureau," Barger and Parry lear that Oliver North had been speaking with their AP boss, Charles J. L( on a regular basis.[19] The English-language AP story, which went o1 December 20, was in effect censored to meet the White House re( "Gone was the reference linking 'virtually all' contra factions tc smuggling, as was any mention of Hull." In their place was a "new ( a CIA report linking a cocaine-financed arms purchase to "one of A top commanders loyal to ARDE leader Eden Pastora," at that t' enemy of Hull, North, and the CIA.[20]

The *Washington Post* ran this curtailed and rewritten AP stor' cember 27, deep inside the paper. The *New York Times* did not all, although in April 1986 (a month after Reagan's broadcast) published a Barger-Parry follow-up story. Then in May the *New 1*

> gave the contras a clean bill of health. Under the headlin( CONTRAS CLEARED ON GUNRUNNING, the unbyli story quoted an unidentified "senior official" of the Just Department as saying that charges that the contras were implicated in gunrunning and drug smuggling were wi( foundation. "There just ain't any evidence," the source turned out, the "senior official" was one Pat Korten, a Justice Department spokesman Terry Eastland. Althou statements to the *Times* were quickly contradicted by the Justice Department and by investigators for the S( Foreign Relations Committee (which was about to be on the gunrunning and drug smuggling charges) the not run a correction. "The confusion was Justice's,"' Shenon, the *Times* reporter who interviewed Korten was accurate. The guy told us what he told us."[21]

Not until late April 1986, nearly five months after the B: did one of the major TV networks air a story on the Con in drug smuggling. Finally, in early 1987, reporters f1 ment press, including Joel Brinkley of the *New York* ' Lardner of the *Washington Post,* collectively added 1 breaking Contra drug story by their own investigativ(

The press's belated achievements in uncovering th( have to be placed in the context of the other delayed mid-1980s: the massive flows of drugs from the Af Pakistani army and the Contra support network's Honduran army, both of which enjoyed de facto p:

information system but as a propaganda system.[28] Although they acknowledge, and indeed rely on, the maverick contrary reporting of such sometime *New York Times* correspondents as T. D. Allman and Raymond Bonner, their monochromatic model of the media too quickly discounts those cases (such as that of Barger and Parry) when the maverick reporters ultimately get their story out. In support of their cynicism, it should be noted that Barger and Parry, and Allman and Bonner before them, all encountered difficulties working for the mass media, which Allman and Bonner have left altogether.

With respect to the drug issue, it is difficult to make absolute judgments about the performance of the United States media. The timidity of Congress in challenging administration big lies on the Contra drug issue arises in no small part from the fear of contradiction and criticism from the powerful establishment media, whose interests all too frequently parallel those of the administration. Although at times the establishment media have given space to corrective stories, and small journals of opinion like the *Nation* are free to run them, such solitary voices raised against the parroting of administration propaganda are not enough to make democracy work.

## Congress and a Total Lie: *"No evidence . . . from hundreds of witnesses"*

The Pat Korten lie to AP and the *New York Times* in May 1986 is rightly listed by the Kerry report in its chronology of events supporting the "sworn testimony from an Assistant U.S. Attorney that officials in the Justice Department sought to undermine the attempts by Senator Kerry to have hearings held on the [Contra drug] allegations."[29] In fact the *New York Times* report was run on May 6, 1986, the day that Republican Committee staff member Rick Messick arranged for a meeting between administration officials and members of Senator Kerry's staff. (It was at this meeting that CIA representatives falsely claimed that no weapons were aboard the March 1985 Contra supply flight of Rene Corvo from Fort Lauderdale.)[30] By similar timing, the *Washington Post,* together with a Democratic congressional staff aide, helped generate the parallel myth, that an exhaustive Congressional investigation, including "reams of testimony from hundreds of witnesses, developed no evidence which would show that the Contra leadership was involved in drug smuggling."[31]

This claim is at the heart of a July 23, 1987, memorandum from Robert A. Bermingham, an investigator for the House Iran-Contra Committee, which was published in the November 1987 Report of the Iran-Contra Committees. The date of that memo is important: it suggests witting exploitation of a lie that had been floated in the July 22 *Washington Post* and that the *Post* itself had retracted on July 24.

One of the authors of this book, Peter Dale Scott, happened to be a witness to the secret nonevent that engendered the lie. He went to Washington for six months in 1987 and was paid by the International Center for Development Policy to tell Congress what he knew about the overlap between U.S. covert operations and the illicit international drug traffic. Thus he was present, on July 21, 1987, at a closed executive session of the House Select Committee on Narcotics Abuse and Control on the explosive issue of alleged Contra involvement in the drug traffic. He and his Washington sponsor (Executive Director Lindsay Mattison of ICDP) submitted a written brief on this subject, as did witnesses from two other groups. They gave instances of Contra leaders and supporters who had been indicted and/or convicted on drug charges. The drug trafficking of one of these Contra leaders, Sebastián "Guachan" González, is now corroborated by the Kerry report; earlier it had been brought to Oliver North's attention by Robert Owen.[32]

The ICDP representatives did not get to speak to their brief; it soon became apparent that no one on the Committee, Democrat or Republican, wished to address the issue. The committee chair, Congressman Charles Rangel, made it clear that he had only called the meeting in response to the persistent demands of his constituents and that he did not have the intention, the means, or the mandate to investigate these charges. He did, however, promise to forward the three briefs, without comment, to the Crime Subcommittee of the House Judiciary Committee.

The next day, the *Washington Post* claimed that Rangel's committee had interviewed "hundreds of witnesses," and quoted Rangel as saying that "none of the witnesses gave any evidence that would show the Contra leadership was involved in drug smuggling."[33] Rangel promptly wrote a four-point letter of denial, but the *Post* declined to publish it; the paper merely corrected the false claim about hundreds of witnesses being interviewed.[34]

Before any correction was printed, however, the "hundreds of witnesses" and the false quotation from Congressman Rangel were enshrined in the Robert A. Bermingham Iran-Contra Committee staff memo of July 23, 1987. As a result the two false and unsupported claims attributed to Rangel were reprinted, without correction, in the Joint Committees' *Iran-Contra Report*.

Although reprinted by the Republicans, and still quoted by them, the Bermingham memo was actually prepared for House Committee Chair Lee Hamilton, a Democrat, and for John Nields, counsel for the Committee's Democratic majority. The Democrats did nothing to repudiate or refute the falsified memo, even after the counsel for the Rangel Committee had complained publicly about it. The counsel, Robert Weiner, told Murray Waas of the *Boston Globe* that "We did indeed find that there is substance to many of the allegations [about Contra drug smuggling]. Mr. Bermingham is wrongly prejudging a congressional committee investigation."[35]

The truth in the *Boston Globe* does not outweigh the error in the *Washington Post*. The latter continues to be solemnly cited as fact, as for example, in Michael Ledeen's book *Perilous Statecraft*.[36]

## The Media and the Kerry Report

The sensitive area of drug trafficking is one where, over and over again, distortions are likely to occur. What is chiefly unusual about the Rangel story is that both the truth of the Contra drug involvement and the falsity of what the *Post* (and the Bermingham memo) wrote about it seem now to be established beyond question.

This distortion was repeated in the press coverage of the Kerry report's treatment of the involvement of drug traffickers in the Contra war. The Kerry report, although cautious, had come up with significant and disturbing facts, such as that "the State Department selected four companies owned and operated by narcotics traffickers to supply humanitarian assistance to the Contras," that when one of these companies in Honduras (SETCO) came under suspicion, along with its allies in the Honduran military, "the DEA office in Honduras was closed in June of 1983," or that "Five witnesses testified that [John] Hull ['a central figure in Contra operations on the Southern Front'] was involved in cocaine trafficking."[37]

Both the drug traffic and the CIA's relationship to it were prominent public issues when the report was released in April 1989. Yet the *New York Times* story on the Kerry report was buried on page 8; the *Washington Post*'s on page 20. Neither John Hull nor the closure of the DEA office was mentioned at all; the State Department story was mentioned only briefly.[38] Thus stories that the *Times* and *Post* had never told continued to be excluded from their columns.

The *Post* in particular devoted far less space to the accounts of Contra involvement ("The report concluded that there was 'substantial' evidence of drug smuggling through the Nicaraguan war zone and that combatants on both sides were involved") than to the subcommittee report's own disclaimers: "The report acknowledges that widely publicized allegations that high-level contras were directly involved in the drug trade could not be substantiated. The report also states that one of the Contras' chief accusers, convicted money launderer Ramon Milian Rodriguez, failed a lie detector test and was found to be 'not truthful.' Another widely quoted contra accuser, Richard Brenneke, never had the Central Intelligence Agency connections he claimed and was found to be otherwise unreliable as well, the report said." Thus the report's twenty-five pages of documentation on the Contras were reduced to a tepid half sentence, while three pages of disclaimers about minor, irrelevant witnesses were given three full sentences.

The *Times* and the *Post,* like the Iran-Contra Committees, were also circumspect in investigating the recurring deals of Oliver North and Richard Secord with drug-linked international arms brokers, such as Manucher Ghorbanifar, Sadeg Tabatabai, and Manzer al-Kassar. Here the press and Congress, so shrill in their demands for a "real war" against drugs, were not covering up for the CIA (which had recommended against dealing with Ghorbanifar); they were covering up for these drug traffickers themselves.

In the same way, Jack Terrell's revelations about the drug aspects of North's illegal Contra support activities, as they slowly found their way into the mainstream U.S. press, were never fully covered. The *Washington Post* ran one story about how more than $100,000 from Secord's Iran-Contra bank accounts had been spent on Robinette efforts against Terrell and others involved in the Christic Institute lawsuit against Secord, a story based largely on Terrell's allegations.[39] But the more such stories proliferated, the more obvious it became that the establishment press was avoiding three central facts: (1) Terrell had told the FBI and other government agencies about major drug smuggling by Contra supporters; (2) the FBI was engaged by North to harass and silence Terrell, an FBI source, along with his political allies; and (3) North's ability to engage the FBI in silencing one of its own witnesses depended on the secret counterterrorism powers of the Operations Sub-Group. (When the Democrats of the Iran-Contra Committees came to issue their report, they too, in their extended treatments of the Terrell story, suppressed these three facts.)

## Intrinsic and Exotic Pressures for Media Conformity on Drugs

Undoubtedly this reluctance to publish arises in part from the phenomenon of pack journalism we have already described, which the press itself has recognized. As the *Los Angeles Times* once observed in a front-page story,

> Former Sen. Eugene McCarthy once likened reporters to
> blackbirds on a telephone wire—when one lands, they all land, he

said; when one takes off, they all take off. Nowhere is this phenomenon more pervasive than in Washington. . . . "Washington is more susceptible to pack journalism than any place I've been," says John Balzar, a political writer for the Los Angeles Times. "I've watched reporters go through the agonies of hell because their stories differed slightly from their colleagues'." . . . "It seems paradoxical to say that competition produces uniformity, rather than diversity," says Howell Raines, Washington bureau chief of the New York Times, but that's exactly what often happens in Washington. One explanation: Washington journalists have many of the same sources, sources who have their own vested interests. They are government aides and spokesmen who function much as political aides and consultants do in a campaign; they are "spin doctors," ready to tell the reporters and commentators just what each event "really means."[40]

In defense of the media, one can point to the unique propaganda campaign mounted by the Reagan administration on behalf of the Contras, with the help of U.S. tax dollars. This campaign itself has been effectively covered up:

Congressional investigators [for the Iran-Contra Committees] did draft a chapter about the domestic side of the scandal for the Iran-*contra* report, but it was blocked by House and Senate Republicans. Kept from the public domain, therefore, was the draft chapter's explosive conclusion: that, according to one congressional investigator, senior CIA covert operatives were assigned to the White House to establish and manage a covert domestic operation designed to manipulate the Congress and the American public. . . . The Administration was indeed running a set of domestic political operations comparable to what the CIA conducts against hostile forces abroad. Only this time they were turned against the three key institutions of American democracy: Congress, the press, and an informed electorate.[41]

CIA Director Casey had created, under State Department cover, an Office of Public Diplomacy (S/LPD), headed by a veteran CIA clandestine operator, Walter Raymond, reporting directly to North and the National Security Council. Under authority of a special National Security Decision Directive, Raymond and North met over seventy times on "public diplomacy" matters. In the course of these, North oversaw the 1984 Barry Seal "sting" operation with its photographs of Federico Vaughan and told McFarlane he planned to influence an upcoming Contra aid vote in Congress by (among other activities) having the Justice Department prepare a "document on Nicaraguan narcotics involvement." Another S/LPD report to the NSC boasted of having "killed" purportedly "erroneous news stories." NPR reporter Bill Buzenberg recalls the head of S/LPD claiming that he had gotten some media chiefs "to change some of their reporters in the field because of a perceived bias."[42]

We agree, however, with author Mark Hertsgaard that the aberrations and excesses of the Reagan years are unfortunately outgrowths of a more fundamental problem: "that the press was part of, and beholden to, the structure of power and privilege in the United States."[43] Former *Newsweek* reporter Bob Parry concurs that when any administration defines its policy priorities so clearly, most media executives are happy to play ball: "In Washington, there is a correspondence between people who run news organizations and people in government. There is this sense of wanting to be respected. . . . [Drug] stories raise too many questions and don't serve the 'national interest.' That is more important to these executives than selling magazines or newspapers. Many news editors and executives are more interested in being respected at cocktail parties than selling newspapers."[44]

Others have pointed to economic as well as psychological bonds that link media chiefs to others with power.

> As ABC's Sam Donaldson acknowledged in his autobiography: "The press, myself included, traditionally sides with authority and the establishment." It is hard to see how it could do otherwise; the press was itself a central part of the American establishment. According to Ben Bagdikian's *The Media Monopoly,* a mere fifty large corporations owned or controlled the majority of media outlets in the United States . . . when Ronald Reagan came to power in 1981. By the time Bagdikian published a new edition of his book in 1987, mergers and acquisitions had shrunk the previous fifty down to twenty-nine. Half of these media moguls ranked among the Fortune 500—itself an elite club whose members, while numbering less than 1 percent of all industrial corporations in the United States, nevertheless accounted for 87 percent of total sales.[45]

Herman and Chomsky also focus on the wealth of the mass media, and the ways in which they "are closely interlocked, and have important common interests, with other major corporations, banks, and government."[46]

This corporate analysis of media oligopoly can easily be oversimplified. Although the media as a whole have been affected by their growing concentration of ownership, the behavior of particular institutions cannot be predicted by their size. Large newspaper chains like Hearst and Knight-Ridder, with relatively independent Washington bureaus, have collectively a far better record on the drug issue than the *New York Times* and the *Washington Post,* which by the yardstick of corporate wealth are smaller. But Hearst and Knight-Ridder newspapers have little circulation among the elites of Washington and New York.

It is true that during Vietnam and Watergate the press had begun to criticize (even if for establishment reasons) the political performance of the U.S. power structure it represented. But this brief drama had led to a prompt backlash for which the academic as well as financial establishments must share responsibility.

> "The most important new source of national power in 1970, as compared to 1950, was the national media," Samuel Huntington, a Harvard professor of political science and frequent government consultant, wrote in 1975. Huntington was one of dozens of scholars hired to explore the theme of "the governability of democracy" for the Trilateral Commission, a private group founded by banker David Rockefeller and composed of highly influential business, political and academic figures from the United States, Western Europe and Japan. It was the Trilateral Commission's view that the United States suffered from an "excess of democracy" which prevented the country from making the difficult and painful choices needed to set things right again. On the specific topic of the press, Huntington asserted, "There is . . . considerable evidence that the development of television journalism contributed to the undermining of governmental authority." Backed by large corporate foundations, right-wing think tanks and other representatives of the American power structure, the attack on the press seemed aimed at convincing both the press itself and the public at large that journalists were out of step with the rest of the country.[47]

In the 1980s, the United States press was open to voices of dissent on policy, but not to questions about the fundamental legitimacy of institutions accused of systematically breaking the law. It is chilling to recognize the extent to which this defense of the status quo entailed, time after time, a protective cover-up of the United States security system's involvement with international drug traffickers, its supposed enemies.

# 12   Conclusion

The history of official toleration for or complicity with drug traffickers in Central America in the 1980s suggests the inadequacy of traditional "supply-side" or "demand-side" drug strategies whose targets are remote from Washington. Chief among these targets have been the ethnic ghettos of America's inner cities (the demand side) and foreign peasants who grow coca plants or opium poppies (the supply side). Experience suggests instead that one of the first targets for an effective drug strategy should be Washington itself, and specifically its own support for corrupt, drug-linked forces in the name of anticommunism.

Since the 1940s these government intelligence connections have opened up unsupervised shipping and plane communications between the United States and drug-growing areas and conferred protection on drug traffickers willing to ally themselves in the war against communism—a process the Kerry subcommittee referred to as "ticket punching."[1] These conditions in turn have created windows of opportunity for drug smugglers to flood America's domestic market with their products.

Such a window was opened wide to cocaine smugglers in Honduras by Washington's support of the Nicaraguan Contras in the 1980s. The resulting "Honduran connection" was built around trafficker allies in the Honduran military, who provided essential support to the Reagan administration's Contra program. Honduras in these years accounted for 20 percent or more of all the cocaine smuggled into the United States. Costa Rica, another center of Contra activity and official corruption, accounted for another 10 percent or more. And Panama, with the CIA-protected Noriega at its helm, supplied drugs, pilots, and banks to service these networks.

The Contra drug connection arose in the context of other drug-related covert operations conducted since the passage of the National Security

Act in 1947, which created the legal justification for a national security bureaucracy that evaded normal constraints of law and congressional review. The cumulative history of such connections suggests that changes in politics, as much as changes in either demand or supply, have driven shifts in the overall pattern of drug flows into the United States.[2]

One clear example is the so-called heroin epidemic of the late 1960s, which followed a decade and a half of CIA collaboration with opium-smuggling gangs and drug-corrupted regimes in the Golden Triangle of Burma, Laos, and Thailand. Historian Alfred McCoy noted that this relationship sparked a "takeoff" in the Southeast Asian opium trade in the 1950s, with Burma's production growing tenfold and Thailand's even more. The addition of American troops and the disruption of the French Connection supplied the conditions for an explosion in heroin shipments across the Pacific.[3]

The revival of covert operations under Reagan was accompanied by the dramatic expansion of another traditional opium region: Southwest Asia's "Golden Crescent." In 1979, the region was not a major heroin supplier to the U.S. market; the drug was virtually unknown in Pakistan. The Afghan war changed all that. By 1984, the year Vice President Bush (Reagan's drug czar) graced Pakistan with an official visit, the border area with Afghanistan supplied roughly 50 percent of the heroin consumed in the United States, and 70 percent of the world's high-grade heroin; and there were 650,000 addicts in Pakistan itself. Heroin was shipped out in the same Pakistani army trucks that brought in covert U.S. aid to the Afghan guerrillas. The only high-level heroin bust in Pakistan was made at the insistence of a Norwegian prosecutor; none was made at the instigation of narcotics officers in the U.S. Embassy.[4]

The Central America drug experience in the 1980s, in short, was not an anomaly but part of a long-standing pattern of intelligence alliances, military intervention, and official corruption. It is a pattern that shows no sign of abating.

## Guatemala: The Pattern Continues

There is no more flagrant example than Guatemala, where U.S. backing for a corrupt and brutal military has recently fostered a booming drug market. Guatemala may not be a drug center on a par with Colombia or Peru, but it has become one of Central America's principal way stations for cocaine bound for the North American market. The largest seizure of cocaine in Central American history, totalling 2,400 kg, took place in Puerto Barrios, Guatemala, in 1987. In 1989, officials seized 4,100 kg of cocaine, only a small fraction of the 500 to 1,000 kg estimated to pass through the country each week.[5] In addition, Mexican traffickers have turned western Guatemala into a major source of opium. Guatemala's poppy fields expanded from 4,500 acres in 1988 to 8,000 in 1989. Opium production, estimated at $1.5 billion annually, could supply about 60 percent of the entire U.S. market.[6]

Guatemala's rugged terrain, backward economy, ineffective law enforcement, and poor radar coverage all attract traffickers. But corruption, above all, accounts for the country's thriving drug trade. Some of that corruption infects the civilian sector. President Vinicio Cerezo's hand-picked candidate for the fall 1990 presidential elections, Alfonso Cabrera, rose from humble circumstances to amass a fortune while serving in various government posts. He campaigned in the helicopter of a suspected Guatemalan drug trafficker. American drug experts believe he tried to cover up the involvement of one of his brothers in a conspiracy to smuggle 54 kg of cocaine to the United States; another brother was convicted on cocaine charges in 1984.[7] Cabrera's main opponent, Jorge Carpio Nicolle of the Union of the National Center, also had an image problem. U.S. Embassy observers said he "has the potential to be even more corrupt than Cerezo and his Christian Democrats."[8] (Yet another accused trafficker chose to run on the Guatemalan Feminist Party ticket.)[9] However, the center of drug corruption in Guatemala is the military, which governed directly from 1954 to 1984 and continues under civilian rule to exercise predominant influence over the country's political direction. The military's role in drug trafficking was spotlighted in mid-1989 with the arrest of Lt. Fernando Minera for trying to load 25 kg of cocaine onto a Miami-bound commercial jet. Minera, a former official with the corruption-fighting Administrative Control Department of the Presidency (DECAP), insisted that he was framed. Besides two prominent civilians (the brothers of President Cerezo and Alfonso Cabrera), Minera leveled drug charges against two army colonels, officers of the G-2 intelligence unit, and the former head of DECAP, Col. Hugo Moran.[10] A huge cocaine bust in May 1990, totalling 634 kg, implicated another army colonel. One of Defense Minister Hector Gromajo's military protégés has also been accused of ties to the drug trade.[11]

What lesson does Washington draw from these facts? According to the *New York Times*, "The United States, losing faith in the civilian government, has turned to [the] military to insure stability and combat growing drug trafficking."[12] More specifically, reports the *Los Angeles Times*, "U.S. agencies are making payments to Guatemalan military officers, particularly in army intelligence, known as the G-2 . . . for their cooperation in combatting drug traffickers' use of Guatemala as a transshipment point for cocaine en route to the United States, and in discouraging the growing of opium poppies in this country."[13]

Given G-2's own record of corruption and the refusal of top military officers to cooperate with Treasury police who handle drug enforcement, these reports raise questions about the nature of Washington's real agenda. One possible clue lies in the military's support for aerial spraying of herbicides over guerrilla-held territory, ostensibly to eradicate opium poppies. Human rights observers charge that the spraying program "is yet another tactic in the 10-year-old counterinsurgency war against the leftist guerrillas," a means of denying them food supplies. This interpretation is supported by the entirely unsubstantiated claims of some U.S. officials that there is an "overlapping of forces" between drug traffickers and the Revolutionary Organization of the People in Arms.[14] As one former top Guatemalan official explained, "the drug issue is the perfect [way] of maintaining aid to the army" in its war against subversion.[15]

The results of growing military aid, including renewed arms shipments, training by U.S. Green Berets, and payments to the G-2, will surely be, as in Honduras, growing drug problems and worsening human rights abuses. Since 1954, the Guatemalan military has been responsible for almost unimaginable brutality, including 100,000 deaths and 40,000 disappearances.[16] In 1989, Amnesty International documented 222 cases of human rights abuses committed by government security forces, but no action was taken—as indeed none had ever been taken against military officers during the preceding decade.[17] In April 1990, Amnesty reported that military-backed death squads were targeting human rights workers, among others, for assassination.[18] The United Nations Human Rights Commission, noting "the increase of assassinations, kidnappings, attempts and threats against people who participate in political activities," approved a resolution on March 7, 1990, asking the Secretary General to "name an independent expert to examine the human rights situation in Guatemala and to continue assisting the government in human rights matters."[19]

Ironically, hard-line elements in the military most supportive of death squads and political violence cited the Cerezo government's "corruption and drug trafficking" as an excuse for failed coup attempts in both 1988 and 1989. Despite the military's own corruption, officers flatter themselves as the nation's "moral reserve," obligated to serve if civilians fail to measure up.[20] A turn by Washington against the civilians and to the military can thus only encourage a return to authoritarian rule.

## From Central America to South America

The problems of military corruption and venality loom larger not only in Central America but throughout Latin America as the Bush administration focuses new attention on aiding national military elites to enlist them in the War on Drugs.[21] Hundreds of millions of dollars will flow to the Colombian, Peruvian, and Bolivian armed forces as part of Bush's Andean Initiative.[22]

The chances of really making a dent in America's drug problem through such aid are almost nonexistent. Millions of peasants, entire national economies, depend on the drug industry. If America's own failure to control the domestic cultivation of marijuana is any test, eradicating drug production from a rugged region one-third the size of the United States will not be possible. And even hard-line law enforcers admit that interdicting drugs that may come by any number of land, sea, or air routes is impossible even with the most advanced technology.

Corruption, moreover, will make the goal of supply-side enforcement all the more remote. Aiding foreign military and intelligence forces in the name of fighting the War on Drugs risks empowering the very forces responsible for protecting organized criminal syndicates.

In Colombia, for example, the attorney general's office had no fewer than 4,200 corruption cases under investigation involving the national police and 1,700 involving the armed forces by late 1989.[23] The attorney general himself, noting how extensively the drug barons had infiltrated the military's ranks, declared, "It was a mistake to bring the Colombian army into this fight and to put it in touch with corruption."[24] Americas Watch reported in 1989 that "there is compelling evidence that regional Army chiefs and high-ranking intelligence operatives are involved in facilitating the commission of atrocious acts by private [drug-financed] armies and death squads."[25]

Washington has nevertheless promoted the Colombian military's role in the drug war with relentless intensity. One top official in Bogotá complained in mid-1990 that his government had received no commitment of increased trade or technical and financial assistance, only more military aid. "The response of the U.S. is the traditional response to these problems," he lamented, "more military, more U.S. troops, more aircraft carriers, not practical solutions on the ground."[26]

Things are little better in Peru. José Blandón, one of the chief witnesses in the U.S. drug case against Manuel Noriega, warned Washington in 1988 that Noriega had "ties with high-ranking officials in the Peruvian armed forces, some of these officers have been involved in well-known drug related cases (case of the chief of police in Lima)."[27] Author James

Mills learned that Juan Ramón Matta Ballesteros bought cocaine from the Paredes family in Peru, which a DEA analyst called "the biggest smuggling organization in Peru and possibly in the world." He wrote that the Paredes family controlled numerous Peruvian officials, including six agents in the Peruvian Investigative Police (PIP), two generals, and a comandante of State Security. The Paredes family was part of an established oligarchy that "controlled not only the roots of the cocaine industry but, to a large extent, the country itself."[28]

A few years later, another trafficker, Reynaldo Rodríguez López, incorporated into his drug ring several generals of the PIP, at whose headquarters Rodríguez maintained an office. He also allegedly corrupted the private secretary of President Fernando Belaunde's minister of interior, a fervent advocate of the thesis that left-wing narcoguerrillas were responsible for the country's drug problem.[29] The truth was quite different. When Belaunde sent the military into the coca-rich Upper Huallaga Valley in 1984, drug production boomed as military commanders allied themselves with powerful traffickers to stamp out Marxist Shining Path guerrillas.[30] "The narco-guerrilla . . . was in part a projection of the Belaunde regime's own internal rot," suggests Rensselaer Lee.[31]

Today the same narcoguerrilla thesis motivates administration requests for tens of millions of dollars in new military aid to Peru. Melvyn Levitsky, the State Department's top narcotics officer, argued in reference to Shining Path that "where the insurgency and the drug traffickers are inextricably bound together, we have to deal with them together. We have an interest in helping them fight that insurgency."[32] Yet he has also admitted that widespread reports of military corruption "have ranged from taking payoffs from the traffickers so that they could go after the Sendero, that is to let the [drug] flights in, to other kinds of collusion."[33] In short, military aid will target guerrillas more reliably than drugs.

Perhaps the most severe example of the cocaine-military symbiosis has been in Bolivia, starting with the explosive growth in state-financed coca production in the mid-1970s under corrupt military rule.[34] The notorious Cocaine Coup in 1980 put a new group of military drug traffickers in power, backed by a syndicate of Bolivia's wealthiest drug lords. The country's return to civilian rule brought less violence but no less corruption among top Army and Navy officers and rural drug police.[35] Daniel Cabezas, chairman of the Bolivian Senate's Commission on Drug Trafficking, may have been too late when he warned in December 1989 against succumbing to American pressure to unleash the military against the drug lords. "There is a serious risk that the armed forces could be corrupted by the cancer of drug trafficking," he observed. "This is too dangerous for such an important institution as the military, which has the responsibility of protecting us."[36]

Under these conditions, the strategy of further militarizing the societies of Latin America promises to be utterly counterproductive, not only for controlling drugs but also for fostering democracy. Surely the latter objective should stand higher in the priorities of both North and South America. It will be achieved not through wholesale destruction of peasant economies and drug wars but rather through strengthening civilian polities and economies.

Washington could better help Latin America by looking more at home than abroad for ways to reduce drug abuse. Rather than export its crime problem, America should start exporting the example of dealing more humanely with the social, psychological, and medical issues of drug use. As Colombian President-elect César Gaviria said in July 1990, "The demand for drugs is the engine of the trafficking problem. If the United States and the industrial countries don't get a way to reduce consumption, we will not solve the problem. It doesn't matter how much we work against the trafficking of drugs, how many lives we lose. It doesn't matter how great our effort, the problem will be there. The United States and industrialized countries need a way to reduce the consumption of drugs."[37]

Instead of addressing the root causes of America's drug demand, however, during the 1980s about 70 percent of federal drug spending went to law enforcement, which even enthusiasts admit can interdict only a small fraction of total drug supplies. Spending priorities must be reversed if any progress toward social healing is to begin. Drug education and support for expanded treatment are essential. So too are broader (if more challenging) programs to rebuild broken communities that breed despair, escapism, and crime. Ultimately, the United States must begin to consider, and experiment with, proposals to take the crime out of drug markets through controlled legalization.

No approach will succeed, however, without urgent political action to end Washington's own complicity with drug traffic. Both Congress and the media, institutions that have served executive power more than they have challenged it, must show more courage. They must simultaneously judge administration foreign policies more critically and exercise more restraint in milking the drug issue for votes and sales. Neither institution is likely to reform entirely from within; only an informed and demanding public can push them to respond as the nation needs and deserves.

# Notes

INTRODUCTION

[1]*Los Angeles Times,* September 14, 1989, citing a *Times-Mirror* poll conducted by Gallup.

[2]James Van Wert, "The US State Department's Narcotics Control Policy in the Americas," *Journal of Interamerican Studies and World Affairs,* 30 (Summer/Fall 1988), 3, citing poll results from 1988.

[3]Elaine Shannon, *Desperados: Latin Drug Lords, U.S. Lawmen, and the War America Can't Win* (New York: Viking, 1988), 85, 362.

[4]*Washington Post Weekly,* September 18–24, 1989.

[5]*Los Angeles Times,* December 15, 1989; *Baltimore Sun,* September 19, 1989.

[6]Some have spoken up. Rep. Peter Kostmayer, a Pennsylvania Democrat, has expressed "grave doubts about the militarization of the Andean anti-narcotics effort" and asked, "Are we getting the United States involved through the back door in fighting guerrilla wars?" See *New York Times,* June 21, 1990.

[7]*San Francisco Examiner,* July 3, 1989; cf. *Baltimore Sun,* June 12, 1989.

[8]Speech at Tufts University conference on drugs and national security, March 1989.

[9]Senate Committee on Foreign Relations, Subcommittee on Terrorism, Narcotics and International Operations, report, *Drugs, Law Enforcement and Foreign Policy* (hereafter Kerry report) (Washington, DC: U.S. Government Printing Office, 1989), 2, 134.

[10]*Newsweek,* July 16, 1990.

[11]*Los Angeles Times,* December 15, 1989.

[12]*Washington Post,* May 28, 1989.

[13]*US News and World Report,* July 31, 1989.

193

[14]*Washington Post,* May 28, 1989.

[15]For a brief synopsis of this history, see Jonathan Marshall, *Drug Wars: Corruption, Counterinsurgency and Covert Operations in the Third World* (Berkeley: Cohan and Cohen, 1991), Chapter 4, and Peter Dale Scott, introduction, in Henrick Krüger, *The Great Heroin Coup: Drugs, Intelligence, and International Fascism* (Boston: South End Press, 1980).

[16]Alfred McCoy, *The Politics of Heroin in Southeast Asia* (New York: Harper & Row, 1972).

[17]Ralph Blumenthal, *Last Days of the Sicilians* (New York: Pocketbooks, 1989), 95.

[18]Ibid., 94.

[19]*Observer* (London), October 6, 1985; cf. *Oakland Tribune,* June 2, 1985.

[20]*San Francisco Chronicle,* December 16, 1983.

[21]*New York Times,* April 10, 1988.

[22]Jaime Malamud Goti, "US National Security, Intervention and the Drug Regime," reprinted in *Drugs, International Security and U.S. Public Policy* (Medford, MA: Tufts University, 1989), 114.

[23]Sporkin testimony before House Iran-Contra Committees, June 24, 1987.

[24]For example, we have avoided relying on the testimony of Ramón Milián Rodríguez, a Cuban-American money launderer who implicated a leading Contra supporter in accepting drug money for the cause; he failed a lie-detector test administered under the auspices of the Kerry subcommittee. The testimony of Richard Brenneke, central to any evaluation of Israel's role in Central America, is too difficult to corroborate and too sweeping for comfort. With regard to the unconfirmed but intriguing story of convicted drug pilot Michael Tolliver—that he flew arms into Honduras and marijuana back to Homestead Air Force base in 1986 on a mission sanctioned by U.S. intelligence agencies—we remain agnostic (for a thorough account, see Leslie Cockburn, *Out of Control* [New York: Atlantic Monthly Press, 1977], 179–85). These witnesses may in fact be perfectly truthful, but prudence dictates turning elsewhere for information. On the other hand, the word of some convicted drug traffickers, like George Morales, has stood up well. Numerous critics from the CIA to author John Dinges have raised questions about the credibility of former Noriega adviser José Blandón, a major Kerry subcommittee witness; because sober investigators who know him best attest to his veracity, we have used his testimony with care.

CHAPTER I

[1]*Dallas Morning News,* December 21, 1985; *Washington Post,* December 27, 1985.

²*Washington Post,* April 17, 1986; Kerry report, 37.

³Kerry report, 37.

⁴Kerry report, 38, 52; *Christian Science Monitor,* June 8, 1987; *Miami Herald,* June 21, 1984.

⁵Kerry report, 38, citing *New York Times,* May 6, 1986, and National Public Radio, "All Things Considered," May 5, 1986; *Christian Science Monitor,* May 9, 1986.

⁶Kerry report, 38.

⁷Kerry report, 39. The CIA used a similar jurisdictional ploy, informing the Kerry subcommittee that "all agency activities in Central America and information it gathers is under close and continuing scrutiny by the House and Senate intelligence committees" (Kerry report, 100). Since those committees had turned over the drug issue to Kerry, however, this excuse was a circular argument.

⁸Footnotes to the report in this book citing pages 145 and beyond refer to these appendices.

⁹Kerry report, 2.

¹⁰Ibid., 36.

¹¹Ibid., 41.

¹²Ibid.

¹³Ibid., 42–43.

¹⁴Ibid., 44.

¹⁵Ibid., 45–46. Milián's credibility is not really in question here, only on matters pertaining to the Contras (and possibly to Noriega).

¹⁶Ibid.

¹⁷Ibid., 47–48.

¹⁸Ibid., 48.

¹⁹Ibid., 41.

²⁰Ibid., 44.

²¹Ibid., 49, citing State Department document 5136c, July 26, 1986.

²²Ibid., 49.

²³Ibid., 51.

²⁴Ibid., 52–53.

²⁵Ibid., 53–54.

²⁶*Washington Times,* January 17, 1989.

²⁷Kerry report, 54.

²⁸Ibid., 56–57.

²⁹*San Francisco Chronicle,* January 14, 1989.

³⁰Agence France Presse, May 18, 1989; *Tico Times* (San José), June 9, 1989.

³¹*Washington Times,* July 24, 1989.

³²Kerry report, 59.

³³Ibid., 60.

³⁴Miami police interview with José Coutin, September 6, 1984, provided to FBI on September 26, 1984; in Kerry report, 371, 374.

[35]FBI interview with Rene Corvo, June 4, 1986, in Kerry report, 416–17. The FBI also knew from other interviews that Corvo had set up a military training camp for anti-Sandinista guerrillas in Florida, financed by Frank Castro and Joseph Marcos (see FBI interview with Joseph Marcos, December 17, 1984, Kerry report, 425–26). The federal investigators should have been aware that both financiers had been indicted in a major 1981 drug conspiracy case, Operation Tick-Talks, although Marcos told the agents that "neither he nor Frank Castro are involved in narcotic or weapons trafficking."

[36]FBI interview with Corvo, March 1, 1985, in Kerry report, 414; on Frigorificos, cf. Kerry report, 365.

[37]Earl deposition, quoted in Kerry report, 61.

[38]Kerry report, 75–78. For more on these episodes, see Chapter 3.

[39]Ibid., 122–33.

[40]*Latin America Weekly Report,* October 13, 1988; *El Pais,* September 14, 1988; *Hoy Internacional* (La Paz), September 12–18, 1988; cf. Federico Aguilob, "El Caso Huanchaca," *Estudios Sociales* II (December 6, 1988). There were also stories in the Argentine press about a European arms dealer and DEA informant named Leif Rasmussen who allegedly bought military supplies (including Chilean fragmentation grenades) in Paraguay for shipment to Iran and who also collected funds to finance the Contras. Rasmussen was allegedly consigned a 115-ton cocaine load smuggled to Brussels by a German rancher in Paraguay close to President Stroessner. See *El Periodista de Buenos Aires,* October 30, 1987, and November 6, 1987. Senator Kerry was aware of this case, although he chose not to mention it in the final report (*Congressional Record,* May 18, 1988).

[41]*Newsday,* July 11, 1987; *Los Angeles Times,* July 17, 1987. The Iran-Contra committees mentioned al-Kassar only in a brief footnote to their final report, omitting even his first name (Iran-Contra report, 337n). His name has since surfaced in connection with the downing of Pan Am Flight 103 in December 1988; a report prepared by a private investigator for Pan Am alleges that al-Kassar used his relationship with the CIA to help smuggle the bomb aboard the plane (Associated Press, November 1, 1989; *Washington Post,* November 2, 1989).

[42]*Newsday,* July 11, 1987; *Los Angeles Times,* July 17, 1987; *Reader's Digest,* August 1986. *Reader's Digest* reported that al-Kassar supplied arms and explosives "for terrorist operations in France, Spain and Holland" and sold "silencer-equipped assassination pistols, rockets and other weapons" to Libya, Iran, South Yemen, and Lebanon. British authorities reportedly want to question him about the sale of timers "for use in terrorist bombs." See *Observer,* April 12, 1987.

[43]*Newsday,* April 19, 1987.

[44]*San Francisco Examiner,* April 20, 1987; *Reader's Digest,* August 1986.

[45] Manfred Morstein, *Der Pate des Terrors* (Munich: Piper Verlag, 1989), 221–22, 227.

[46] Kerry hearings, III, 237.

[47] Kerry report, 49.

[48] Gerard Colby, *DuPont Dynasty* (Secaucus, NJ: Lyle Stuart, 1984), 778, 786 regarding the CIA and Thailand; *Nation,* June 13, 1987, on the Contras.

[49] Owen to North, February 10, 1986, exhibit RWO11, in Iran-Contra Committees, *Joint Hearings on the Iran-Contra Investigation,* Testimony of Robert C. McFarlane, Gaston J. Sigur, Jr., and Robert Owen (Washington, DC: U.S. Government Printing Office, 1987), 817, 438–39; cf. Kerry hearings, III, 56–57.

[50] *San Francisco Examiner,* April 14, 1988.

[51] *Los Angeles Times,* April 7, 1988; Kerry hearings, III, 202.

[52] *Miami Herald,* February 16, 1987; cf. Kerry report, 366. In an open letter to fellow Cuban exile militants, dated June 17, 1985, Vidal admitted that some financing for his operations in Costa Rica came from Frigorificos principals Moisés Nuñez and Frank Chanes.

[53] *Miami Herald,* February 16, 1987.

[54] Costa Rica Asamblea Legislativa, Comision Especial Nombrada Para Investigar Los Hechos Denunciados Sobre Narcotrafico, *Informe Final,* July 20, 1989, 61.

[55] House Select Committee on Narcotics Abuse and Control memo, June 26, 1985.

[56] Leslie Cockburn, *Out of Control* (New York: Atlantic Monthly Press, 1987), 89.

[57] Kerry report, 156.

[58] *Newsday,* January 21, 1987; cf. *Newsweek,* January 26, 1987; *San Francisco Chronicle,* January 20, 1987; *New York Times,* August 23, 1987. An FBI spokesman described the informant as previously "reliable." *New York Times,* February 24, 1988.

[59] *San Francisco Chronicle,* January 20, 1987.

[60] *San Jose Mercury,* April 13, 1987; *Washington Times,* March 27, 1987; *Oregonian,* August 20, 1988. One of those who used the bank's good offices for drug money laundering on a huge scale was Ramón Milián Rodríguez, a business partner of General Noriega and a professed financial supporter of the Contras. (See *San Antonio Light,* June 11, 1985, reprinted in Kerry report, 501.) His CIA-trained client Carlos Soto, a founder of Frigorificos, also laundered money through the same bank (Kerry report, 298, 303). The former campaign fundraiser for President Arias of Costa Rica, Ricardo Alem, was accused by a legislative commission of laundering drug money through Banco de Iberoamerica. So, too, was Steven Samos, a Panamanian drug money launderer. (See *Wall Street Journal,* January

8, 1987, and April 17, 1986; Roberto Velez, *The Eisenmann Connection* [Panama: Editora Renovacion, 1987], 59).

[61]Interview with Jack Blum, November 26, 1990.

CHAPTER 2

[1]See Peter A. Lupsha, "Towards an Etiology of Drug Trafficking and Insurgent Relations: The Phenomenon of Narco-Terrorism," *International Journal of Comparative and Applied Criminal Justice,* XIII (Fall 1989), 60–74.

[2]A spokesman for the unconventional warfare community, Special Forces commander Col. John D. Waghelstein, argued that the narcoterrorist theme could overcome the public's strong disinclination to support military intervention against guerrilla movements in Latin America:

> A melding in the American public's mind and in Congress of this connection would lead to the necessary support to counter the guerrilla/narcotics terrorists in this hemisphere. . . . Congress would find it difficult to stand in the way of supporting our allies with the training, advice and security assistance necessary to do the job. Those church and academic groups that have slavishly supported insurgency in Latin America would find themselves on the wrong side of the moral issue. Above all, we would have the unassailable moral position from which to launch a concerted offensive effort using Department of Defense (DOD) and non-DOD assets. . . . Instead of responding defensively to each insurgency on a case-by-case basis, we could act in concert with our allies. Instead of wading through the legislative snarl and financial constraints that characterize our security assistance posture, we could act with alacrity to the threat. Instead of debating each separate threat, we can begin to see the hemisphere as a whole and ultimately develop the vision that has been sorely lacking. (*Military Review,* February 1987, 46–47)

[3]Carl Channell and Richard Miller, "Action Plan for 1986 Programs of the American Conservative Trust and The National Endowment for the Preservation of Liberty," in Iran-Contra Report, Appendix A, 686.

[4]Quoted in Shannon, *Desperados,* 175, 159.

[5]February 10, 1986, speech, reprinted in Department of State, Current Policy Paper 792.

[6]*El Periodista de Buenos Aires,* January 19, 1989; January 26, 1989.

[7]*Miami Herald,* January 23, 1976.

[8]*Miami Herald,* August 6, 1981; July 26, 1983.

[9]Interview with Jerry Sanford, former assistant U.S. attorney, July 13, 1987; interview with Daniel Cassidy, assistant U.S. attorney, November 6, 1986; interview with Miami detective D. C. Diaz, January 25, 1990; *Miami Herald,* July 26, 1983.

[10]Owen letter to North, November 5, 1984, supplied by Christic Institute.

[11]Owen letter to North, August 2, 1985, supplied by Christic Institute.

[12]FBI 302, August 10, 1987, reprinted in Kerry report, 458. Castro's colleague, Porfirio Bonet, was indicted with Castro in Operation Tick-Talks.

[13]*New York Times,* August 23, 1988; cf. FBI 302, August 20, 1987, interview with Frank Castro in Kerry report, 459. His fellow guerrilla camp financier was José Marcos, also indicted in Tick-Talks (interview with Miami detective D. C. Diaz, January 25, 1990). A Florida judge ruled in July 1989 that the presidential authorization of covert operations against Nicaragua made the Neutrality Act inapplicable in this case.

[14]*Houston Post,* February 18, 1990.

[15]Kerry report, 60–61. The report refers only to a committee request to the Justice Department for information on Castro.

[16]*BNDD Bulletin,* September–October 1970; cf. Hank Messick, *Of Grass and Snow* (Englewood Cliffs, NJ: Prentice-Hall, 1979), 6.

[17]Quoted in Warren Hinckle and William Turner, *The Fish Is Red* (New York: Harper & Row, 1981), 314.

[18]John Cummings, "Omega 7," *Parapolitics/USA,* No. 5.

[19]Hinckle and Turner, *Fish Is Red,* 314.

[20]*St. Petersburg Times,* December 29, 1980.

[21]Messick, *Of Grass and Snow,* 6; *Miami Herald,* November 15, 1979.

[22]*St. Petersburg Times,* May 30, 1982.

[23]Donald Goddard, *Easy Money* (New York: Farrar, Straus & Giroux, 1978), 310.

[24]Morales was an informant for Raul Diaz, a controversial officer with the Metro Dade police department (Paul Eddy, *The Cocaine Wars* [New York: Norton, 1988], 85). In January 1985, Diaz introduced the drug-money launderer Ramón Milián Rodríguez to his friend Félix Rodríguez, a former CIA officer who became a central organizer of the Contra logistics effort. Milián claims that he offered and Rodríguez accepted $10 million to help the Contra cause in return for his freedom; Rodríguez says he merely passed to agents of the CIA and FBI Milián's offer of a deal to implicate the Sandinistas. Diaz refused to testify on this matter before the Kerry committee (Kerry report, 61–62; Kerry hearings, IV, 322–24, 330–32). Morales was killed in 1982, shortly before he was due to testify about the finances of one of Diaz's enemies (*Arizona Republic,* February 20, 1983).

[25]Lucien Conein memo, May 25, 1976. This document, and several in citations that follow, was released under the Freedom of Information Act to the National Organization for Reform of the Marijuana Laws and supplied to the authors by John Hill.

[26]"Report of June 18, 1975 to the Attorney General, Subject: Additional Integrity Matters," (known as Defeo report), 8–9.

[27]"Project Buncin: Summary, September 1972–March 1973."

[28]"Overall Assessment of Project DEACON 1," December 2, 1974.

[29]"Project Buncin: Summary, September 1972–March 1973."

[30]Ibid.

[31]*Washington Post,* June 13, 1976; interview with José Antonio Fernandez, October 10, 1990.

[32]*Miami Herald,* January 24, 1989; Associated Press, December 16, 1987; April 13, 1989.

[33]Associated Press, January 23, 1989.

[34]*St. Petersburg Times,* May 30, 1982.

[35]Interview with José Antonio Fernandez, October 10, 1990.

[36]FBI interview with Rafael Torres Jimenez, December 17, 1984, in Kerry report, 431.

[37]Besides Castro and Morales, these include Eduardo Garcia, Diego Morales, Rubén Perez, and Juan Novaton. See *Houston Chronicle,* January 9, 1983; DEA report, August 17, 1981.

[38]DEA report, op. cit., on Villoldo, Diego Morales, and Rubén Perez; *Progressive,* May 1987. Oliver North's notebooks contain an entry for May 12, 1984: "contract indicates that Gustavo is involved w/ drugs." See Kerry report, 146.

[39]He was also a suspected front man for Guillermo Hernandez Cartaya, yet another Bay of Pigs veteran and the proprietor of the WFC finance conglomerate, widely reputed to have handled drug funds. See James Ring Adams, *The Big Fix* (New York: Wiley, 1990), 79–81, 137.

[40]Interview with Daniel Cassidy, July 28, 1988.

[41]Kerry report, 45–46, 150, 299–319, 362. The marijuana supplier was Carlos Soto.

[42]Indicted with the others was Steven Kalish, who later testified about Panamanian Gen. Manuel Noriega's involvement in the drug trade. Interview with Daniel Cassidy, July 28, 1989 (Castro); *Houston Chronicle,* July 13, 1983 (Fernandez and Grouper); *Miami News,* April 27, 1978; June 10, 1978; Senate Committee on Government Operations, Permanent Subcommittee on Investigations, hearing, "Drugs and Money Laundering in Panama," January 28, 1988 (Washington, DC: U.S. Government Printing Office, 1988) (Kalish).

[43]Morales testimony to Florida Assistant State Attorney Rina Cohan, December 16, 1980; *Miami Herald,* August 12, 1981; cf. Eddy, *Cocaine Wars,* 89.

[44]Interview with Orlando Bosch, *New Times,* May 13, 1977.

[45]Armando López Estrada, quoted in CBS special report, June 10, 1977.

[46]These founding members were Frank Castro, Luis Posada, Jose Dionisio Suarez, Armando López Estrada, and Juan Perez Franco. See *Wall Street Journal,* January 16, 1977.

[47]Quoted in John Cummings, "Miami Confidential," *Inquiry,* August 3, 1981, 20; cf. Penny Lernoux, *In Banks We Trust* (Garden City, NY: Anchor Press, 1984), Ch. 8.

[48]Other associates had Contra ties as well. According to a federal agent, one of Hernandez Cartaya's aides was Ramón Milián Rodríguez. Hernandez Cartaya's friend from university days, Carlos Perez, became a leading fundraiser for the Contras. He was endorsed in a primary race for Congress by Oliver North at a reception hosted by Richard Nixon's confidant Bebe Rebozo. See *Miami Herald,* May 4, 1986; July 1, 1989. He lost the primary to Ileana Ros-Lehtinen, an outspoken defender of CORU founder Orlando Bosch and wife of the U.S. attorney in Miami. She went on to win the race against an attorney for the CIA-linked international arms dealer Sarkis Soghanalian.

[49]*Providence Sunday Journal,* June 22, 1980.

[50]John Dinges and Saul Landau, *Assassination on Embassy Row* (New York: Pantheon, 1980), 251 and 251n. Emphasis in original.

[51]*Miami News,* July 17, 1986.

[52]Jonathan Marshall, Peter Dale Scott, and Jane Hunter, *The Iran-Contra Connection: Secret Teams and Covert Operations in the Reagan Era* (Boston: South End Press, 1987), 131.

[53]Félix Rodríguez testimony before Iran-Contra Committees, May 28, 1987; Kerry hearings, IV, 345.

[54]Kerry hearings, IV, 345–46; *Miami Herald,* August 26, 1987.

[55]Cummings, "Miami Confidential."

[56]*Miami Herald,* February 12, 1977.

[57]CBS News, June 10, 1977 (Merida); *Covert Action Information Bulletin,* July 1978; Hinckle and Turner, *Fish Is Red,* 341–342 (Lopez Estrada trial); Marshall, Scott, and Hunter, *Iran-Contra Connection,* 43, 143 (Costa Rica).

[58]John Cummings, "U.S. Intelligence and International Terrorism," *Parapolitics/USA,* No. 2.2.

[59]Taylor Branch and Eugene Propper, *Labyrinth* (New York: Viking, 1982), 185.

[60]Cummings, "U.S. Intelligence and International Terrorism."

[61]*San Francisco Chronicle,* April 15, 1978.

[62]These three were Guillermo Novo, Virgilio Paz, and José Dionisio Suarez.

[63]Cummings, "Omega 7." The CNM leadership also had at least an oblique connection with Restoy's drug partner Mario Escandar through their work with the CIA agent and drug trafficker Enrique Castro (FBI transcript of Eduardo Arocena telephone conversation, December 19, 1982). Castro was a partner of Union City crime boss and Bay of Pigs veteran José Miguel Battle, who in turn had ties to Escandar (*Miami News,* December 28, 1979).

[64]Interview with Dan Benitez, April 6, 1981.

[65]Dinges and Landau, *Assassination on Embassy Row,* 264n.

[66]House Select Committee on Narcotics Abuse and Control, memo, June 26, 1985. This was the Frogman ring, described in Chapter 6.

[67]*Miami Herald,* July 1, 1988. Suarez was later arrested on the Letelier charges (*New York Times,* April 12, 1990).

[68]*St. Petersburg Times,* May 30, 1982; Branch and Propper, *Labyrinth,* 529.

[69]Branch and Propper, *Labyrinth,* 530, 534.

[70]Jonathan Marshall, in *Parapolitics/USA,* No. 2.

[71]*Washington Post,* November 7, 1978; *Proceso,* April 17, 1989 (Ismael Zambada).

[72]*Washington Post,* November 7, 1978; James Mills, *The Underground Empire: Where Crime and Governments Embrace* (New York: Dell, 1986), 85, 360.

[73]Mills, *Underground Empire,* 360–61, 357, 521, 548, 73, 619.

[74]Mills, *Underground Empire,* 608–9.

[75]Justice Department informant report; Cummings, "U.S. Intelligence and International Terrorism."

[76]Victor Marchetti and John Marks, *The CIA and the Cult of Intelligence* (New York: Knopf, 1974), 131 (Murray); *Washington Post,* October 26, 1986 (Villoldo, Rodríguez). Villoldo, we have seen, had definite narcotics connections.

[77]*Arizona Daily Star,* April 13, 1984; September 5, 1984; September 7, 1984; Guillermo Garcia letter, May 15, 1984 (Murray, Nazar, Durazo); *Washington Post,* July 24, 1979 (Durazo). Durazo established a political police organization, the Directorate of Investigations for the Prevention of Delinquency, that earned a reputation for brutality and corruption but which would have been a valued source of information to more than one American agency. See *San Jose Mercury News,* January 15, 1983.

[78]"Background Establishing a Clandestine Collection Gathering Effort Within DEA," memo to George Belk, October 8, 1974.

[79]*New York Times,* April 1, 1985. DEA informant Lawrence Harrison claimed that Nazar had been on the CIA payroll "for 10 years. He was their chief agent" (DEA debriefing of Harrison, September 26, 1989).

[80]Shannon, *Desperados,* 180.

[81]Quoted in Cummings, "U.S. Intelligence and International Terrorism"; cf. *New York Times,* March 28, 1982.

[82]Shannon, *Desperados,* 180–83; *Washington Post Weekly,* February 13, 1989; *Washington Post,* April 6, 1982.

[83]Terrence Poppa, *Druglord* (New York: Pharos Books, 1990), 145.

[84]Quoted in Shannon, *Desperados,* 65.

[85]*New York Times,* December 24, 1980; cf. Dominick DiCarlo, assistant secretary of state for international narcotics matters, testimony to House

Select Committee on Narcotics Abuse and Control, June 22, 1983; cited in Shannon, *Desperados,* 130.

[86]*International Study Missions,* Summary Report, 1984, 4–6; cf. Shannon, *Desperados,* 132.

[87]*Oakland Tribune,* February 26, 1985.

[88]Shannon, *Desperados,* 2–3.

[89]Ibid., 128–29.

[90]*Washington Post,* May 12, 1985. This account notes that the State Department wanted to play down these inconvenient facts.

[91]*New York Times,* November 23, 1984.

[92]*Proceso,* April 17, 1989.

[93]*Oregonian,* August 14, 1988; Shannon, *Desperados,* 62–63; *Time,* April 7, 1986.

[94]"Report of a Staff Study Mission . . . to the Committee on Foreign Affairs," House of Representatives, *US Narcotics Control Programs Overseas: An Assessment,* February 22, 1985; Frank Forrestal, "The Sinai-American Connection," *MERIP Reports,* No. 63, 20.

[95]Shannon, *Desperados,* 109.

[96]Ibid., 67 69; *Peninsula Times Tribune,* February 18, 1980, citing an exposé in the *San Diego Union; Newsweek,* December 16, 1985.

[97]"Report of a Staff Study Mission . . . to the Committee on Foreign Affairs," 37–38.

[98]Mills, *Underground Empire,* 550.

[99]Ibid., 1157; Kerry hearings, IV, 93.

[100]Poppa, *Druglord,* 68; *New York Times,* October 20, 1986; Shannon, *Desperados,* 291; *Washington Post,* June 4, 1988.

[101]Mills, *Underground Empire,* 101.

[102]Shannon, *Desperados,* 67; cf. *Proceso,* April 17, 1989.

[103]*New York Times,* April 21, 1985.

[104]Shannon, *Desperados,* 179.

[105]Ibid., 8.

[106]*Los Angeles Times,* June 7, 1985.

[107]Shannon, *Desperados,* 294.

[108]*Time,* March 17, 1988; cf. Shannon, *Desperados,* 186–87. The use of tanker trucks to smuggle marijuana was one of Sicilia Falcón's great innovations.

[109]Shannon, *Desperados,* 294; trial memorandum, *United States of America v. Rafael Caro Quintero et al.,* United States District Court for the Central District of California, CR 87-422(f)-ER.

[110]Quoted in Shannon, *Desperados,* 186. For evidence of Zorrilla's ties to drug lord Rafael Caro Quintero, a principal suspect in the Camarena murder, see *Excelsior* (Mexico City), August 1, 1989. Zorrilla has also been accused of the murder of muckraking Mexican journalist Manuel Buendia (*Los Angeles Times,* June 13, 1989).

[111]Shannon, *Desperados,* 132.

[112]Ibid., 9.

[113]Lotz was also a pilot for Robert Vesco in Costa Rica in the mid-1970s. See Kerry hearings, IV, 666.

[114]*Los Angeles Times,* August 19, 1988, and August 31, 1988; DEA debriefing of Werner Lotz, November 20, 1987.

[115]A judge ruled the testimony hearsay or irrelevant. See *Los Angeles Times,* July 8, 1990. The witness, Lawrence Harrison, also told the DEA that another kingpin of the Guadalajara cartel, Ernesto Fonseca, "felt betrayed" when the DEA arranged a raid on the Chihuahua marijuana plantation in 1984, having "had a reason to believe that they should not be bothering him" (DEA debriefing, September 26, 1989).

[116]*Los Angeles Times,* July 5, 1990; July 8, 1990; DEA debriefing of Harrison, February 13, 1990. Harrison's information about the training camp appears to have been second- or third-hand.

[117]*Washington Post,* July 8, 1990.

[118]Michael Levine, *Deep Cover* (New York: Delacorte Press, 1990), 151, 179, 184, 306.

[119]*Wall Street Journal,* November 20, 1986; Shannon, *Desperados,* 61; United Press International, June 30, 1980; *Newsweek,* May 13, 1985; United Press International, June 30, 1988.

[120]Krüger, *Great Heroin Coup,* 213; *New York Times,* August 10, 1980.

[121]Future CORU founders Gaspar Jimenez, Orlando Bosch, and Luis Posada were implicated in the murder of Cuban diplomats in Argentina. See *Miami Herald,* February 12, 1977; October 18, 1977 (Jimenez); "Declaration of the Acting Associate Attorney General," June 23, 1989 (summary released in Bosch immigration case); *Miami Herald,* August 14, 1976. (Posada). House Select Committee on Assassinations, appendix to hearings, *Investigation of the Assassination of President John F. Kennedy,* X (Washington, DC: U.S. Government Printing Office, 1979), 44.

[122]Interview with Leandro Sanchez Reisse, *Somos* (Buenos Aires), February 25, 1987.

[123]Ibid.

[124]*Los Angeles Times,* April 29, 1989; *La Repubblica,* June 8, 1984.

[125]*El Periodista de Buenos Aires,* April 9, 1987, quoting Antonio Troccoli; cf. Marshall, Scott, and Hunter, *Iran-Contra Connection,* 24, 69–76, 80.

[126]Lernoux, *In Banks We Trust,* 189.

[127]*El Periodista de Buenos Aires,* April 9, 1987; interview with Miami detective D. C. Diaz, January 25, 1990. One such trainer was Juan Martin Ciga Correa, an active member of the AAA's appendage Milicia, which was financed by the military intelligence agency SIDE and which took part in the DINA-directed assassination of Chilean General Prats on September 30, 1974.

[128]*La Repubblica,* June 8, 1984.

[129]*Latin America,* December 19, 1975.

[130]*San Francisco Examiner,* January 27, 1987.

[131]Interview with Jack Blum, August 25, 1989.

[132]*Los Angeles Times,* August 31, 1980.

[133]Magnus Linklater, Isabel Hilton, and Neal Ascherson, *The Nazi Legacy* (New York: Holt, Rinehart, and Winston, 1984), 280. The specialist was Major Hugo Raul Miori Pereira.

[134]*Miami Herald,* July 30, 1980. The adviser was Lt. Col. Julio Cesar Duran.

[135]*Los Angeles Times,* August 31, 1980.

[136]*Stern,* May 17, 1984; May 24, 1984; June 7, 1984; *Granma,* June 21, 1987; Linklater, Hilton, and Ascherson, *Nazi Legacy,* 281, 288; *EFE* (Madrid), May 23, 1987; June 14, 1987; and April 6, 1988. When arrested in Brazil, Mingolla admitted that he had worked as an adviser to the military dictatorships of Argentina, Bolivia, and Guatemala but said he was now working as a liaison between drug syndicates and such left-wing guerrilla organizations as Colombia's M-19 and Peru's Shining Path.

[137]Branch and Propper, *Labyrinth,* 305–27; Linklater, Hilton, and Ascherson, *Nazi Legacy,* 212–13. CNM took responsibility under its cover name Cero.

[138]Linklater, Hilton, and Ascherson, *Nazi Legacy,* 278–79. Delle Chiaie had close connections with the P2 lodge in both Italy and Argentina, including José López Rega (211–12).

[139]Ibid., 280–82.

[140]*Sunday Times* (London), August 10, 1980.

[141]*Sunday Times,* June 29, 1980.

[142]*Los Angeles Times,* August 31, 1980.

[143]*Newsweek,* November 23, 1981.

[144]*Miami Herald,* October 14, 1981; *Latin America Regional Reports/ Andean Group,* RA-80-07, August 29, 1980.

[145]Morales testimony to Florida Assistant State Attorney Rina Cohan, December 16, 1980.

[146]*L'Espresso,* October 24, 1982; Linklater, Hilton, and Ascherson, *Nazi Legacy,* 289ff.

[147]Joachim Fiebelkorn, quoted in Martin Lee and Kevin Coogan, "The Agca Con," *Village Voice,* December 24, 1985.

[148]The alleged assassin, Cap. Alvaro Saravia, was arrested in the United States on drug charges (*El Periodista de Buenos Aires,* August 27, 1987). On the CAL meeting, see also Marshall, Scott, and Hunter, *Iran-Contra Connection,* 68–69.

[149]Scott Anderson and John Lee Anderson, *Inside the League* (New York: Dodd, Mead, 1986), 147–48, 197, 204.

[150]*Corriere della Sera,* March 30, 1987; Lee and Coogan, "The Agca Con."

[151]*New Leader,* June 27, 1988; *San Francisco Examiner,* May 22, 1988.

[152]*Panorama* (Milan), November 10, 1985; cf. *La Razon* (Buenos Aires), November 21, 1986.

[153]*Los Angeles Times,* November 9, 1988; *San Francisco Examiner,* July 8, 1990.

[154]Marshall, Scott, and Hunter, *Iran-Contra Connection,* 59. Alvarez studied under Jorge Rafael Videla, leader of that country's junta in the late 1970s. Anderson and Anderson, *Inside the League,* 224.

[155]Anderson and Anderson, *Inside the League,* 176; *Albuquerque Journal,* December 15, 1985. The information on CAL and Argentina's secret police comes from Francisco Guirola.

[156]*Kansas City Star,* May 22, 1985; Craig Pyes and Laurie Becklund, "Inside Dope in El Salvador," *New Republic,* April 15, 1985; *Miami Herald,* April 29, 1985.

[157]Jonathan Marshall, "The Foreign Minister of the New Right," *City Paper,* 7 (June 19–25, 1987), 17; Anderson and Anderson, *Inside the League,* 206; cf. Marshall, Scott, and Hunter, *Iran-Contra Connection,* 76–77.

[158]Roy Gutman, *Banana Diplomacy* (New York: Simon and Schuster, 1988), 22, 51–52. The diplomat was Gerardo Schamis.

[159]John Prados, *Presidents' Secret Wars* (New York: William Morrow, 1986), 380–81; *Latin America Weekly Report,* February 12, 1982.

[160]A third party in this operation was said to be Francisco Aguirre, a CIA-connected Nicaraguan exile who frequently does business in Argentina. See *El Periodista de Buenos Aires,* December 17, 1988; Gutman, *Banana Diplomacy,* 49–51.

[161]Gutman, *Banana Diplomacy,* 20, 22, 36, 51–52, 54.

[162]Ibid., 55–57.

[163]Marshall, Scott, and Hunter, *Iran-Contra Connection,* 11.

[164]Prados, *Presidents' Secret Wars,* 381.

[165]*Latin America Weekly Report,* February 12, 1982. Gen. Alberto Valin was the ambassador.

[166]Marshall, Scott, and Hunter, *Iran-Contra Connection,* 132–34, 141; Anderson and Anderson, *Inside the League,* 177, 225.

[167]Anderson and Anderson, *Inside the League,* 177.

[168]Interview with Jack Blum, August 25, 1989; *Somos,* February 25, 1987.

[169]*Miami Herald,* December 28, 1981; *Asian Outlook,* June 1977; Anderson and Anderson, *Inside the League,* 248.

[170]Peter Maas, *Manhunt* (New York: Random House, 1986), 202 (Suarez); Félix Rodríguez, *Shadow Warrior* (New York: Simon and Schuster, 1989), 203–6; *Los Angeles Times,* October 16, 1986; *New York Times,* December 10, 1986 (Rodríguez). The information on Suarez comes from Rafael Quintero, who may have heard it directly from Rodríguez, later

his partner in the Contra supply operation and, like Suarez, a colleague of the CIA's former station chief Theodore Shackley.

[171]*El Periodista de Buenos Aires,* November 27, 1988.

[172]He was accused of the kidnapping of Uruguayan businessman Carlos Koldobsky. See *El Periodista de Buenos Aires,* August 27, 1987. Sanchez Reisse escaped from a Swiss prison where he was held on charges relating to these kidnappings. The only other escapee from that prison was Licio Gelli, founder of the P2 lodge of which Suarez Mason was a member. Both Gelli and Sanchez Reisse shared the same attorney, Dominique Poncet. Sanchez Reisse's other attorney, Phillipe Neyrou, represented Albert Hakim, a principal in North's "Enterprise." See *El Periodista de Buenos Aires,* December 25, 1987.

[173]*El Periodista de Buenos Aires,* November 27, 1988; December 17, 1988; August 27, 1988.

[174]Interview with Jack Terrell, August 27, 1989.

[175]Gutman, *Banana Diplomacy,* 105.

[176]*San Francisco Chronicle,* January 19, 1984.

[177]*Washington Post,* June 2, 1985.

[178]*New Leader,* June 27, 1988; *El Periodista de Buenos Aires,* March 25, 1988.

CHAPTER 3

[1]Anderson and Anderson, *Inside the League,* 218–30. Alvarez allegedly founded a military intelligence unit, Battalion 316, that tortured or murdered more than 130 victims between 1981 and 1983. See *Nation,* January 23, 1988, and February 20, 1988.

[2]Kerry report, 75.

[3]Frederic Sondern, *Brotherhood of Evil* (London: Panther Books, 1959), 51; cf. Fred Cook, *Mafia!* (Greenwich, CT: Fawcett, 1973), 33; Dwight Smith, Jr., *The Mafia Mystique* (New York: Basic Books, 1975), 30.

[4]David Leon Chandler, *Brothers in Blood* (New York: Dutton, 1975), 49, 97–98; Thomas Karnes, *Tropical Enterprise* (Baton Rouge: Louisiana State University Press, 1978), 4, 10; Thomas McCann, *An American Company* (New York: Crown, 1976), 16.

[5]Chandler, *Brothers in Blood,* 98.

[6]Karnes, *Tropical Enterprise,* 2, 6, 104; cf. Peter Dale Scott, *Crime and Cover-Up* (Berkeley: Westworks, 1977), 16, 55.

[7]Leonard Katz, *Uncle Frank* (New York: Drake, 1973), 99–101.

[8]Ibid.

[9]John Davis, *Mafia Kingfish* (New York: McGraw-Hill, 1989), 36.

[10]William Walker, III, *Drug Control in the Americas* (Albuquerque: University of New Mexico Press, 1989), 86.

[11]Scott, *Crime and Cover-Up,* 16, 46; Maurice Helbrant, *Narcotics Agent* (New York: Vanguard, 1941), 265–81.

[12]Walker, *Drug Control in the Americas,* 146.

[13]James Morris, *Honduras: Caudillo Politics and Military Rulers* (Boulder: Westview, 1984), 8–9.

[14]Walker, *Drug Control in the Americas,* 90, 145.

[15]Ibid., 142–44.

[16]Karnes, *Tropical Enterprise,* 41, 44–45; McCann, *An American Company,* 18–20; Walker, *Drug Control in the Americas,* 263n. Walker notes that Maloney's intervention in 1932 was aided by arms shipments for pro-Carias forces arranged by TACA.

[17]Messick, *Of Grass and Snow,* 174–78; Lernoux, *In Banks We Trust,* 152–53; *Tampa Tribune,* June 9, 1974. Somoza claimed he was being "framed" by all the evidence at Stancel's trial.

[18]Walter LaFeber, *Inevitable Revolutions* (New York: Norton, 1983), 264; *San Francisco Chronicle,* June 6, 1974; November 16, 1975.

[19]Penny Lernoux, *Cry of the People* (London: Penguin Books, 115–17).

[20]Ibid., 117; *San Francisco Chronicle,* May 17, 1988; *New York Times,* May 25, 1988; Kerry report, 78. Regalado Lara is the half-brother of Gen. Humberto Regalado Hernandez, former armed forces chief of Honduras.

[21]"Honduras: Challenging Castle & Cooke," *NACLA Report,* March/April 1978, 43–44; Lernoux, *Cry of the People,* 118–19. Another patron of the Contras in the region, Gen. Manuel Noriega, got his start in military intelligence spying on unions organized by banana workers at United Fruit's plantations in Panama. See *Wall Street Journal,* October 18, 1989; Frederick Kempe, *Divorcing the Dictator* (New York: Putnam, 1990), 57.

[22]Matta was later "absolved through the Honduran legal system" (Mark Rosenberg, "Narcos and Politicos," *Journal of Interamerican Studies and World Affairs,* XXX, [Summer/Fall 1988], 148).

[23]*Latin America Political Report,* April 28, 1978; June 9, 1978; June 21, 1978; August 11, 1978; *Honduras Update,* March/April 1988; May 1988.

[24]Mills, *Underground Empire,* 944.

[25]Government sentencing memorandum, December 21, 1989, in *United States of America v. Juan Ramón Matta-Ballesteros,* CR 85-606-PAR.

[26]Mills, *Underground Empire,* 943.

[27]Shannon, *Desperados,* 115; *New York Times,* April 6, 1988.

[28]*Facts on File,* August 11, 1978.

[29]The Kerry report wrongly suggests, on the basis of José Blandón's testimony, that the Honduran military was introduced to narcotics trafficking in 1981 by Panama's General Noriega (73–74).

[30]*New York Times,* February 12, 1988. *High Times,* May 1979, reported that Paz had turned Honduras into a smuggling bridge between Colombia and Florida.

[31]Gutman, *Banana Diplomacy,* 55–57.

[32]Hector Aplicano, head of G-2 from October 1984 to mid-1986, had a close association with Matta's airline SETCO through his assistant Captain Leonel Luque, according to Jack Terrell. And the head of G-2 in 1988, Col. Roberto Nuñez Montes, has also been named as a drug protector (*New York Times,* April 15, 1988). He was appointed head of the antidrug unit (House Foreign Affairs Committee hearing, *Narcotics Review in Central America* [Washington, DC: U.S. Government Printing Office, 1988], 80).

[33]Kerry report, 44.

[34]John Dillon and Jon Lee Anderson, "Who's Behind the Aid to the Contras," *Nation,* October 6, 1984, 318.

[35]*New York Times,* April 10, 1988.

[36]Kerry report, 75.

[37]*Los Angeles Times,* February 13, 1988. One step in the process that led to Zepeda's removal may have been the selection of Ed Heath, a cautious DEA bureaucrat known for his sensitivity to Washington politics, to head the Mexico City station, which supervised the agency's Central American field agents. Heath's appointment in mid-1983 coincided exactly with the closing of Zepeda's listening post in Honduras. Once in charge, Heath reportedly played down the significance of the "Guadalajara connection" of which Matta was a significant supplier. See Shannon, *Desperados,* 126; interview with DEA public affairs chief Con Daugherty, July 1989. Heath's career suggests a pattern of accommodation to local leadership interests. In 1972, Heath was chosen to reopen the BNDD's Panama office as a conciliatory gesture to the country's leader, Gen. Omar Torrijos, whose brother had been indicted on drug trafficking charges (John Dinges, *Our Man in Panama* [New York: Random House, 1990], 67). In the mid-1970s, Heath apparently ran the DEA station in Mexico City (Mills, *Underground Empire,* 525); it was around this time that DEA-CON 1 informant Carlos Hernandez Rumbaut was reportedly on the payroll of that station (see Chapter 2). In his book *Deep Cover,* former DEA undercover agent Michael Levine supplies an unflattering portrait of Heath as attempting to protect high-ranking Mexican officials and military personnel from U.S. justice (269, 282–83, 285, 288).

[38]*Los Angeles Times,* February 13, 1988.

[39]Mort Rosenblum, "Hidden Agendas," *Vanity Fair,* March 1990, 120.

[40]*Metro* (San Jose), October 13, 1988.

[41]Kerry hearings, IV, 724–25.

[42]Kerry report, 75.

[43]Ibid., 286.

[44]Ibid., 44–45; cf. 296.

[45]Ibid., 280–81, 284.

[46]Ibid., 285.

[47]Ibid., 45, 297; Cockburn, *Out of Control,* 234; Associated Press, April 17, 1987; April 3, 1987; April 18, 1987; April 22, 1987; May 1, 1987.

[48]Iran-Contra exhibit RWO-11.

[49]Robert Owen memo to Oliver North, March 17, 1986, Iran-Contra exhibit RWO-13.

[50]*Washington Post,* February 26, 1987.

[51]*Iran-Contra Report,* 50–51.

[52]Congressional Quarterly, *Iran-Contra Puzzle* (Washington, DC: *Congressional Quarterly,* 1987), 97; *Washington Post,* February 26, 1987.

[53]North diary, July 12, 1985; partly reprinted in Kerry report, 147.

[54]*Newsweek,* May 23, 1988.

[55]Cockburn, *Out of Control,* 227.

[56]Interview with Jack Blum, May 13, 1990.

[57]Owen to North, March 17, 1986. North's diaries for July and August 1986 reflect his concern over leaks about the Secord operation by both Félix Rodríguez and former CIA agent Carl Jenkins (one of the men Owen listed as "bad mouthing" Secord).

[58]North diary, June 23, 1986 (Villoldo and Dellamico) and May 12, 1984 (Villoldo and drugs).

[59]North diary, June 24, 1986, released under the Freedom of Information Act to the National Security Archive.

[60]*Washington Post,* February 26, 1987. Félix Rodríguez confirmed to the Kerry subcommittee that in 1980 he had worked with Dellamico in Guatemala and that he knew George Bush through Don Gregg, an old friend and colleague from his service in Vietnam, who became Bush's national security adviser in the 1980s (Kerry hearings, IV, 368–69 [Dellamico]; 328 [Gregg]; 357–60 [Bush]). Secord testified that Rodríguez's real loyalty was to Ronald Martin: "Felix was working for Ronald Martin. I was also paying Felix." Gregg was reportedly responsible for sending both Rodríguez and Villoldo to Central America.

[61]Cockburn, *Out of Control,* 227.

[62]*Boston Globe,* June 27, 1988. Congressman Les Aspin noted in the Iran-Contra hearings that the "numbers did not check out" in the Contra accounts; the available funds shown were insufficient to pay for the known arms purchases. The final report of the Iran-Contra Committees notes that the cutoff of U.S. support in October 1984 "did not cause any immediate crisis for the Contras," and refers to "the $1 million-a-month pledged by Country 2 [Saudi Arabia]" which would "bridge the gap." (See *Iran-Contra Report,* 42.) But Saudi Arabia supplied Adolfo Calero with only $7.5 million from July 1984 to February 1985, little more than

half the $14 million the administration privately estimated that his move-
ment needed (*Iran-Contra Report,* 37–41; Appendix A, 1, 209, 212, 236).
Any other major sources of support are unknown.

[63]Jacqueline Sharkey, "The Contra-Drug Trade-Off," *Common Cause
Magazine,* September-October 1988, 29 (Efrain Diaz).

[64]The Cuban exile trafficker José Antonio Fernandez recalls being told
in late 1979 by Gustavo Villoldo of Bueso Rosa's role as a protector of
smugglers (interview with Fernandez, October 10, 1990).

[65]*Ma'ariv* (Tel Aviv), November 27, 1986; *New York Times,* February
23, 1987.

[66]*World Paper,* February 1985; Anderson and Anderson, *Inside the
League,* 232–33.

[67]*Nation,* January 23, 1988.

[68]*Oakland Tribune,* January 16, 1989; Jack Anderson, *San Francisco
Chronicle,* January 13, 1984; Anderson and Anderson, *Inside the League,*
228–30.

[69]*Time,* November 12, 1984; *New York Times,* November 4, 1984;
*Miami Herald,* November 3, 1984.

[70]*New York Times,* November 3, 1984. The name of the police chief is
not given. The coconspirator was Faiz Sikaffy, a partner in corruption of
former Honduran President Paz, Matta's protector and one of the Contras' first patrons. See *Central America Report,* November 9, 1984. Sikaffy
was later indicted for shipping more than a ton of marijuana into the
United States (*Dallas Morning News,* November 17, 1984). He may have
been paying off a debt to the Marcello crime syndicate in Louisiana (*New
York Times,* November 3, 1984).

[71]Kerry report, 76.

[72]The officials were Gen. Robert Schweitzer, retired from the National
Security Council, where he had supported Argentina's role in anti-Sandinista operations, and who later became an international arms dealer;
and Col. Nestor Pino, a Bay of Pigs veteran. See Francis McNeil, *War
and Peace in Central America* (New York: Scribner's, 1988), 229; Gutman,
*Banana Diplomacy,* 45–48; *New York Times,* February 23, 1987.

[73]Quoted in *Metro* (San Jose), October 13, 1988.

[74]John Martin to William Weld, September 30, 1986, *Iran-Contra
Report,* Appendix A, 776; McNeil, *War and Peace in Central America,*
230.

[75]The other officials were Ambassador John Negroponte, Gen. Paul
Gorman of the U.S. Southern Command, and CIA officer Duane Clarridge.

[76]His belief that he could "walk free" may have stemmed from Matta's
success in walking out of the same prison—Eglin Air Force Base—after
his 1971 conviction for immigration violations.

[77]North electronic PROF message to Poindexter, September 17, 1986,
*Iran-Contra Report,* Appendix A, 775. Besides Gorman and Clarridge,

North's "cabal" included Elliott Abrams from the State Department and two Justice Department officials.

[78]Poindexter PROF to North, September 18, 1986, *Iran-Contra Report,* Appendix A, 784.

[79]McNeil, *War and Peace in Central America,* 230–31; *Iran-Contra Report,* 110.

[80]Kerry hearings, III, 48.

[81]U.S. policy toward Honduras in this period combined subtle intimidation with not so subtle bribery. According to a document admitted into evidence at the trial of Oliver North, the high-level Crisis Preplanning Group agreed on February 7, 1985, that in order to extract greater support from Honduras for the Contras at a time of growing congressional opposition to the Contra war, "a Presidential letter should be sent to President [Roberto] Suazo of Honduras and to provide several enticements to Honduras in exchange for its continued support of the Nicaraguan Resistance." Besides delivery of U.S. military and economic assistance, the "enticements" included "increased support from the CIA on several projects being conducted by the Agency in Honduras." See stipulation of admitted facts in *United States of America v. Oliver L. North,* 20; cf. Theodore Draper, "Revelations of the North Trial," *New York Review of Books,* August 17, 1989, 59.

[82]*Honduras Update,* March/April 1988; May 1988.

[83]*New York Times,* May 25, 1988.

[84]Thomas Zepeda testimony, Kerry hearings, IV, 724–25.

[85]Bruce M. Bagley, "Colombia and the War on Drugs," *Foreign Affairs* (Fall 1988), 83; reprinted in Kerry report, 239. Cf. *New York Times,* May 21, 1988: "The Colombian-Mexican relationship, developed by Juan Ramón Matta Ballesteros, a Honduran with close ties to the Medellín groups, led to an explosion of cocaine shipments through Mexico, with cocaine seizures in that country rising from 2.3 tons in 1985 to 9.3 tons in 1987."

[86]*Washington Post,* December 7, 1987.

[87]Mort Rosenblum, "Hidden Agendas," *Vanity Fair,* March 1990, 120.

[88]*Washington Times,* July 6, 1989, on arraignment in Miami of Luis Santacruz Echeverri, linked to July 1987 seizure of 2.5 tons of cocaine shipped to Miami on a Honduran freighter.

[89]Rosenblum, "Hidden Agendas," 102, 118.

[90]*Miami Herald,* November 26, 1987; *Latin America Regional Reports,* RM-86-09, October 30, 1986; *NACLA Report on the Americas,* January/ February 1988, 19–20.

[91]House Committee on Foreign Affairs, hearing, *Narcotics Review in Central America,* 14, 26, 30–33 (Abrams), 77 (Matta and permits); *Central America Report,* August 5, 1988; Robert Collier, "Honduras Drug Traffic Quietly Overlooked," Pacific News Service, May 20, 1988; *Los*

*Angeles Times,* February 13, 1988; *New York Times,* April 15, 1988 and October 15, 1989; *El Periodista de Buenos Aires,* April 15, 1988. General Regalado has since been accused by senior Honduran officers of misappropriating and trafficking in millions of dollars' worth of U.S. military aid (*New York Times,* October 15, 1989). The Honduran Special Drug Trafficking Investigating Commission did not implicate him in narcotics smuggling (*El Heraldo* [Tegucigalpa], December 14, 1989). However, he was denied reelection as chief of the armed forces (*Central America Report,* October 27, 1989). As for Col. Riera Lunati, the State Department declared proudly that he "attended the International Drug Enforcement Conference in Guatemala City in March 1988, showing his support for international drug law enforcement." See House Foreign Affairs Committee, *Narcotics Review in Central America,* 80.

⁹²Quoted in ACAN, December 17, 1989.

⁹³*New York Times,* February 15, 1988.

⁹⁴Kerry hearings, IV, 382.

⁹⁵Rosenblum, "Hidden Agendas," 106.

⁹⁶*Central America Report,* August 5, 1988; Robert Collier, "Honduras Drug Traffic Quietly Overlooked," Pacific News Service, May 20, 1988, *Los Angeles Times,* February 13, 1988; *New York Times,* April 15, 1988; October 15, 1989; *El Periodista de Buenos Aires,* April 15, 1988.

CHAPTER 4

¹Testimony of José Blandón, Kerry hearings, III, 14–15.

²Asamblea Legislativa, *Informe Final,* 67.

³Seymour Hersh, "Our Man in Panama," *Life,* March 1990, 81–84; Kempe, *Divorcing the Dictator,* 51.

⁴House Foreign Affairs Committee hearing, *Narcotics Review in Central America* (Washington, DC: U.S. Government Printing Office, 1988), 91; Hersh, "Our Man in Panama," 87; Dinges, *Our Man in Panama,* 58–64.

⁵Report of Senate Select Committee on Intelligence, quoted in letter of Michael Shaheen, Jr., Justice Department counsel, to Rep. Edward Roybal, August 15, 1978; Michael DeFeo, et al., "Report of June 18, 1975 to the Attorney General, Subject: Additional Integrity Matters," 11; cf. Dinges, *Our Man in Panama,* 63–64.

⁶Dinges, *Our Man in Panama,* 67.

⁷Kempe, *Divorcing the Dictator,* 28–30; Dinges, *Our Man in Panama,* 90; *New York Times,* June 12, 1986; September 27, 1988.

⁸Hersh, "Our Man in Panama," 88.

⁹Kempe, *Divorcing the Dictator,* 26, 162.

¹⁰*Newsweek,* January 15, 1990; *New York Times,* January 17, 1990.

¹¹Kempe, *Divorcing the Dictator,* 162, citing José Blandón.

[12]Kerry report, 85, 94–96; Kempe, *Divorcing the Dictator*, 158–60; Dinges, *Our Man in Panama*, 252–53; *San Francisco Chronicle*, May 19, 1990; Memorandum of Facts offered at trial of Oliver North; diary entries released under the Freedom of Information Act to the National Security Archive in Washington, DC.

[13]*Los Angeles Times*, July 17, 1987; *Washington Times*, March 27, 1987; Morstein, *Der Pate des Terrors*.

[14]Kempe, *Divorcing the Dictator*, 165.

[15]Kerry hearings, II, 204; cf. *Oakland Tribune*, February 15, 1990.

[16]*Tico Times*, June 16, 1989. The alleged recipient of the money, Rafael Angel Calderon, Jr., vigorously denied the charge as politically inspired. He was elected president of Costa Rica in 1990.

[17]*Tico Times*, July 28, 1989; cf. *Tico Times*, April 21, 1989.

[18]*Miami Herald*, March 22, 1987; *Washington Post*, July 22, 1987; *Los Angeles Times*, April 7, 1987; Kerry report, 126–27; Kerry hearings, III, 196ff.

[19]Senate Government Operations Committee, Permanent Subcommittee on Investigations, *Drugs and Money Laundering in Panama* (Washington, DC: U.S. Government Printing Office, 1988), 6–12, 31.

[20]Dinges, *Our Man in Panama*, 212.

[21]Kerry hearings, II, 186ff.; cf. *Miami Herald*, February 25, 1990.

[22]*La Nacion* (San José), November 24, 1986.

[23]Kerry hearings, II, 208–9; *Tico Times*, May 25, 1989 and July 28, 1989; Asamblea Legislativa, *Informe Final*, 54. The legislative report notes that Viales got his orders from Enrique Chacon, Vice Minister of Public Security under Benjamin Piza, himself a close collaborator with CIA station chief Joseph Fernandez.

[24]Ibid.; Kerry hearings, II, 115–17, 205–6; Dinges, *Our Man in Panama*, 211.

[25]*Miami Herald*, February 25, 1990; Kerry report, 48.

[26]Quoted in Kerry report, 92.

[27]Mills, *Underground Empire*, 1132.

[28]Kerry report, 12.

[29]House Foreign Affairs Committee, staff report, *US Narcotics Control Programs Overseas: An Assessment* (Washington, DC: U.S. Government Printing Office, 1985), 31.

[30]*New York Times*, June 12, 1986.

[31]*Executive Intelligence Review*, September 16, 1988.

[32]Kerry report, 94–96. Murphy and Park borrowed a plane from Sarkis Soghanalian, a CIA-linked arms dealer who appears to have shipped weapons to the Contras, as he had for Somoza several years before. See Kerry hearings, IV, 253–55; United Press International, March 23, 1987; North diary, February 7, 1984 ("Sarkis—delivered weapons gratis!").

[33]*San Francisco Chronicle*, May 19, 1990; Kempe, *Divorcing the Dictator*, 160.

[34]Dinges, *Our Man in Panama*, 253; *Iran-Contra Report*, Appendix B, XII, 550–54. The public relations firm was International Business Communications.

[35]Dinges, *Our Man in Panama*, 159, 253.

[36]Mills, *Underground Empire*, 1132.

[37]Kerry report, 79–80, 99ff., 123.

[38]Kerry report, 79.

[39]Testimony of Ambassador Francis McNeil, Kerry hearings, III, 42.

[40]*Washington Post*, October 23, 1988.

[41]*New York Times*, June 10, 1990.

[42]*New York Times*, February 6, 1990; Kerry hearings, II, 215; House Foreign Affairs Committee, hearing, *Narcotics Review in Central America*, 93.

[43]*El Siglo* (Panama City), August 23, 1990; *San Francisco Examiner*, October 24, 1990.

[44]*Oakland Tribune*, January 5, 1990; *Atlanta Constitution*, April 22, 1989, February 2, 1990, February 13, 1990; February 23, 1990; *New York Times*, January 14, 1990.

[45]*Oakland Tribune*, January 5, 1990 and January 22, 1990; *La Republica* (Panama), December 5, 1988; *Boston Globe*, February 5, 1990; House Select Committee on Narcotics Abuse and Control, hearing, *Panama* (Washington, DC: U.S. Government Printing Office, 1987), 27–28. Panama's new attorney general, Rogelio Cruz, fired his special prosecutor after the latter accused Cruz of being a drug trafficker (*La Prensa* [Panama City], June 10, 1990).

[46]Kempe, *Divorcing the Dictator*, 3–4, 204.

[47]*San Francisco Examiner*, October 22, 1989.

[48]*Miami Herald*, January 19, 1988; United Press International, January 18, 1988; *Independent*, March 19, 1988; *New York Post*, July 11, 1988.

[49]*Hadashot* (Tel Aviv), September 4, 1989.

[50]*Ha'aretz* (Tel Aviv), August 31, 1989.

[51]*Israeli Foreign Affairs*, February 1990 and April 1990.

[52]Kerry report, 84–85.

[53]Kerry hearings, III, 18–19.

[54]Kempe, *Divorcing the Dictator*, 163.

[55]*San Francisco Chronicle*, May 16, 1988; cf. *Newsweek*, May 23, 1988.

[56]ABC News, April 7, 1988.

[57]Jane Hunter, "Cocaine and Cutouts: Israel's Unseen Diplomacy," *Link*, January–March 1989; *Newsweek*, May 23, 1988.

[58]Kerry report, 130–32. Several independent journalists have cast substantial doubt on Brenneke's veracity (*Oregonian*, May 17, 1988; *Boston Globe*, May 17, 1988; *New Republic*, June 13, 1988). Brenneke was, however, acquitted of lying at the trial of Heinrich Rupp when he testified about secret meetings of top Reagan campaign aides in 1980 with Iranian

representatives in Paris. The jury in Brenneke's trial chose not to believe testimony from Donald Gregg (*Oakland Tribune*, May 5, 1990).

[59]Kerry hearings, IV, 291–93.

[60]Jon Lee Anderson, "Loose Cannons," *New Outlook*, February 1989.

[61]*Latin America Regional Reports*, RM-87-02, February 19, 1987; Jane Hunter, "Cocaine and Cutouts."

[62]Reuters, April 15, 1988; *Israeli Foreign Affairs*, July 1987; June 1988. Brenneke has claimed that Saada was also a silent partner in the arms supermarket of Martin, McCoy, and Dellamico (Hunter, "Cocaine and Cutouts").

[63]Kerry report, 301.

[64]*New York Times*, August 26, 1989. One of the most intriguing reports of an Israeli-Colombian drug connection was the story in *Hadashot* that the Cali cartel "employs Israelis, especially in transferring funds from drugs sales in the U.S. to the bank accounts of the heads of the cartel in Colombia and Panama. They are also assisted by banking services in Israel" (September 1, 1989). The newspaper alleged that the Cali cartel is run by Colombian Jews; actually, they are only involved in its money-laundering operations. Jews who emigrated from Europe in the 1930s established banking and money-changing channels exploited by the drug entrepreneurs in the 1970s and 1980s (interview with a federal agent, November 15, 1989). One of the chief Cali money launderers was Isaac Kattan, a drug associate of both Alberto Sicilia-Falcón and Juan Ramón Matta Ballesteros (Mills, *Underground Empire*, 168; Kerry report, 286–88). Kattan boasted that he invested his millions in Israel bonds (*Newsweek*, July 20, 1981). Kattan had connections to Nicaraguans through the cocaine-trafficking Espinosa brothers (*New York Times*, February 28, 1981) and the Popular Bank and Trust, owned by a prominent Nicaraguan exile and used as a conduit for Contra and State Department humanitarian funds (*Miami Herald*, June 14, 1987; *Village Voice*, July 1, 1986). In 1988, federal authorities broke up a nationwide money-laundering ring serving the Cali cartel. It was run by two Israelis who won the cooperation of a network of Hassidic Jews and a former Israeli Air Force captain by claiming they were moving the money on behalf of Mossad to finance "anti-Communist guerrillas in Central America," presumably the Contras. (Ibid.; *Kol Ha'ir*, April 14, 1989; *Northern California Jewish Bulletin*, January 13, 1989; United Press International, March 17, 1989.)

[65]Quoted in *Washington Post Weekly*, June 18–24, 1990.

[66]*La Repubblica*, August 26, 1989; *Los Angeles Times*, August 30, 1989; *San Francisco Chronicle*, August 29, 1989.

[67]*New York Times*, September 8, 1989 (Col. Amatzia Shuali). Ben-Or, in turn, reportedly arranged three shipments of arms to the Contras through Honduras and had introduced Gerard Latchinian to Mario Dellamico of the Arms Supermarket. See *Ma'ariv*, December 13, 1985; *Miami Herald*, December 1, 1986.

[68]*La Repubblica*, August 26, 1989.

[69]Israel Radio, August 25, 1989 (Zvi Zamir).

[70]Jerusalem Press Service, September 1, 1989.

[71]*Israeli Foreign Affairs*, October 1989, 2.

[72]*Yediot Ahronot*, August 29, 1989.

[73]*Israeli Foreign Affairs*, October 1989, 6.

[74]Jerusalem Television, May 12, 1990, in Foreign Broadcast Information Service, May 14, 1990.

[75]*Miami Herald*, May 7, 1990; *Israeli Foreign Affairs*, May 1990, June 1990.

[76]*Israeli Foreign Affairs*, June 1990, 1–2; Deutsche Presse Agentur (Hamburg), April 19, 1990.

[77]*Israeli Foreign Affairs*, October 1990; quoted in *Israeli Foreign Affairs*, June 1990, 4.

[78]Associated Press, May 31, 1990.

[79]Israeli "military security experts" joined other foreign mercenaries in the coup, possibly at the request of the Argentine military, which enjoyed close relations with the Israeli government in this period. Israel then joined a handful of other countries—including South Africa and the dictatorships of Guatemala, the Philippines, South Korea, and Taiwan—in giving the new military rulers in Bolivia aid and diplomatic support. See *Stern*, June 7, 1984; *New York Times*, August 6, 1980; *Los Angeles Times*, August 31, 1980; "Israel and Bolivia," *Israel & Palestine*, October 1984, 15–18. On Israel's arms deals with the Argentine junta, see *Middle East*, February 1986; *Washington Post*, December 12, 1982; Ignacio Klich, "Israel y America Latina," *Le Monde Diplomatique* [Spanish edition], February 1983. According to the political scientist Amos Perlmutter, after the Falklands War Israeli officials conceived of turning Argentina into a South Atlantic power by selling it several billion dollars' worth of weapons (*New York Times*, December 5, 1986).

[80]*Hadashot*, September 3, 1989.

[81]*Telegraph* (London), May 13, 1990.

[82]*Sunday Telegraph*, March 5, 1989.

[83]Ibid.

[84]Kempe, *Divorcing the Dictator*, 290 (Herrera). It was Herrera who held talks with Klein over the possibility of training on Antigua.

CHAPTER 5

[1]James Mills, *The Underground Empire: Where Crime and Governments Embrace* (Garden City, NY: Doubleday, 1986), 811.

[2]Rensselaer W. Lee III, *The White Labyrinth: Cocaine and Political Power* (New Brunswick, NJ: Transaction, 1988), 8–9.

[3]Mills, *Underground Empire*, 1142–43. Mills's list of countries includes Bolivia, Brazil, Colombia, Costa Rica, Cuba, Honduras, Mexico, Nicaragua, Panama, and Peru.

[4]Chapter 6 shows that traffickers in Cali also supplied the cocaine for at least two of the networks involving the families of Contra leaders, including the ring in the Frogman case in San Francisco. The role of the Cali traffickers in the Frogman case was covered up in Reagan press releases.

[5]Frederick Kempe, *Divorcing the Dictator*, 4.

[6]Kerry report, 287; *Miami Herald*, February 8, 1987; Mills, *Underground Empire*, 881.

[7]Kerry report, 287; Guy Gugliotta and Jeff Leen, *Kings of Cocaine: Inside the Medellín Cartel* (New York: Simon and Schuster, 1989), 68. The *New York Times* also called Kattan "the biggest money launderer for major narcotics trafficking organizations in South America" (February 28, 1981).

[8]Kerry report, 285.

[9]Mills, *Underground Empire*, 883 (Torrijos), 893 (Cali); cf. 581–87.

[10]Ibid., 581ff. (Sicilia), 1151 (Félix).

[11]Ibid., 608, 1157; see also Chapter 2.

[12]Ibid., 567, 575–76.

[13]Ibid., 897; *Miami Herald*, February 8, 1987.

[14]Mills, *Underground Empire*, 585, 811.

[15]Ibid., 584–87 (Rivera); 876–79 (Paredes).

[16]Ibid., 584, 862, 876–79.

[17]Lee, *White Labyrinth*, 106.

[18]Ibid., 177.

[19]Mills, *Underground Empire*, 365, 576, 590, 863.

[20]Krüger, *Great Heroin Coup*, 109. Among those extradited were Ricord, Christian David, Claude-André Pastou, and Michel Nicoli. About this time, Rivera became the manager of a Coca-Cola bottling company in Guayaquil, Ecuador. The operators of third-world Coke and Pepsi bottling plants (such as future Contra leaders Adolfo Calero and Donald Lacayo in Somoza's Nicaragua) are not infrequently local agents of U.S. corporate and/or CIA influence; cf. Lernoux, *In Banks We Trust*, 164; McCoy, *Politics of Heroin*, 186.

[21]Krüger, *Great Heroin Coup*, 7.

[22]"It was the opinion of Centac agents and intelligence analysts that Cornejo may have provided liaison between associates of Ricord and Sarti and Alfonso Rivera's International Narcotics Organization" (Mills, *Underground Empire*, 813).

[23]Blumenthal, *Last Days*, 95–96.

[24]Mills, *Underground Empire*, 554–55.

[25]Peter Dale Scott, in Krüger, *Great Heroin Coup*, 4–5, citing Philip M. Williams, *Wars, Plots, and Scandals in Post-War France* (Cambridge: Cambridge University Press, 1970), 115, 118–19.

[26]Krüger, *Great Heroin Coup*, 83–84; Alain Jaubert, *Dossier D . . . comme drogue* (Paris: Alain Moreau, 1973), 296.

[27]Blumenthal, *Last Days*, 95.

[28]Mills, *Underground Empire*, 363.

[29]Jean-Pierre Charbonneau, *The Canadian Connection* (Ottawa: Optimum, 1976), 87, 207–10.

[30]The involvement of Sicilian Mafia families (Cuntrera and Caruana) in creating a new global center for the heroin and cocaine traffic is particularly suggestive of continuity. These families appear to be an extension of the old Montreal Cotroni connection that passed on so much Corsican and Sicilian Mafia heroin in the 1950s and 1960s (*Business Week*, April 18, 1988, 48–51). In like manner, the so-called Steve Kalish drug operation, which supplied the evidence for Noriega's indictment in Tampa, appears on the basis of Kalish's own Congressional testimony to be an extension of the old Detroit Teamster connection that received and distributed the heroin from Montreal. The Corsicans, Sicilians, and Detroit Teamsters have all been linked to CIA covert operations as well as to each other and to the Cuban exiles in Miami (McCoy, *Politics of Heroin*, 15–52; Jim Hougan, *Spooks: The Haunting of America* (New York: Morrow, 1978), 107–9; Krüger, *Great Heroin Coup*, 14–15, 143).

[31]Krüger, *Great Heroin Coup*, 85 (Ricord); Marshall, Scott, and Hunter, *Iran-Contra Connection*, 70–71 (CAL, CORU).

[32]Marshall, Scott, and Hunter, *Iran-Contra Connection*, 68–70; cf. 76–78. In May 1980 DEA officials in Miami seized 854 pounds of cocaine base and arrested two high-level Bolivian drug traffickers of the Roberto Suarez drug organization, which financed the June 1980 Cocaine Coup. DEA officer Michael Levine, who arranged the sting, has recently charged that one of the suspects, Jose Roberto Gasser, son of WACL associate Erwin Gasser, "was almost immediately released from custody by the Miami U.S. attorney's office, without the case being presented to the grand jury. . . . Within weeks of the Miami arrests, with the financing of the Suarez organization and Erwin Gasser, and the support of our CIA, a bloody coup was begun. . . . Bolivia soon became the principal supplier of cocaine base to the then fledgling Colombian cartels, making themselves the main suppliers of cocaine to the United States. And it could not have been done without the tacit help of DEA and the active, covert help of the CIA" (Levine, *Deep Cover*, 17–18, 103–104).

[33]Christopher Dickey, *With the Contras: A Reporter in the Wilds of Nicaragua*, (New York: Simon and Schuster, 1985), 87. Gen. Álvarez Martínez of Honduras, another key figure in the germination of the Contras, had connections both to Argentina and to CAUSA, the political arm of the Sun Myung Moon Unification Church that also played a role in the 1980 Bolivian Cocaine Coup. (Kai Herrmann, "Klaus Barbie: A Killer's Career," *Covert Action*, Winter 1986, 18–19.) CAUSA became an important backer of the FDN in the United States.

[34]Gutman, *Banana Diplomacy*, 40. The source of Pallais's largesse (estimated at $300,000 or more) is unclear. Some have speculated that his

cousin Somoza was financing continental counterterrorism through Argentina and WACL-CAL (Krüger, *Great Heroin Coup*, 11, 217; cf. Marshall, Scott, and Hunter, *Iran-Contra Connection*, 77). Others have guessed that the money came from cocaine profits from Bolivia after the Cocaine Coup.

[35]Gutman, *Banana Diplomacy*, 40, 49–52; Marshall, Scott, and Hunter, *Iran-Contra Connection*, 76–77. Carbaugh attended the 1980 CAL conference in Buenos Aires, met d'Aubuisson there, and made many trips in 1980–81 between the Argentine government in Buenos Aires, d'Aubuisson, and General Alvarez in Honduras (Anderson and Anderson, *Inside the League*, 227). Another early backer of the Contras under Carter in 1980 was Maj. Gen. Robert Schweitzer, then the U.S. Army's Director of Strategy, Plans, and Policy (Gutman, *Banana Diplomacy*, 45–49). Later Schweitzer recruited Oliver North for Reagan's NSC; still later, in retirement, Schweitzer became an arms supplier to the Contras in partnership with John Singlaub of WACL.

[36]Marshall, Scott, and Hunter, *Iran-Contra Connection*, 22.

[37]Anderson and Anderson, *Inside the League*, 245.

[38]Dickey, *With the Contras*, 87, 90, 92; Kerry hearings, II, 142 (testimony of José Blandón). CIA links to the MCRL and WACL in Costa Rica appeared to go back to the 1960s, when the CIA's drug-trafficking Cuban terrorist, Manuel Artime, with the help of Nicaraguan dictator Luis Somoza, established his base of military operations against Cuban shipping on another MCRL ranch (Hinckle and Turner, *Fish Is Red*, 149). See Marshall, Scott, and Hunter, *Iran-Contra Connection*, 140–41, 273–74.

[39]Mills even records the speculation of an FBI agent on the Sicilia Falcón case whether Sicilia Falcón (a Cuban exile from Miami), along with one of his killers and also the ex-CIA operative working in the DEA effort to catch Sicilia—whether all of them "had been—were still—CIA operatives? And that when [Sicilia] Falcón became too powerful, too ambitious, when it appeared that he might be on his way to controlling the Mexican government, the CIA had surfaced [the killer] to 'do' him?" (Mills, *Underground Empire*, 386).

[40]Ibid., 859, 886.

[41]Ibid., 899 and passim; Gugliotta and Leen, *Kings of Cocaine*, 191.

[42]Ibid., 882.

[43]Ibid., 889.

[44]Ibid., 884.

[45]Ibid., 1089, 917–20. In the words of Mills's source (1089): "There's not one Centac-21 agent assigned to work the Latin American end of that Centac anymore, not one of the core members that knew what the organizational structure was in South America. Foreign prosecutions have virtually ceased. The avenues we opened in Mexico, El Salvador, Colombia, and Peru have all but closed."

[46]"The linkages between the Colombian security forces and the drug traffickers remained essentially intact throughout the López presidency [of 1974–78]. In 1975 the DAS [security police] even became involved in shoot-outs against other Colombian anti-narcotics units" (Bruce M. Bagley, "Colombia and the War on Drugs," *Foreign Affairs* (Fall 1988), 79; reprinted in Kerry report, 235). See also Marshall, *Drug Wars*.

[47]*Latin American Regional Report: Andean Area*, June 24, 1983; *Le Devoir* (Montreal), March 24, 1984.

[48]Gugliotta and Leen, *Kings of Cocaine*, 93. Most accounts of MAS, including the Kerry report's, mention only Jorge Ochoa (Kerry report, 27, 232; Eddy, *Cocaine Wars*, 287; Shannon, *Desperados*, 104). While the Kerry report locates the MAS meeting in a suburb of Medellín (Kerry report, 27, 232), other well-informed sources locate the MAS meeting in Cali (Eddy, *Cocaine Wars*, 287; cf. Gugliotta and Leen, *Kings of Cocaine*, 92). Certainly Cali's links to the Colombian military are older and stronger than Medellín's.

[49]Lee, *White Labyrinth*, 117–18.

[50]Gugliotta and Leen, *Kings of Cocaine*, 94–96; Bruce Bagley, "Colombia and the War on Drugs"; Kerry report, 85–86, 233.

[51]Lee, *White Labyrinth*, 111.

[52]Ibid., 131; Gugliotta and Leen, *Kings of Cocaine*, 108–10. An associate of Escobar in the Colombian Congress displayed a photocopy of an endorsed check to Lara Bonilla for one million pesos ($12,281) from Evaristo Porras Ardila, a trafficker who in the fall of 1989 was arrested in Ecuador and extradited to Colombia.

[53]Amnesty International USA News Release, October 11, 1989.

[54]Lee, *White Labyrinth*, 164–65.

[55]Ibid., 160–61.

[56]Jenny Pearce, "The Dirty War," *NACLA Report on the Americas*, April 1990, 25.

[57]Gugliotta and Leen, *Kings of Cocaine*, 218.

[58]Kerry hearings, II, 51.

[59]Gerald Loeb, Report to FBI, January 8, 1986; Kerry hearings, II, 419–26.

[60]Kerry hearings, II, 50. In 1987 personnel from three airlines (Pan Am, Texas Air/Eastern, and Delta) were arrested at New York's Kennedy Airport for drug-trafficking offenses (*Wall Street Journal*, March 11, 1987).

[61]Kerry hearings, II, 50, 57. The detective agency refused to accept a Kerry subcommittee subpoena (Kerry report, 61–62, 169). It was headed by Raúl Díaz, a veteran of the Miami police and a DEA Centac Task Force who "chose to quit the police force, and, in some people's eyes, joined the other side. . . . [Kerry subcommittee counsel Jack] Blum became convinced that he had identified . . . the 'cut out' between those nether worlds

of espionage and drug trafficking, the 'link man' between the Cartel and the CIA—former police lieutenant, Raúl Díaz." Díaz was also extremely close to Félix Rodríguez of the Ilopango air base, and admits to having been in the Executive Office Building ("next door to Oliver North's office") the day Félix Rodríguez phoned the White House to report that the Hasenfus plane had been shot down (Eddy, *Cocaine Wars*, 338–39).

[62]Scott, *War Conspiracy* (Indianapolis and New York: Bobbs-Merrill, 1972), 210–11 (Helliwell); McCoy, *Politics of Heroin*, 130, 138, 141, 144 (Sea Supply).

[63]*Wall Street Journal*, April 18, 1980; Sterling Seagrave, *The Marcos Dynasty* (New York: Harper & Row, 1988), 336, 361–67.

[64]Scott, *War Conspiracy*, 210–11; cf. Marshall, Scott, and Hunter, *Iran-Contra Connection*, 80–81.

[65]R.T. Naylor, *Hot Money and the Politics of Debt* (New York: Linden/ Simon & Schuster, 1987) 292; citing *Latin-American Weekly Report*, August 29, 1980.

[66]Jonathan Kwitny, *The Crimes of Patriots* (New York: Norton, 1987), 315–16 and passim.

[67]Ibid., 294. Former CIA Director William Colby apparently billed Nugan Hand for legal work on this project and another involving the Turks and Caicos Islands (290).

[68]Lernoux, *In Banks We Trust*, 52–53. "City National had a murky history. It was suspected of being used for the deposit of illegal 'skim' money from casinos in the Bahamas during the late 1960s. One of the bank's directors, Max Orovitz, was a buddy of Mob financier Meyer Lansky and had been convicted for stock fraud in New York" (47n). Duque's man on the board of City National, José Luis Castro, was represented by Hugh Culverhouse, a business partner of Marvin Warner (*Miami Herald*, June 11, 1983) and director of Major Realty, founded by Max Orovitz in 1961.

[69]Kwitny, *Crimes of Patriots*, 356.

[70]Naylor (*Hot Money*), 291; Kwitny, *Crimes of Patriots*, 294.

[71]*Wall Street Journal*, August 22, 1985; Naylor, *Hot Money*, 432.

[72]Naylor, *Hot Money*, 295–96, 312–13.

[73]Ibid.; *Miami Herald*, February 12, 1986.

[74]Lernoux, *In Banks We Trust*, 147–48, 153; Marshall, Scott, and Hunter, *Iran-Contra Connection*, 44.

[75]Kerry report, 287; Kwitny, *Crimes of Patriots*, 293–94; Lernoux, *In Banks We Trust*, 128–29; interview with Jack Terrell, June 24, 1989. (Vaughan).

[76]Mills, *Underground Empire*, Gugliotta and Leen, *Kings of Cocaine*, 27.

[77]Gugliotta and Leen, *Kings of Cocaine*, 273; Mills, *Underground Empire*, 883, 893. Harold Rosenthal, a former Atlanta bail bondsman con-

victed for the shipment, was called a leader of the "largest cocaine trafficking ring in the nation's history" (*Miami Herald*, February 8, 1987).

[78]Kerry report, 287; *Miami Herald*, February 1987; Gugliotta and Leen, *Kings of Cocaine*, 68 (Kattan-Cali).

[79]Bruce Bagley, "Colombia and the War on Drugs"; reprinted in Kerry report, 233.

[80]Gugliotta and Leen, *Kings of Cocaine*, 274.

[81]Shannon, *Desperados*, 146 (Casey); Gugliotta and Leen, *Kings of Cocaine*, 104 (Tambs).

[82]Eddy, *Cocaine Wars*, 189.

[83]Eddy, *Cocaine Wars*, 148; Gugliotta and Leen, *Kings of Cocaine*, 30.

[84]Gugliotta and Leen, *Kings of Cocaine*, 63; cf. NBC News, September 5, 1983, reprinted in Kerry report, 24: "Authorities say Vesco's Colombian cocaine supplier is this man, Carlos Lehder"; *Fortune*, November 10, 1986, 38: "With the assistance of fugitive American financier Robert Vesco, Lehder's men struck a deal with Fidel Castro's officials to let drug-laden planes fly through Cuban air space unimpeded for two hours a day. . . . He fancies himself a Marxist revolutionary."

[85]Gugliotta and Leen, *Kings of Cocaine*, 113; cf. Shannon, 139: "[After the Lara Bonilla assassination of 1984], one of the first extradition orders was for Carlos Lehder, a leader of the Medellín cocaine cartel." For the record, Lehder's response to the murder of Lara Bonilla (a liberal opponent of U.S. policies in Central America) was to denounce it as a DEA or CIA plot against himself.

[86]Eddy, *Cocaine Wars*, 187; Gugliotta and Leen, *Kings of Cocaine*, 114.

[87]Shannon, *Desperados*, 172–73.

[88]Lee, *White Labyrinth*, 158.

[89]Ibid., 175.

[90]Ramón Milián Rodríguez, trained as a money launderer by the CIA's Cuban protégé Manuel Artime, went on to launder funds for the Colombian factions, including Gilberto Rodríguez Orejuela of the Cali group and relatives of both the Ochoas and Pablo Escobar (Kerry report, 450–51).

[91]The 1983 Customs report on Matta and Santiago Ocampo also shows the importance of Matta to West Coast cocaine shipments (Kerry report, 287).

[92]Gugliotta and Leen, *Kings of Cocaine*, 336; cf. 337: "Those who believed in the War of the Cartels blamed the Cali group for fingering Ochoa [in his arrest] at the El Cerrito tollbooth in November 1987 and for murdering some higher-ups in his organization."

[93]Shannon, *Desperados*, 143; Eddy, *Cocaine Wars*, 298 (documents); Gugliotta and Leen, *Kings of Cocaine*, 211 (Cali).

[94]Mills, *Underground Empire*, 1125–26.

[95]Eddy, *Cocaine Wars*, 299–301; Shannon, *Desperados*, 166–67; Gugliotta and Leen, *Kings of Cocaine*, 173–77.

[96]Shannon, *Desperados*, 144–45; cf. Gugliotta and Leen, *Kings of Cocaine*, 133–34.

[97]Gugliotta and Leen, *Kings of Cocaine*, 134.

[98]*New York Times*, March 21, 1984.

[99]Bagley, "Colombia and the War on Drugs"; reprinted in Kerry report, 240.

[100]"Intrigued by the Tranquilandia raid and the related seizures, CIA director William Casey ordered his analysts to examine the 'narcoterrorism' question in depth. . . . In the case of Latin America, the CIA analysis came back with much less evidence of a narcoterrorism merger than Casey had expected. So he scrapped the study and ordered a second one. This effort produced a mild white paper that asserted, in the words of one official, that the terrorists and traffickers 'fed at the same trough.' That is, these groups coexisted in rural areas in a number of countries, exploited the state of anarchy in these areas, and sometimes shared facilities such as landing strips" (Shannon, *Desperados*, 145–46).

[101]Lee, *White Labyrinth*, 172.

[102]Ibid., 218.

[103]Some have accused DEA agents of using pressure to develop the concept of a Medellín-Sandinista narcoguerrilla alliance: "In 1984, Jorge Luis Ochoa . . . was taken into custody in Spain. According to a report in *The Nation*, the DEA told him that it would arrange for his release if he agreed to implicate the Sandinistas in drug-smuggling, but he refused, saying the Sandinistas were not involved. Months later, Spain refused to extradite him because of the political nature of the request and sent him to Colombia" (*New York Times*, March 15, 1987). "Ochoa . . . told reporters that the idea of implicating Nicaragua had been given to him after his arrest by a US DEA agent who was a former CIA man" (Naylor, *Hot Money*, 180, citing *El País*, June 6, 1985; *Cambio*, January 21, 1985; *Latin American Weekly Report*, August 9, 1985). DEA officials have rejected these charges, which in our view are unproven.

[104]Kerry hearings, IV, 724 (testimony of Thomas Zepeda, DEA chief in Tegucigalpa).

[105]Kerry report, 285–86.

[106]John Cummings and Ernest Volkman, "Snowbound," *Penthouse* (July 1989), 66. Cummings and Volkman claim that "Seal was recruited to find pilots" for "the C.I.A.'s secret Black Eagle operation," which they describe as the Contra arms-supply network authorized by CIA Director Casey in 1982 and set up through Panama and Noriega by "an essential Casey contact, Micha 'Mike' Harare [Harari]." They also claim that Casey, "concerned that the operation be as far removed from the C.I.A. as possible, hit upon the idea of using the Vice President's office as a 'cover,' arranging it via Bush's [National Security Adviser], Donald Gregg, a former C.I.A. officer. Gregg, in turn, knew the right man to oversee the

job: Félix Rodríguez." This claim correlates with the earlier public charges from José Blandón that the Harari network supplied the Ilopango Air Force Base, and Félix Rodríguez in particular, from 1982 to 1986; and that Casey accordingly placed Noriega on the CIA payroll (Kerry hearings, III, 18; PBS, "Frontline," May 17, 1988). It is not clear how much of Blandón's story should be believed. Both Gregg and Rodríguez have flatly denied the charges. The last election produced numerous self-professed insiders talking about Bush, Gregg, and Rodríguez's links to the Contras and drugs, and some of these statements are not only exaggerated but possibly perjured (Kerry report, 61–62).

[107]Details in the 1983 Customs report corroborate at least part of the Cummings-Volkman story and suggest that Moss, Seal, and Matta were in fact part of a single network. The Customs report shows that Seal was under investigation by the Louisiana State Police; Cummings and Volkman report that in the early spring of 1982, when two members of the Louisiana State Police narcotics unit tried to recruit Seal as an informant, he replied, "Well, before I do that, I'll have to check with some people," suggesting that "perhaps those rumors about Seal running guns for the C.I.A. . . . were true"; Kerry report, 285; Cummings and Volkman, 64–66.

[108]Robert Parry and Peter Kornbluh, "Iran-Contra's Untold Story," *Foreign Policy* (Fall 1988), 4.

[109]Gugliotta and Leen, *Kings of Cocaine*, 148–49.

[110]Shannon, *Desperados*, 149.

[111]Ibid.; Gugliotta and Leen, *Kings of Cocaine*, 149–50; Eddy, *Cocaine Wars*, 304.

[112]Gugliotta and Leen, *Kings of Cocaine*, 219.

[113]Ibid., 152.

[114]Shannon, *Desperados*, 149–52.

[115]Kerry report, 121.

[116]Kerry report, 68–69; *Miami Herald*, July 29, 1988. There are other problems. Seal never explained to anyone's satisfaction how 700 kg of cocaine would clear U.S. Customs. Seal in fact solved the problem by landing the CIA-prepared plane at Homestead Air Force Base, but he could hardly have alleviated the concerns of the Ochoas by telling them this.

[117]*Iran-Contra Report*, Appendix B, 12, 830; cf. 829.

[118]Kerry hearings, IV, 157.

[119]North diary entry for July 31, 1984. One DEA-assisted book claims that the photos show Pablo Escobar and Gonzalo Rodríguez Gacha (Gugliotta and Leen, *Kings of Cocaine*, 163), and another, Pablo Escobar alone ("Seal said that . . . Gonzalo Rodríguez Gacha was off camera," Shannon, *Desperados*, 152).

[120]Gugliotta and Leen, *Kings of Cocaine*, 162.

[121]Shannon, *Desperados*, 156.

[122]North diary for June 26, 1984, quoted in Gugliotta and Leen, *Kings of Cocaine*, 167; cf. North diary, June 26, 1984 (released by Kerry subcommittee): "Clarridge: [redacted]."

[123]Gugliotta and Leen, *Kings of Cocaine*, 168, Cf. Shannon, 153: "Within a few days of Seal's return from Managua, DEA agents heard that CIA officials had sent the president enlargements of the pictures." For other North diary entries, see Kerry report, 146.

[124]North diary entry for July 17, 1984; partly reprinted in Kerry report, 146.

[125]Shannon, *Desperados*, 175–76. Since then the most recent Colombian investigation has blamed the local military for most of the killings in the incident (Penny Lernoux, *Los Angeles Times Book Review*, September 10, 1989). Cf. Lee, *White Labyrinth*, 175.

[126]Lee, *White Labyrinth*, 181.

CHAPTER 6

[1]North American readers may be confused by the many appearances of the extended Chamorro family, one of Nicaragua's traditional ruling families, among the Contras. Here, our discussion of the family is restricted to Fernando "El Negro" Chamorro and his brother Ermundo. For our purposes, Adolfo "Popo" Chamorro (with his first cousins Alfredo and Octaviano César) represents a different branch of the family. Adolfo "Popo" Chamorro was the cousin of Contra leader Pedro Joaquín Chamorro (the son of Nicaraguan president Violeta Barrios de Chamorro), while Alfredo César, a close ally of Violeta Chamorro, is also distantly connected to her by marriage. Contra leaders Ernesto "Tito" Chamorro and Edgar Chamorro come from still other family branches.

[2]*San Francisco Examiner*, March 16, 1986; reprinted in Kerry report, 432; cf. Marshall, Scott, and Hunter, *Iran-Contra Connection*, 137.

[3]Kerry report, 58, citing *San Francisco Examiner*, March 16, 1986.

[4]FBI teletype of November 8, 1982, from San Francisco to Director; Kerry report, 400. The court records had mentioned only Horacio Pereira, not Troilo and Fernando Sánchez.

[5]United Press International, April 26, 1986; quoted in Marshall, Scott, and Hunter, *Iran-Contra Connection*, 137–38; cf. Justice Department summary in Kerry report, 826. The Contra Leonardo Zeledon Rodríguez was allegedly beaten and threatened by Bermúdez (cf. Kerry report, 868). The Frogman bust had already been linked to the Contras by sealed court records, including a letter from Francisco Aviles Saenz "as international relations secretary of UDN-FARN, a contra military unit." The Kerry subcommittee staff found the signature of Aviles certifying a humanitarian aid receipt signed by "Risa," a Contra leader praised by Owen and linked

by him to his project with Frigoríficos (Kerry report, 411; Owen memo to North, August 2, 1985).

[6]Owen memo to North, March 17, 1986 (Iran-Contra exhibit RWO-13). In a 1986 memo prepared for the Kerry investigation, Jack Terrell noted that Aristides Sánchez and his brother "Cuco" were said to have run "gambling, prostitution and narcotics operations in Managua" in the Somoza era.

[7]Marshall, Scott, and Hunter, *Iran-Contra Connection*, 137, summarizing *San Francisco Examiner*, June 23, 1986. Terrell also alerted the Kerry subcommittee staff to Norwin Meneses and reported that Meneses had allegedly supplied a house in Miami for the wife and family of Enrique Bermúdez, another holdover from the Somoza era. Another Somoza-era figure in the case is Carlos Cabezas, one of the two principal smugglers convicted in San Francisco, who was, according to his federal probation report, a former member of Somoza's air force (*San Francisco Examiner*, March 16, 1986; reprinted in Kerry report, 433).

[8]*San Francisco Examiner*, June 23, 1986.

[9]Letter from Joseph P. Russionello, U.S. Attorney, Northern District of California, March 19, 1986; Kerry report, 396–98.

[10]State Department Document 5136c, July 26, 1986, reprinted in Kerry report, 268; FBI teletype of November 8, 1982, reprinted in Kerry report, 401.

[11]Kerry report, 58–59. The report's source for calling Troilo and Fernando Sánchez "relatives" and "marginal participants in the Contra movement" is a "staff interview with Carlos Cabezas, March 1988, and with former Contras in San Francisco and Miami."

[12]Dickey, *With the Contras*, 153–56. Fernando "El Negro" Chamorro also allegedly received Argentine money in 1981 (139).

[13]Anderson and Anderson, *Inside the League*, 179–82. One of the Anderson brothers was in Guatemala in 1982 with the former CIA contract agent Mitch WerBell, who was there to help Sandoval and Sisniega in a coup attempt against the new military strongman, Efraín Ríos Montt. This was WerBell's last known coup attempt; he died soon afterwards. Sisniega is now a fugitive in Honduras, wanted by Guatemalan authorities for terrorism.

[14]Marshall, Scott, and Hunter, *Iran-Contra Connection*, 78.

[15]Naylor, *Hot Money*, 167, 169, 410; *New York Times*, May 17, 1983.

[16]So, until early 1984, did the chief Argentine protégé and Contra supporter in Honduras, Gen. Gustavo Álvarez Martínez, who himself had been trained by members of the Argentine junta and enjoyed WACL backing (Anderson and Anderson, *Inside the League*, 227–32).

[17]Horacio Pereira was arrested in Miami in December 1982. Carlos Cabezas, Julio Zavala, and many others were arrested in February 1983 (*San Francisco Examiner*, March 16, 1986; reprinted in Kerry report, 432–33).

[18]Kerry report, 59; Kerry hearings, II, 121, 133; Dinges, *Our Man in Panama*, 191, 279.

[19]Kerry hearings, II, 133. According to Blandón, this drug support was "part of what led to the Spadafora [murder] incident later." Dinges writes that Spadafora informed DEA about the drug activities of "Guachan" González, "one of his most bitter rivals in ARDE," who he believed had been contracted by Noriega to assassinate him in 1984. See Dinges, *Our Man in Panama*, 191, 214, 239.

[20]Kerry hearings, III, 141.

[21]Kerry hearings, III, 18; Dinges, *Our Man in Panama*, 112–14; Kempe, *Divorcing the Dictator*, 16. The Kerry report says that the arms delivered to overthrow Somoza (by Rodríguez and Carlton) "were purchased in Europe by Michael Harari and Jorge Krupnick, who worked with Noriega"; a footnote at this point cites the published testimony of Blandón (Kerry report, 84). Both Blandón and Carlton actually testified that the arms were purchased, in Eastern Europe and on the black market, by Krupnick (Kerry hearings, II, 139, 192); neither responded affirmatively to Senator Kerry's question about whether the arms also came from Harari. Elsewhere Blandón testified to "the arms resupply network that Noriega had, in which they obtained arms in different countries with the network of César Rodríguez and that of Harrare [Harari]" (Kerry hearings, III, 18). As of this writing (September 1990) Bilonick was under indictment with Noriega in Miami.

[22]Kerry report, 43. DIACSA was partly owned by the Guerra family of Costa Rica, whose airstrips had been used by Rodríguez and Carlton in their arms flights to El Salvador and the Contras (Kerry report, 47; Dinges, *Our Man in Panama*, 113).

[23]Kempe, *Divorcing the Dictator*, 236–57; Dinges, *Our Man in Panama*, 243–50; Kerry report, 342ff. A third indictee was Antonio Aizprua, one of the four members of the Rodríguez-Carlton group identified by Blandón (Kerry hearings, II, 115; cf. IV, 685).

[24]Kerry hearings, II, 115; III, 27; Mills, *Underground Empire*, 881–93. Carlton himself initially confirmed that his suppliers were from Cali, then changed his testimony and said he was supplied by Luis Jose Ospina of the "Pereira cartel," a Colombian trafficking group allegedly headed by Carlos Octavio Piedrahita Tabares, which laundered funds through the Great American Bank of Miami (Kerry hearings, II, 205–06; Dinges, *Our Man in Panama*, 211). Mills interviewed an American, John Allen, who smuggled for the Cali-based airline owner Santiago Ocampo.

[25]"Guachan" González may have been turned in to the Costa Rican intelligence agency DIS by his old rival Hugo Spadafora. Spadafora contacted DIS in 1984, after he heard that "Guachan" was plotting to assassinate him on Noriega's behalf. Spadafora told his wife that "he had recently received information that Wachan was involved in drug traffick-

ing—carrying drugs to the United States on the same planes and from the same Costa Rican airstrips used to land supplies for ARDE" (Dinges, *Our Man in Panama*, 191, 205, 213).

[26]Terrell tesified under oath, in a Costa Rica libel suit brought by John Hull against journalists Tony Avirgan and Martha Honey, that he heard Felipe Vidal say in 1985 of Edén Pastora, "We put a bomb under him the first time, but it didn't work because of bad timing" (Cockburn, *Out of Control*, 76; cf. Tony Avirgan and Martha Honey, *La Penca: On Trial in Costa Rica* (San Pedro, Montes de Oca: Editorial Porvenir, 1987), 88; Kerry report, 723. Terrell also testified that Vidal told him that Amac Galil, the suspected assassin in the La Penca bombing, was from the Israeli intelligence agency Mossad (Kerry report, 723; Avirgan and Honey, *La Penca: On Trial*, 87).

[27]Avirgan and Honey, *La Penca: On Trial*, 47; Avirgan and Honey, "La Penca: Report of an Investigation" (Washington, DC: Christic Institute, n.d.), 28.

[28]Kerry report, 54–55; Kerry hearings, II, 115–17; 205–7; cf. IV, 693–94. Carlton was told "that one of the murderers was a Contra activist named Carlos Eduardo Zapporoli [Zapparolli], who had the drugs flown to a strip on the farm owned by John Hull. . . . The Costa Rica officer who was Carlton's source said Zapporoli used the money from the drugs to buy weapons for the Contras" (Dinges, *Our Man in Panama*, 211; cf. Kempe, *Divorcing the Dictator*, 238). Blandón (not Carlton, as the report states) also testified to the truth of the story, told earlier to the subcommittee by Terrell, that the Cali cartel kidnapped Hull's daughter in an attempt to force the return of the cocaine.

[29]A Robert Owen memo of August 2, 1985, corroborates his sworn testimony that César's Southern Opposition Block (BOS) was not receiving funds from North or Calero (deposition of Robert Owen, October 1, 1987, 65; *Iran-Contra Report*, Appendix B, 20, 852).

[30]Morales testimony; Kerry hearings, III, 298.

[31]Kerry hearings, I, 57, 66, 68; III, 257, 262.

[32]Kerry report, 458; *Miami Herald*, August 6, 1981.

[33]Kerry hearings, I, 76–80, 192.

[34]In August 1983 Morales's pilot Gary Betzner flew one of Morales's planes from Miami to a U.S. naval air station at Boca Chica in southern Florida, and from there with a load of ship mines to the tightly controlled Ilopango base in El Salvador. He returned with a shipment of drugs ("marijuana or Quaaludes") from Riohacha in Colombia (Kerry hearings, I, 57, 68 [Morales]; III, 256–57 [Betzner]).

[35]Frank Castro was a part-owner, with Porfirio Bonet, of a travel agency in Hialeah (in northern Miami) that Castro, a resident of the Dominican Republic, used as his Miami address. Hull's neighbor, Bill Crone, testified that on his mid-1983 trip to Miami "the gentleman from the travel

agency" in northern Miami, who had visited Costa Rica, took him to Corvo's camp; Crone also discussed "with the gentleman at the travel service . . . a DC-3 they was wanting to get into Costa Rica" (Kerry hearings, I, 155–57). Another FBI witness, Joseph Marcos, told the FBI that he, Rene Corvo, and Frank Castro, had established the camp. Jorge Morales testified that John Hull and two Contra pilots, Marcos Aguado and Gerardo Duran, came to his office in Opalocka, Florida, in mid-1983, but that he avoided meeting Hull because of his CIA connections (Kerry hearings, I, 76–77).

[36]Owen memo to North, November 5, 1984.

[37]Cockburn, *Out of Control*, 170.

[38]Kerry hearings, I, 55, 191. Hull and Duran were also reimbursed for their Miami expenses by Aguado, presumably on behalf of ARDE or the CIA (Kerry hearings, I, 199).

[39]Kerry report, 458 (Castro), 425 (Marcos); Kerry hearings, I, 150–57 (Crone); I, 79; III, 310 (Morales); *Iran-Contra Report*, Appendix B, 20, 641 (Owen); Ben Bradlee, Jr., *Guts and Glory: The Rise and Fall of Oliver North* (New York: Fine, 1988), 201 (Rivas). Crone told the Kerry subcommittee that he and Rivas came to Washington "because we were very upset with Pastora" (Kerry hearings, I, 151).

[40]In January 1985 Owen set up his own Council for Democracy, Education, and Assistance, drawing on funds from the conservative activist Carl Channell to lobby on behalf of the UNO. Besides Owen, the CDEA's three directors include retired U.S. Air Force Gen. John P. Flynn, whom Owen met through John Hull, and Robert Wall, whose name appears in North's notebook.

[41]According to an Owen memo to North of April 1, 1985, Hull's friend Luis Rivas then claimed to represent politically the small residue of troops ("43 men") still loyal to "El Negro" Chamorro, but actually commanded by José "Chepon" Robelo.

[42]Kerry hearings, III, 278. It has been suggested, but not proved, that the motive for Manuel Noriega's gift of $100,000 in July 1984 to "a Southern Front Resistance leader" may have been to restore the broken Noriega-Pastora connection through the new Pastora–Octaviano César alliance.

[43]Kerry hearings, I, 54–55; III, 278–80; Cockburn, *Out of Control*, 169–70. Pastora had just heard in Washington from a CIA officer, "Alberto Fenton," that his CIA aid had been cut off (*Washington Post*, July 3, 1986).

[44]Kerry hearings, III, 308, 330–31; Cockburn, *Out of Control*, 170. Those on the plane were Morales, Marcos Aguado, "Popo" Chamorro, and Octaviano César.

[45]Kerry hearings, I, 57, 68; III, 256–57.

[46]Kerry report, 55; Kerry hearings, III, 262–67.

[47]*Miami Herald*, October 12, 1990.

[48]Kerry hearings, III, 261–68; *Miami Herald*, October 12, 1990; see also George Morales, at Kerry hearings, III, 300–303.

[49]Kerry hearings, III, 307.

[50]Eddy, *Cocaine Wars*, 332: "To the chagrin of the DEA, Morales was allowed bond—initially of $2 million—his trial was endlessly delayed, and he was given extraordinary freedom by the court to travel abroad. He was granted permission to travel to the Bahamas, Cuba (twice), the Dominican Republic, Panama, and Mexico."

[51]Cockburn, *Out of Control*, 170.

[52]Eddy, *Cocaine Wars*, 335.

[53]Kerry hearings, I, 96–97. A witness has said that in an earlier briefing Morales had talked of giving political contributions in the United States as well.

[54]*Tulsa World*, April 7, 1990. The witness also named "Popo" Chamorro and Octaviano César as two of the Contra leaders involved. He said there were others, but the U.S. Attorney on the case persuaded the judge "that naming the other contras would damage on-going federal investigations into the matter."

[55]*Miami Herald*, October 12, 1990.

[56]Kerry hearings, IV, 680–81 (testimony of Werner Lotz); cf. Kerry report, 47–48, 342. DIACSA's chief owner, Alfredo Caballero, "was an important supplier of airplanes and equipment to the Contras" (Dinges, *Our Man in Panama*, 212). In 1983–84 Caballero supplied Pastora (Kerry hearings, II, 204), but in 1984 he apparently shifted his allegiance to the FDN when he became a friend of the FDN supply chief Mario Calero. "During 1984 and 1985 . . . the FDN chose DIACSA for 'intra-account' transfers. The laundering of money through DIACSA concealed the fact that some funds for the Contras were through deposits arranged by Lt. Col. Oliver North" (Kerry report, 48). Other personnel from DIACSA in Costa Rica were associated with the Jorge Morales cocaine connection.

[57]Telephone conversation with Jonathan Winer, October 9, 1990.

[58]Joel Millman, "Narco-Terrorism: A Tale of Two Stories," *Columbia Journalism Review* (September–October 1986), 50; *Washington Post*, December 27, 1985. See Chapter 11.

[59]Eddy, *Cocaine Wars*, 333; Kerry hearings, I, 85; III, 309–10, 328. Originally the plane had been loaded with 420 kg; all but eighty disappeared at Great Harbour in the Bahamas at the time of seizure.

[60]Cockburn, *Out of Control*, 171.

[61]Memo of April 1, 1985; Kerry report, 42.

[62]Christic Institute deposition of Alberto Guevara Bonilla, 32.

[63]In this deteriorating situation the Morales operation appears to have become increasingly competitive with that of the Miami-based Cubans; by 1986 Morales and a former Cuban American ally, Luis "Kojak" Garcia,

were threatening each other's life (Eddy, *Cocaine Wars*, 334; cf. Kerry hearings, I, 81).

[64]Eddy, *Cocaine Wars*, 332–37.

[65]Kerry report, 49–53. In April 1986, "Popo" Chamorro was arrested in Costa Rica on arrival from Miami and was returned to the United States (*San Francisco Examiner*, April 24, 1986). One month earlier the U.S. Embassy in Costa Rica reported that "'Popo' Chamorro is alleged [deletion] to be involved in drug trafficking" (deposition of Tómas Castillo, exhibit 9, *Iran-Contra Report*, Appendix B, Vol. 3, 553; CIA Cable from San Jose to Washington, March 26, 1986).

[66]Gutman, *Banana Diplomacy*, 203: "With North's help, Secord sold arms to the rebels starting in 1984, delivered them in the course of 1985, and took over the entire resupply operation in 1986."

[67]Kerry report, 45; citing grand jury statements of Carlos Soto on file with *U.S. v. Rodriguez*, 88-0222, USDC, Northern District of Florida, September 29, 1987, and Kerry hearings, II, 260–61; cf. Kerry report, 298–341. Soto told the grand jury of his acquaintance with Wilfred Navarro, a former CIA Cuban associated with an Angola coup plot directed by former Watergate burglar Frank Sturgis (341; *Parapolitics/USA* No. 6, 32).

[68]Kerry report, 45.

[69]Owen memo to North, March 17, 1986. According to Martha Honey, Steven Carr, now dead, told her that Nuñez was at this time working on a stratagem to extract money from NHAO for boats that could be used for drug smuggling.

[70]Without that deletion, Owen could hardly have claimed, as he did under oath in the Iran-Contra hearings, that the Christic Institute case "is absolutely scurrilous and there's no truth to it" (testimony of Robert Owen, May 19, 1987, U.S. Congress, *Iran-Contra Investigation*, Joint Hearings, 100-2, 402).

[71]Kerry report, 61; cf. 374; cf. Owen deposition, May 6, 1987, 5; *Iran-Contra Report*, Appendix B, Vol. 20, 734.

[72]Kerry report, 415–24. The plane's arrival at the Hull ranch (when Richard Secord was trying to replace the drug-linked arms suppliers) was witnessed by Robert Owen, who to his credit recognized the shipment as a "problem" and reported it promptly to North (Owen deposition, May 4, 1987, 30; *Iran-Contra Report*, Appendix B, Vol. 20, 665; Owen memo to North, March 26, 1985; March 27, 1985).

[73]The assurances of CIA legislative liaison John Rizzo are recorded not only by Kerry's staff but also by Thomas Marum, a member of the Justice Department who was present (Kerry report, 159, 1008, 1012–13; cf. 804, 864).

[74]*Oakland Tribune*, February 15, 1990.

[75]Kerry report, 374.

[76]Marshall, Scott, and Hunter, *Iran-Contra Connection*, 47, 134–36.

[77]Kerry report, 458–59.

[78]Kerry report, 414, 365–70, 301.

[79]Kerry report, 416–19.

[80]Kerry report, 849; cf. 865; Cockburn, *Out of Control*, 156–57.

[81]Kerry report, 61 (*United States v. Rene Corvo*, SD Florida, August 1988); Kerry report, 45 (*United States v. Luis Rodriguez*, 87-01044, ND Florida; *United States v. Luis Rodriguez*, 88-0222 CR-King, SD Florida).

[82]Kerry report, 388 (North diary, September 4, 1984, Q0543); Owen memo of November 26, 1985.

[83]Owen memo of March 17, 1986. According to this memo, "a fishing company is now being formed in Limon, Costa Rica to provide cover for the boats." A later Owen memo of April 7, 1986, confirms that the shrimp-boat operation had established a cover in Limon. Jack Terrell told Washington investigators that in 1986 Vidal and two associates were briefly detained in Limon in connection with the discovery of cocaine on board an airplane. He also claimed that a partner with Chanes in the Limon fishing company was Watergate burglar Eugenio Rolando Martinez, whom Howard Hunt identified in a congressional hearing as an informant to the CIA on Cuban exile narcotics involvement (Nedzi hearing, 543); and who has been named by others as a government informant in the CORU-linked narcoterrorist case of the World Finance Corporation (cf. Messick, *Of Grass and Snow*). Martinez is a long-time ally of Félix Rodríguez, with whom he served in the CIA's Operation 40, closed down in the early 1970s because of its cocaine involvement (Marshall, Scott, and Hunter, *Iran-Contra Connection*, 37, 45). Martinez is also said to be extremely close to his former son-in-law Raul Díaz, the Miami detective (and friend of Félix Rodríguez) whose agency was allegedly hired by Eastern Airlines to "fabricate information" against their pilot who went to the FBI (Eddy, *Cocaine Wars*, 339; Kerry hearings, II, 57). Kerry subcommittee counsel Jack Blum was allegedly persuaded by his investigations that Díaz was "the 'cut out' between those nether worlds of espionage and drug trafficking, the 'link man' between the Cartel and the CIA" (Eddy, *Cocaine Wars*, 339). If so, Diaz would appear to have inherited the mantle of his father-in-law.

[84]Cockburn, *Out of Control*, 89. This portion of Fernandez's testimony (given under the name of Tómas Castillo) was censored.

[85]*Miami Herald*, February 16, 1987. Martha Honey and Tony Avirgan interviewed ARDE officials and investigators in Costa Rica who recalled Vidal as someone who "had spoken in both Miami and Costa Rica about the need to 'liquidate' Pastora" ("La Penca Report," 28).

[86]*Iran-Contra Report*, 106–9; deposition of Kevin W. Currier, Executive Session, May 5, 1987, 6, 46–47; *Iran-Contra Report*, Appendix B, Vol. 8, 199, 237, 238.

[87]Kerry report, 442–45.

[88]Kerry report, 378; *Miami Herald*, August 6, 1981; Lernoux, *In Banks We Trust*, 116; Eddy, *Cocaine Wars*, 89–91, 178–80.

[89]Kerry report, 371–81, Currier deposition, May 5, 1987, 6, 8; *Iran-Contra Report*, Appendix B, Vol. 8, 199, 201.

[90]Kerry report, 460 (Luis Crespo), 413, 425, 460 (Perez). Luis Crespo lost his right hand in March 1974, when a bomb he was preparing in Miami exploded prematurely; his companion, Humberto Lopez, Jr., lost an eye. Humberto Lopez had been part of a goon squad that Watergate burglar Bernard Barker brought to Washington to attack Daniel Ellsberg in 1972; he was also the founder of the Frente Nacional por la Liberacion de Cuba, later expanded into CORU by Frank Castro (Hinckle and Turner, *Fish Is Red*, 318; Carlos Rivero Collado, *Los Sobrinos del Tio Sam* [Havana: Editorial de Ciencias Sociales, 1976], 335–36). At the time of the March 1974 FNLC explosion, the Frente was based in Somoza's Nicaragua. Rafael Perez, alias Torpedo, and the *pragmatistas* (founded by Eduardo Paz) had been responsible for the April 1972 bombing of the Cuban commercial office in Montreal (ibid., 331); both Paz and Perez joined El Negro Chamorro on the Contra Southern Front. Other *pragmatistas* (after Perez had split with them) are said to have murdered former Brigade 2506 president Juan Peruyero in January 1977, after he had begun to talk to a Miami Grand Jury about CORU (cf. *Miami Herald*, December 30, 1983).

[91]Kerry report, 460 (Ramon Sánchez). For details of the incident, see Hinckle and Turner, *Fish Is Red*, 201.

CHAPTER 7

[1]National Public Radio, "All Things Considered," May 5, 1986; Kerry report, 438. Terrell even reported the exact gauge of the 20-millimeter cannon on Corvo's flight; cf. Kerry report, 423.

[2]National Public Radio, "All Things Considered," May 5, 1986; Kerry report, 440; cf. 159. See Chapter 11.

[3]Kerry report, 374 (Miami FBI information received September 26, 1984: Francisco Chanes "is a narcotics trafficker and . . . was giving financial support to anti-Castro groups and the Nicaraguan Contra guerrillas; the monies comes from narcotic transactions"); Cockburn, *Out of Control*, 40 (Carr). Cf. *Avirgan and Honey v. Hull et al.*, in the United States Court of Appeals for the Eleventh Circuit (henceforth Christic Appeal), No. 88-5720, exhibit 6. Terrell in his report to the FBI in New Orleans alleged that Chanes met with Tom Posey (*Iran-Contra Report*, Appendix B, Vol. 21, 127); Owen later confirmed his own presence at the meeting in Calero's house with Posey and Chanes (*Iran-Contra Report*, Appendix B, Vol. 20, 799).

⁴Kerry report, 61 (*United States v. Rene Corvo*, SD Florida, August 1988); Kerry report, 45 (*United States v. Luis Rodriguez*, 87-01044, ND Florida; *United States v. Luis Rodriguez*, 88-0222 CR-King, SD Florida).

⁵A month later a Costa Rica judge signed an extradition order for Hull on the murder charge (*New York Times*, March 1, 1990).

⁶Peter Dale Scott interviewed Terrell extensively in 1987 while working with Terrell at the International Center for Development Policy in Washington.

⁷Terrell has hinted that the money came from CIA contacts (*Iran-Contra Report*, Appendix A, Vol. 1, 837–39). Robert Owen told North that Terrell's funds came from a rich Texas oilman, "Mako" Stewart, with whom Terrell was indicted in 1988 (Owen memo to North, January 31, 1985, Owen exhibit RWO-2).

⁸*Iran-Contra Report*, 41.

⁹Steven Emerson, *Secret Warriors* (New York: Putnam, 1988), 134–35.

¹⁰*United States v. Oliver L. North*, government stipulation no. 1; Emerson, *Secret Warriors*, 134.

¹¹*Washington Post*, September 15, 1984; Emerson, *Secret Warriors*, 134; *Iran-Contra Report*, 39.

¹²*Memphis Commercial Appeal*, April 13, 1986; cf. Kerry report, 854.

¹³Pegasus/Camper Report of December 12, 1984; reprinted in Kerry report, 519–24.

¹⁴Bob Woodward, *Veil* (New York: Simon & Schuster, 1987), 361–62.

¹⁵Woodward, *Veil*, 388.

¹⁶Kerry report, 522–23; Kerry hearings, IV, 295. Terrell later claimed that Posey leaked the story (*Iran-Contra Report*, Appendix A, Vol. 1, 837).

¹⁷Telephone interview with Terrell, as reported by Bradlee, *Guts and Glory*, 261. See also Cockburn, *Out of Control*, 74.

¹⁸Owen deposition, April 20, 1987; *Iran-Contra Report*, Appendix B, Vol. 20, 648–52.

¹⁹Pegasus/Camper Report of 12 Dec 1984; reprinted in Kerry report, 524. With the exposure of Pegasus, North proposed to McFarlane that the British mercenary David Walker establish "an arrangement with the FDN for certain special operations expertise aimed particularly at destroying HIND helicopters" (North memo of December 4, 1984; McFarlane exhibit RCM-32; quoted and discussed in *Iran-Contra Report*, 44).

²⁰Bradlee, *Guts and Glory*, 261–62.

²¹Cockburn, *Out of Control*, 76. Terrell testified to Vidal's remarks under oath in the Costa Rica libel suit brought by John Hull against Avirgan and Honey (*La Penca: On Trial*, 88; Kerry report, 723).

²²Owen deposition, October 1, 1987, 13; *Iran-Contra Report*, Appendix B, Vol. 20, 800: "To my knowledge, that never took place. That was a pure lie."

[23]Owen memo to Adolfo Calero, March 27, 1985 (submitted at Owen's Christic suit deposition). Posey and Adams confirmed to Bradlee that "there was a plot against Pastora" (Bradlee, *Guts and Glory*, 262).

[24]North diary entry for November 27, 1984.

[25]Owen memo to North, January 31, 1985, Owen exhibit RWO-2. Cf. Owen memo to North, April 1, 1985, Owen exhibit RWO-7.

[26]National Public Radio, "All Things Considered," May 5, 1986; Kerry report, 438.

[27]Owen depositions, October 1, 1987; June 5, 1987; *Iran-Contra Report*, Appendix B, Vol. 20, 799, 733.

[28]Deposition of Tom Posey; *Iran-Contra Report*, Appendix B, Vol. 21, 58–59: "How would a person from California know about a meeting in Houston, when I just found out about it the same day, fascinated me." Owen deposition, October 1, 1987; *Iran-Contra Report*, Appendix B, Vol. 20, 824: "I . . . told Ollie eventually that I thought he was using bad judgment in associating with him . . . I didn't trust him" (at this point Owen asked to go off the record). Cf. Owen memo to North, January 27, 1985: "Do you want me to go south to watch over Spivey?" (Posey deposition; *Iran-Contra Report*, Appendix B, Vol. 21, 204).

[29]FBI Internal Memo of April 1987 for Senate Select Committee on Intelligence, forwarded with letter of April 22, 1987, in connection with confirmation hearing for director-designate of Central Intelligence William Webster (henceforth "Webster letter").

[30]Webster letter. In mid-January Spivey traveled to Washington with Posey, now the hero of his proposed documentary, and the two men met with Robert Owen (Owen deposition, October 1, 1987; *Iran-Contra Report*, Appendix B, Vol. 20, 799, 820). Spivey later claimed "that in early 1985 he saw Miami-based FBI reports on the Contra drug charges in North's office" (Bradlee, *Guts and Glory*, 405).

[31]North's notebook for January 5, 1985, Clarridge exhibit DRC-31: "1905—Call to [deleted] FBI/1930—Call from Adolfo [Calero]—Cuban Americans—Terrell, Jack—was w[ith] CIA—6 Years—worked out of Africa—says he knew Denton—joined CMA after September." Cf. North's notebook for March 18[?], 1985, Shultz exhibit GPS-76/3249: "CMA—Flaco/Jack Terrell . . . STAY AWAY."

[32]Webster letter; cf. *Chicago Tribune*, August 30, 1987.

[33]Posey deposition; *Iran-Contra Report*, Appendix B, Vol. 21, 60–61. According to Revell, on January 5, 1985, FBI agent Michael Boone in Los Angeles, who had been charged to locate and interview Spivey, received a call from Spivey about Terrell and Tom Posey shortly before he received the call from North (Webster letter; *Iran-Contra Report*, 648). Posey told the committees that the phone call occurred just before the meeting at Calero's house on January 5. Others date the Calero house meeting December 20, which could move the Kiszynski-Spivey contact back to before Spivey's call of December 21 to the State Department.

North's notebooks show a call from Spivey about Terrell on January 2, followed by a discussion of Spivey with Owen, which could very well have set up the January 5 Miami meeting. Kiszynski's cable to FBI Headquarters after this interview (apparently on January 8) relays Spivey's opinion that Posey is "well-meaning," while Terrell "is unstable and could jeopardize U.S. interests in Central America" (Kiszynski cable on "Neutrality Matters," Miami File 2-696, reproduced in *United States v. Jack Terrell et al.*, Defense Motion of October 1988 to Dismiss the Indictment. U.S. District Court, SD Florida, 88-6097-Cr-Judge Roettger). A Select Committee document confirms that Kiszynski interviewed Tom Posey on January 5, 1985 (deposition of Jeffrey Feldman, April 30, 1987, 91; *Iran-Contra Report*, Appendix B, Vol. 10, 120).

[34]For years Kiszynski had worked with the ex-CIA Cuban operatives in Miami. His relations to them had come under suspicion in 1979–80 during a police investigation of how information on a sensitive police investigation of CORU terrorists had ended up in the hands of the terrorists themselves. In 1979 a Miami police informant had alleged that two Cubans from the terrorist network CORU (Coordination of United Revolutionary Organizations) had plans to blow up an airline flying to Cuba and that the terrorists had obtained police documentation on the case. Although a 1980 police investigation into this matter was inconclusive, it did establish that Miami police had given the informant's report to FBI agent Kiszynski, who managed this network of former CIA operatives, and more importantly that Kiszynski had subsequently left his briefcase with the suspected terrorist team for several hours (*Miami Herald*, December 15, 1983).

[35]FBI interview of Oliver North, July 22, 1986; *Iran-Contra Report*, Appendix A, Vol. 1, 855.

[36]*Washington Post*, December 27, 1985. For the difficulties of Brian Barger and Bob Parry publishing this story, see *Rolling Stone*, September 10, 1987, and Chapter 11.

[37]Deposition of Kevin W. Currier, May 5, 1987, 6–7; *Iran-Contra Report*, Appendix B, Vol. 8, 199–200. Cf. *Iran-Contra Report*, 106; Kerry report, 377.

[38]Currier deposition, May 5, 1987, 6; *Iran-Contra Report*, Appendix B, Vol. 8, 199.

[39]Kerry report, 371–81.

[40]Currier deposition, 23–24; *Iran-Contra Report*, Appendix B, Vol. 8, 215–16; Kerry report, 866; deposition of Mark Richard, August 19, 1987, 76; *Iran-Contra Report*, Appendix B, Vol. 23, 76. The two Cuban exiles Coutin and Corvo had originally been allies in the Contra support operation; they subsequently had a falling-out, allegedly after two of Coutin's men ran across evidence of the operation's involvement with drug smugglers in Costa Rica (Kerry report, 373–74; Cockburn, *Out of Control*, 43).

[41]Feldman memo of May 14, 1986 (as leaked to selected journalists); Feldman deposition, April 30, 1987, 21; Currier deposition, 27; *Iran-Contra Report*, Appendix B, Vol. 8, 219; Vol. 10, 50.

[42]See for example, Feldman deposition, April 30, 1987, 21; deposition of Richard D. Gregorie, July 17, 1987, 19; deposition of Leon Kellner, April 30, 1987, 30, 97, 107; *Iran-Contra Report*, Appendix B, Vol. 10, 50; Vol. 12, 1165; Vol. 14, 1054, 1121, 1131.

[43]*Iran-Contra Report*, 106–9.

[44]Poindexter deposition exhibit 45 (FBI SECRET/ORCON Letterhead Memorandum of July 18, 1986, "JACK TERRELL"), 1; emphasis added.

[45]FBI teletype of July 1986; *Iran-Contra Report*, Appendix A, Vol. 1, 861; emphasis added.

[46]Currier deposition, 14; *Iran-Contra Report*, Appendix B, Vol. 8, 206. Ambassador Tambs also testified that Feldman and his FBI agents "said they were investigating some Cuban Americans who apparently had connections between gun-running and also some—perhaps narcotics dealings . . . I was under the impression the whole thing was going to go to the grand jury" (U.S. Congress, *Iran-Contra Investigation*, Joint Hearings, 100–3; testimony of Lewis Tambs, May 28, 1987, 414–15).

[47]Deposition of FBI Executive Assistant Director Oliver B. Revell, July 15, 1987, 17; *Iran-Contra Report*, Appendix B, Vol. 22, 949. Former public defender John Mattes has said that agents Currier and Kiszynski told him in 1986 that "we're investigating these people [Corvo, Chanes et al.] for drugs" ("The Kwitny Report," Public Broadcasting System, April 1989). Cf. Deposition of "C/CATF" Alan Fiers, 29; *Iran-Contra Report*, Appendix B, Vol. 3, 1106.

[48]Memo from John M. Poindexter to the president, drafted by Oliver L. North, "Terrorist Threat: Terrell," July 28, 1986, Poindexter deposition exhibit 45; *Iran-Contra Report*, Appendix A, Vol. 2, 1323.

[49]For the details, see Cockburn, *Out of Control*, 53–68. Of chief interest for this story is that the abandoned briefcase of Saum, an apparent informant and provocateur, contained many telephone numbers, including that of CMA chief Tom Posey and of Lt. Col. Doug Menarchik, Vice President Bush's chief representative at the Working Group meetings of the Vice President's Task Force on Combating Terrorism. Colonel Menarchik has confirmed knowing the name of Alan Saum; but when one of the authors asked Menarchik if he knew Major Saum, "S(for Stephen),A,U,M," he twice replied, "I do not know a Mr. Faum." According to Leslie Cockburn, Saum, in an April 1987 letter "with a Swedish postmark and a return address in Bet Shemesh, Israel, . . . described his current assignment as identifying pro-Soviet activists among Swedish writers and artists" (*Out of Control*, 67).

[50]Feldman's recollection was "that Leon told me Justice had called him and requested a continuance in the Garcia sentencing" (Feldman deposition, 31; *Iran-Contra Report*, Appendix B, Vol. 10, 60). Kellner agreed

that "it would have had to come from" himself and Mark Richard (Kellner deposition, 10; *Iran-Contra Report*, Appendix B, Vol. 14, 1034). Mark Richard testified that the call "may very well have come from me. I don't recall it. I do recall that the sentencing was postponed" (Richard deposition, 72; *Iran-Contra Report*, Appendix B, Vol. 23, 72). However, Lowell Jensen, then Deputy Attorney General, testified that "I think probably I had talked with Kellner" about it (Jensen deposition, 57, cf. 53; *Iran-Contra Report*, Appendix B, Vol. 14, 589; cf. 585).

[51]*Iran-Contra Report*, 371, citing DEA Agent #1 deposition, 158; Appendix B, Vol. 8, 588.

[52]In June 1988 the court dismissed the suit, with an order granting summary judgment; a supplementary order awarded the defendants costs and attorneys' fees. As of this writing (September 1990), both judgments are being appealed.

[53]*Iran-Contra Report*, 107; Currier deposition, May 5, 1987, 37–40; Revell deposition, July 15, 1987, 6; *Iran-Contra Report*, Appendix B, Vol. 8, 229–32; Vol. 22, 938.

[54]*Iran-Contra Report*, 107.

[55]Jensen deposition, 55–57; *Iran-Contra Report*, Appendix B, Vol. 14, 587–89. Revell testified that both the memo and the Poindexter interview arose because "Lowell [Jensen] had asked me to give him a briefing and also he asked me for a document that he could use in discussing it with the NSC" (Revell deposition, July 15, 1987, 4; *Iran-Contra Report*, Appendix B, Vol. 22, 936). However, Jensen denied this under oath:

Q: Do you recall contacting Mr. Revell?

A: No; I don't think so. I don't know that I contacted him directly. I think I spoke with the Criminal Division people.

Q: So, to the best of your recollection, you did not contact the FBI directly?

A: No.

(Jensen deposition, 495, *Iran-Contra Report*, Appendix B, Vol. 14, 581). Revell meanwhile gave a quite different and less disturbing account of what concerned Jensen about the Miami case, testifying that it was the alleged threat against Ambassador Tambs (Revell deposition, July 15, 1987, 4; *Iran-Contra Report*, Appendix B, Vol. 22, 936).

[56]*Iran-Contra Report*, 107; Jensen deposition, 58; Richard deposition, August 19, 1987, 54–56; *Iran-Contra Report*, Appendix B, Vol. 14, 590; Vol. 23, 54–56; Meese exhibit EM-73. As we have seen, Kellner had been consulting with Washington on the Corvo investigation even before Richard's phone call to Kellner on March 24.

[57]Feldman testified that he came away from the Terrell interview with "a bigger picture of Tom Posey's involvement with the FDN [Contras] and CMA's attempts to put mercenaries into Costa Rica," than Garcia's earlier story of an assassination plot had revealed (Feldman deposition, 38, cf. 39–40; *Iran-Contra Report*, Appendix B, Vol. 10, 67; cf. 68–69).

[58]*Iran-Contra Report*, 107.

[59]Currier deposition, May 5, 1987, 35; cf. Feldman deposition, April 30, 1987, 60–61; *Iran-Contra Report*, Appendix B, Vol. 8, 227; Vol. 10, 89–90. See also *Iran-Contra Report*, 107.

[60]"The Kwitny Report," Public Broadcasting System, April 1989. According to Feldman, Hull told him that the U.S. Embassy had not advised him concerning the interrogation, a claim contradicted by the Embassy employee's statement the following day.

[61]Owen memo to Oliver North, April 7, 1986, Owen exhibit RWO-15; Cockburn, *Out of Control*, 135. Fernandez later denied under oath that he had talked to Owen about Feldman or that he could recall seeing the diagram (U.S. Congress, *Iran-Contra Investigation*, Joint Hearings, 100–4, Testimony of "Tómas Castillo," May 29, 1987, 69).

[62]Terrell claimed to have seen John Hull in the company of Robert Owen at the December 1985 meetings in Houston and Miami.

[63]Currier deposition, May 5, 1987, 26; *Iran-Contra Report*, Appendix B, Vol. 8, 218. CIA Station Chief Joe Fernandez, alias Tómas Castillo, later allegedly "admitted to the congressional Iran-contra committees in secret testimony that Vidal and Corvo were 'our people' (CIA) and had a 'problem with drugs,' but that the agency had to 'protect' them" (Cockburn, *Out of Control*, 89). Felipe Vidal has been charged in Miami with drug running (*Miami Herald*, February 16, 1987), as have others named by Terrell in the Cuban Contra support network. In 1989 John Hull was briefly arrested and indicted in Costa Rica on drug-trafficking charges (see Chapter 1).

[64]*Iran-Contra Report*, 115, emphasis added. North notebook page Q2078 in *Iran-Contra Report*, Appendix A, Vol. 1, 732.

[65]Poindexter deposition exhibit 1, 41.

[66]*Iran-Contra Report*, 108; Kellner deposition, 27–28; *Iran-Contra Report*, Appendix B, Vol. 14, 1051–52. Meese testified that he asked about the case because it had received attention by the press (*Iran-Contra Report*, 108; Meese deposition, July 8, 1987, 219–24; *Iran-Contra Report*, Appendix B, Vol. 18, 220–25).

[67]*Iran-Contra Report*, 108; Feldman draft memo of May 14, 1986; *Iran-Contra Report*, Appendix A, Vol. 1, 774.

[68]Cockburn, *Out of Control*, 138.

[69]Gregorie deposition, 48; Kellner deposition, 17–20; David Leiwant deposition, 14; *Iran-Contra Report*, Appendix B, Vol. 12, 1194; Vol. 14, 1041–44; Vol. 16, 18; *Iran-Contra Report*, 108.

[70]"The Kwitny Report," Public Broadcasting System, April 1989.

[71]Kerry report, 147–48; cf. 636, 652–53.

[72]Kerry report, 982–83; memo of May 23, 1986, from Bergquist to Trott. Jack Terrell was the only witness to testify directly in the Costa Rica trial. Steven Carr had been scheduled to appear for the defense, but at the last minute was spirited out of Costa Rica with the collusion of

John Hull and U.S. Embassy personnel in "flagrant violation of Costa Rican law" (Cockburn, *Out of Control*, 141–44, 148). His information was transmitted in part by Martha Honey as a witness in her own defense and in part by British fellow mercenary Peter Glibbery. The information of Jesus Garcia was provided to the court by his public defender John Mattes, who later became the attorney defending Jack Terrell.

[73]North notebook.

[74]Feldman deposition, 92; *Iran-Contra Report*, Appendix B, Vol. 10, 121; cf. *The Iran-Contra Report*, 109; *Village Voice*, July 14, 1987; "The Kwitny Report," Public Broadcasting System, April 1989. According to "The Kwitny Report," Kenneth Bergquist of the Justice Department was advised by the Office of the Independent Counsel that he was under criminal investigation for unauthorized disclosure of the rewritten Feldman memo. See Chapter 9.

[75]Kellner deposition, 109; *Iran-Contra Report*, Appendix B, Vol. 14, 1133. On June 5, 1986, North took another step that suggested his true interest in Terrell; he went to consult with Tom Green, Richard Secord's lawyer.

[76]Revell deposition, July 15, 1987, 19; *Iran-Contra Report*, Appendix B, Vol. 22, 951.

[77]*Iran-Contra Report*, 112; FBI Washington Field Office teletype of June 11, 1986; *Iran-Contra Report*, Appendix A, Vol. 1, 802–5; Kerry report, 162.

[78]FBI Washington Field Office teletype of June 11, 1986; *Iran-Contra Report*, Appendix A, Vol. 1, 802–3; Revell deposition, July 15, 1987, 49–51; *Iran-Contra Report*, Appendix B, Vol. 22, 981–83.

[79]Glenn Robinette memo of July 15, 1986; *Iran-Contra Report*, Appendix A, Vol. 1, 832.

[80]Terrell-Grothaus book proposal, 10–11; *Iran-Contra Report*, Appendix A, Vol. 1, 843–44; cf. 880, 823.

[81]FBI teletype of July 1986; *Iran-Contra Report*, Appendix A, Vol. 1, 863: "Terrell is believed to be a star witness in a civil suit naming Secord." Cf. FBI teletype of July 23, 1986; *Iran-Contra Report*, Appendix A, Vol. 1, 869: "Terrell is believed by Secord to be star witness in civil suit."

CHAPTER 8

[1]*Newsweek*, October 21, 1985, 26 (Flashboard). Those involved in the Iran arms deals appear to have used "Flash" messages on this secure system as late as October 31, 1986 (Robert Earl exhibit 3–8, May 30, 1987).

[2]Five members of the Senior Review Group of the Vice President's Task Force on Combating Terrorism now joined North to constitute the new Operations Sub-Group. (The five, all given counterterrorism respon-

sibilities, were Charles Allen of the CIA, Robert Oakley of the State Department, Noel Koch of the Defense Department, Lt. Gen. John Moell-
ering from the Joint Chiefs of Staff, and Oliver Revell of the FBI.) In
January 1986, by virtue of the Task Force Report and of the resulting
National Security Decision Directive NSDD-207, North was also given a
new Office to Combat Terrorism, which was kept secret even from many
other NSC members. Two key members of Bush's Task Force staff, Robert
Earl and Craig Coy, moved over to staff North's new office. Earl and Coy
spent much of the next year working on the Iran arms sales and Contra
support operation, making it easier for North to travel. Earl testified that
he spent between a quarter and a half of his time on Iran matters; his
colleague Coy "knew everything . . . about Democracy Incorporated,"
the Contra support operation (Earl deposition, May 30, 1987, 98–99,
35; *Iran-Contra Report*, Appendix B, Vol. 9, 1034–35, 971). Earl and
Coy also handled the domestic propaganda of Carl Channell and Richard
Miller, the suppression of potentially embarrassing investigations by other
government agencies (that "might ruin a greater equity of national security"), and, for the White House, right-wing contributions to illegal
Contra arms purchases (Earl deposition, May 30, 1987, 33–37 [investi-
gations]; May 15, 1987, 117–21 [Channell and Miller]; May 15, 1987,
118–19, 131 [right-wing contributors]; *Iran-Contra Report*, Appendix B,
Vol. 9, 969–73, 679–83, 693). Earl and Coy also took the minutes of
the OSG (Coy deposition, March 17, 1987, 24–25; cf. Earl deposition,
May 2, 1987, 22–23; *Iran-Contra Report*, Appendix B, Vol. 7, 961–62;
Vol. 9, 574–75). For the details, see Peter Dale Scott, "Northwards Without North," *Social Justice*, XVI, 2 (Summer 1989), 1–30; Peter Dale Scott,
"The Terrorism Task Force," *Covert Action Information Bulletin*, 33 (Win-
ter 1990), 12–15.

[3]Revell deposition, July 15, 1987, 11; *Iran-Contra Report*, Appendix
B, Vol. 22, 943.

[4]Secord's anxiety about what Terrell knew also led to a meeting between
Glenn Robinette and Robert Owen and then to subsequent meetings
between Owen, Robinette, and Moisés Nuñez of Frigorificos de Puntarenas. Owen admitted under oath to these meetings and to having been
first introduced to Nuñez "several years ago . . . by, I believe, John Hull."
Under advice of counsel, Owen declined to reveal what was discussed at
the meetings, except that they involved "the matters of defense of the
Avignone [Avirgan]-Honey lawsuit."(Owen deposition, May 6, 1987, 4–
7; *Iran-Contra Report*, Appendix B, Vol. 20, 733–36); cf. Kerry report,
61.

[5]*Iran-Contra Report*, 112; Revell deposition, July 15, 1987, 25, 28;
*Iran-Contra Report*, Appendix B, Vol. 22, 957, 960.

[6]Terrell had contacted one of these two men some months earlier, taping his phone conversation and giving it to the FBI. On July 18 the FBI put the two Nicaraguans under surveillance along with Terrell.

[7]Revell deposition, July 15, 1987, 28; *Iran-Contra Report*, Appendix B, Vol. 22, 960.

[8]*Iran-Contra Report*, Appendix B, Vol. 20, 837–38:

> Q: Were you aware of any FBI information regarding a possible assassination plot by Mr. Terrell against Ambassador Tambs or the President?
> A: I did hear about that. That was through Glenn Robinette. I know that Glenn had conversations with the FBI about it.

Cf. the sworn deposition of Oliver Revell (*Iran-Contra Report*, Appendix B, Vol. 22, 963): "I believe that Robinette knew Terrell had been in contact with both sides, the Sandinistas and contras . . . and thought he had made himself available to the Sandinistas for mercenary purposes." This information corroborates North's memo of the same day, saying that Robinette had evaluated Terrell as "extremely dangerous" and "possibly working for the security services of another country." The two Robinette memos on Terrell from July 15 and July 17 give a quite different picture of Terrell.

[9]FBI Washington Field Office teletype, July 17, 1986; *Iran-Contra Report*, Appendix A, Vol. 1, 823; FBI interview of Oliver North, July 22, 1986, Appendix A, Vol. 1, 880; Revell deposition, July 15, 1987, 28; *Iran-Contra Report*, Appendix B, Vol. 22, 960. Many parts of Terrell's book proposal help explain North's decision to alert Poindexter to Terrell, above all the revelation that Terrell was talking to the DEA, FBI, and Senator Kerry's staff about Contra-CIA collaboration with drug traffickers. See *Iran-Contra Report*, Appendix A, Vol. 1, 842, 851:

> [Terrell] met with FDN leader Adolfo Calero . . . and a CIA operative from Costa Rica who helped the Cubans in both the drug trade and in their dream of freedom fighting . . . . Terrell is currently cooperating here in the United States with the FBI, the DEA, Federal attorneys from Miami, and the Costa Rican government, all of whom are investigating a web of drug traffic, assassination attempts plotted in the United States with CIA approval, anti-neutrality violations, and stacks of conspiracy allegations involving the FDN Contras and their American supporters. On April 5, 1986, at the request of and under the aegis of Senator Kerry, . . . he was escorted by armed guard to a safe house near Annapolis, where further debriefing will take place and a decision made as to his testimony.

[10]"Notes on J. Terrell—Operational Use/Threat," unaddressed memo from Glenn Robinette, July 17, 1986.

[11]"Notes on J. Terrell," unaddressed memo from Glenn Robinette, July 17, 1986.

[12]Poindexter deposition exhibit 44 (memo from North to Poindexter, "Terrorist Threat: Terrel[l]," July 17, 1986; *Iran-Contra Report*, Appendix A, Vol. 2, 1321. The phone calls North complained about were not anti-Contra calls, as his memo might suggest, but pro-North phone calls harassing *Washington Post* editor Leonard Downey for having allowed "the use of North's name" (despite appeals from North and the White House) in a *Post* story (Bradlee, *Guts and Glory*, 283). North brought up the phone calls again to the FBI on July 22: "While Terrell's name has not come up, North mentioned that in March, 1986, *Washington Post* Managing Editor Leonard Downey received obscene calls at night in which the caller used North's name. Downey wrote North a letter advising him that if the activity did not stop, he would prosecute" (FBI FD-302, July 25, 1986; *Iran-Contra Report*, Appendix A, Vol. 1, 856).

[13]Poindexter deposition exhibit 44 (memo from North to Poindexter, "Terrorist Threat: Terrel[l]," July 17, 1986; *Iran-Contra Report*, Appendix A, Vol. 2, 1321. The relationship between the July 17 memos of Robinette and North is confirmed by their document and (Bates) page numbers as released to the Select Committees. North's memo was numbered document 14042 for the Committees, with Bates page numbers N 45918–19; Robinette's was numbered document 14043, with Bates page numbers N 45920–21. Both documents were released by the administration on June 22, 1987, the day before Robinette's testimony.

[14]Robinette memo of July 15, 1986; *Iran-Contra Report*, Appendix A, Vol. 1, 832.

[15]Poindexter deposition exhibit 45, FBI SECRET/ORCON Memo from Office of the Director, July 18, 1986, "JACK TERRELL." The FBI memo also spoke of Terrell's efforts to ingratiate himself with Manuel Cordero of the Nicaraguan Embassy, which Terrell had recorded for the FBI's benefit, and mentioned that Terrell told Cordero he planned to come to Washington and "testify at a committee hearing . . . against the Contras."

[16]Poindexter deposition exhibit 45 (memo from Poindexter to the president, July 28, 1986, drafted by North July 25, 1986, "Terrorist Threat: Terrell"); *Iran-Contra Report*, Appendix A, Vol. 2, 1322.

[17]Poindexter deposition exhibit 45 (memo from Poindexter to the president, July 28, 1986, drafted by North July 25, 1986, "Terrorist Threat: Terrell"); *Iran-Contra Report*, Appendix A, Vol. 2, 1322. The memo continued, "Since it is important to protect the knowledge that Terrell is the subject of a criminal investigation, none of those with whom he has been in contact on the Hill have been advised." In other words, North

and Revell had decided not to advise Senator Kerry of the harassment of his witness.

[18]North in July 1986 was concerned he might be ousted from the NSC or at least relieved of his Contra responsibilities. That North linked Terrell to the efforts to oust him is indicated by the advice someone gave Robinette to contact Leonard Garment. On July 11, North himself had obtained Garment's help in maintaining his NSC position. Poindexter, according to Michael Ledeen, "informed North that he was taking him off the Central American 'account,' and put it in the hands of a member of the NSC Intelligence Directorate, Vince Cannistraro. But North had unexpected strength. He went first to his conservative friends—Andy Messing and Spitz Channell among others. . . . He also spoke, at my suggestion, to Leonard Garment, one of the most influential Republican lawyers in Washington. The result of all this political activity was a barrage of phone calls to Poindexter, demanding that North be kept in his post. Poindexter was steamrollered by this political machine and abandoned the idea of replacing North" (Michael A. Ledeen, *Perilous Statecraft: An Insider's Account of the Iran-Contra Affair* [New York: Scribner, 1988], 197–98). North's meeting with Garment, at which Ledeen was present, took place on July 11, 1986 (Shultz exhibit GPS-74/3343; cf. Coy deposition, June 1, 1987, 46; *Iran-Contra Report*, Appendix B, Vol. 7, 1117). On July 18, the *Wall Street Journal* ran an article by Suzanne Garment (Leonard's wife) attacking "senior officials" who would "turn their back on a man with Colonel North's record at a time when he is under outside attack" (Bradlee, *Guts and Glory*, 427).

[19]Bradlee, *Guts and Glory*, 426. This internecine squabble explains North's complaint to FBI agents on June 3 about their failure to contact "National Security Officer Fred Colcon for any information concerning drug charges leveled against North" (FBI teletype of 11 June, 1986; *Iran-Contra Report*, Appendix A, Vol. 1, 804). Cf. *Iran-Contra Report*, 112: "He complained that the FBI had never contacted an NSC staffer who supposedly was the source of allegations linking North to drug traffic."

[20]Bradlee, *Guts and Glory*, 431.

[21]*Iran-Contra Report*, 113.

[22]FBI teletype of 17[?] July, 1986; *Iran-Contra Report*, Appendix A, Vol. 1, 820; cf. 821.

[23]Poindexter deposition exhibit 45 (memo from Poindexter to the president, July 28, 1986, drafted by North, July 25, 1986, "Terrorist Threat: Terrell"); *Iran-Contra Report*, Appendix A, Vol. 2, 1321. Robert Oakley told Bob Parry of *Newsweek* that OSG-TIWG (which he cochaired with North) "never discussed Terrell" (*Newsweek,* September 21, 1987, 7). But Revell testified under oath that he believed he did tell the OSG about Terrell's "threat" (Revell deposition, July 15, 1987, 36; *Iran-Contra Report*, Appendix B, Vol. 22, 968).

[24]Compare the FD-302, July 25, 1986 (*Iran-Contra Report*, Appendix A, Vol. 1, 829–31) with the earlier teletype of July 18 [?], 1986 (*Iran-Contra Report*, Appendix A, Vol. 1, 821–23). The *Iran-Contra Report* also misdates the interview as "July 15" (112).

[25]FBI FD-302, July 25, 1986 (*Iran-Contra Report*, Appendix A, Vol. 1, 854). That this occurred on July 18 is confirmed by Robinette's diary for that day.

[26]Revell deposition, July 15, 1987, 32–35; *Iran-Contra Report*, Appendix B, Vol. 22, 964–67.

[27]FBI memo of July 18, 1986 (*Iran-Contra Report*, Appendix A, Vol. 1, 813).

[28]Revell deposition, July 15, 1987, 26; *Iran-Contra Report*, Appendix B, Vol. 22, 958.

[29]*Iran-Contra Report*, 113.

[30]*Forbes*, November 13, 1989.

CHAPTER 9

[1]For their analogous actions against another antidrug witness, Joseph Kelso, see Chapter 10.

[2]FBI memo of July 18, 1986; *Iran-Contra Report*, Appendix A, Vol. 1, 812.

[3]FBI memo of July 18, 1986; FBI teletypes of July 17[?], 1986; July 22, 1986; July 23, 1986; *Iran-Contra Report*, Appendix A, Vol. 1, 813, 820, 865–66, 869–71. The FBI also began to investigate the Council on Hemispheric Affairs, where David MacMichael had a second appointment. In paying Terrell, the ICDP was following an evolving practice among public-interest groups. Under budget-cutting restrictions imposed in the mid-1980s, Congress itself could no longer reimburse key witnesses, and private groups stepped into the breach. This practice of paying witnesses has naturally engendered controversy, but Terrell's testimony has been amply corroborated.

[4]Kerry report, 585; FBI teletype of July 1986; *Iran-Contra Report*, Appendix A, Vol. 1, 862.

[5]Kerry report, 584–86 (Kellner deposition).

[6]Revell deposition, July 15, 1987, 34; *Iran-Contra Report*, Appendix B, Vol. 22, 966.

[7]Revell deposition, July 15, 1987, 36; *Iran-Contra Report*, Appendix B, Vol. 22, 968.

[8]Three ICDP employees were interviewed directly by the FBI about their foreign contacts: Melinda Rorick about a Cuban, Bill Loker about a Soviet Embassy employee, and David MacMichael about Nicaraguan Embassy employees. A fourth ICDP employee, Margarita Suarez, was not located by the FBI, who instead interviewed her roommate about a Cuban.

[9]Hull's letter enclosed affidavits from Carr and Glibbery "retracting some of their prior statements regarding gun-running and Contra support" (*Iran-Contra Report*, 109). In August Terrell had helped persuade Glibbery not to play along with John Hull's offers to get him out of Costa Rica in exchange for retracting his earlier statements about gunrunning. Glibbery then repudiated his own retraction.

[10]Kellner deposition, 60–64; cf. Richard deposition, 87–90; *Iran-Contra Report*, Appendix B, Vol. 14, 1084–88; Vol. 23, 87–90.

[11]*Iran-Contra Report*, 109.

[12]Kerry report, 147, 636.

[13]Kerry report, 167, 528; cf. 631 (Feldman deposition). Neither Feldman nor the Kerry report specifies the day of this October 1986 meeting, but the notes of it were marked "10/14/86" (Kerry report, 633).

[14]Kerry report, 1017. In contrast, Mark Richard, who called the meeting, told the Iran-Contra Committees that "most of our time [was spent] on the humanitarian aid case, after which Richard said, 'Let's wait a few minutes and discuss . . . the Posey case, the Costa case' " (Richard deposition, 82; *Iran-Contra Report*, Appendix B, Vol. 23, 82).

[15]Richard deposition, 23, 201; *Iran-Contra Report*, Appendix B, Vol. 23, 201; FBI teletypes of May 16, 1986, and July 1986; *Iran-Contra Report*, Appendix A, Vol. 1, 798, 821 (cf. 829).

[16]Undated staff memorandum to Senator Kerry [April 1986], reprinted in Kerry report, 861–63; cf. 147, 158. The agenda is included as "Enclosure Two" to a Justice Department memo of May 13, 1986, from Ken Bergquist in the Department's Office of Legislative Affairs to Assistant Attorney General Steve Trott, the same official who told his subordinate Mark Richard to advise the U.S. Attorney's Office in Miami that decisions in the Corvo investigation "should be run by you [i.e., Richard]" (*Iran-Contra Report*, 107). The Bergquist memo, with its enclosures, was in turn reprinted in the Kerry report as an appendix to Feldman's testimony (857–78). Feldman's initials are visible on both the Bergquist memo and the Kerry staff agenda.

[17]Kerry report, 864–68; cf. 159, 1007–8. The minutes also are appended to the Bergquist memo.

[18]Kerry report, 147, 608–888.

[19]Even the investigation of Frigorificos was narrowed. By May 1986, the Kerry staff had asked for an investigation of Francisco Chanes, Frank Castro, and Ocean Hunter, a shrimp company owned by Luis Rodríguez and Francisco Chanes. The Kerry report (46) noted that "Ocean Hunter imported seafood it bought from Frigorificos and used the intercompany transactions to launder drug money"; it also observed that Frigorificos had continued to receive State Department humanitarian funds until the Senate Foreign Relations Committee raised questions with the Justice Department (Kerry report, 46–47, 60–61, 849; cf. 374). No reference is

made to the 1986 allegation, later publicized by CBS and Leslie Cockburn, that "funds from cocaine sales [are] said to be used to purchase weapons for contras"; and that a witness, Steven Carr, had seen three kg of cocaine at the house where he picked up the Corvo arms (Kerry report, 849; cf. 865; Cockburn, 156–57).

[20] Kerry report, 167–69.

[21] Ibid., 158.

[22] Ibid.

[23] North diary; Kerry report, 158, 160; cf. 647, 830.

[24] Kerry report, 629–30.

[25] Ibid., 636.

[26] Ibid., 830; cf. 638, 647, 859.

[27] North notebook, June 2, 1986.

[28] FBI teletype of June 11, 1986; *Iran-Contra Report*, Appendix A, Vol. 1, 805.

[29] Kerry report, 161.

[30] Sam Watson diary, April 21, 1986.

[31] Kerry report, 158; North notebook.

[32] Murray Waas, *Village Voice*, July 14, 1987.

[33] U.S. Department of Justice, Office of Professional Responsibility, *Annual Report to the Attorney General, 1988*, 7; Murray Waas, *Village Voice*, July 14, 1987; Kerry report, 653–58 (Feldman testimony). According to Maas, Messick used the rewritten Feldman memo to give the press the false impression that one of Feldman's chief witnesses, Jesus Garcia, had been "inconclusive" and "deceptive" in his answers to a polygraph examination.

[34] Kerry report, 150.

[35] Hull letter of September 8, 1986, to "R. O[wen]"; Owen exhibit at Appendix B, Vol. 20, 856; cf. 826.

[36] *Iran-Contra Report*, 109. This was becoming a game of hardball. In August Terrell had helped persuade Glibbery to repudiate his own retraction. On this trip Terrell's life was threatened.

[37] Kerry report, 152; cf. 169.

[38] Cockburn, *Out of Control*, 57.

[39] Ibid., 238.

[40] Ibid. The third autopsy, performed for the family in Florida, differed from the earlier ones by ruling that marks behind Carr's left elbow "were needle marks from an injection."

[41] Avirgan and Honey, *La Penca: On Trial*, 15.

[42] Cockburn, *Out of Control*, 236. Carr's death occurred the night after the first major news story about him, in the *Miami Herald*, December 12, 1986.

[43] Cockburn, *Out of Control*, 141–45, 148.

[44] Kerry report, 10–11, 18, 23.

[45]The U.S. government stated at the trial that in 1984 Noriega had passed $100,000 to a Contra leader.

[46]Kerry report, 11; Kerry hearings, II, 29.

[47]Its grander allegations about a thirty-year conspiracy by a "secret team" remain much more controversial.

[48]*Avirgan and Honey v. John Hull* et al., *Opinion Granting Summary Judgments*, United States District Court, SD Florida, Case No. 86-1146-CIV-KING, 5 (cited hereafter as *Opinion*), citing 18 U.S.C. §§ 1961–1968.

[49]Ibid.

[50]Ibid., 30–34: "The plaintiffs have not . . . produced evidence that the defendant Hansen was paid by, worked with, associated with, or conspired with any of the other defendants."

[51]Ibid., 35. Cf. Avirgan and Honey, *La Penca: On Trial*, 88.

[52]*Opinion*, 36.

[53]In his appeal of Judge King's dismissal, Christic counsel Daniel Sheehan argues that this exclusion was an abuse of the court's discretion: "The Court Abused Its Discretion by Excluding as Inadmissible Plaintiffs' Evidence Relevant to Causation Where the Defendants Failed to Object to the Evidence and the Courts Failed to Give Plaintiffs the Opportunity to Be Heard on Any Issue: . . . Defendants made no objections to the form or the admissibility of any affidavits or exhibits submitted by plaintiffs. Where a party fails to object to the form or admissibility of evidence in affidavits submitted to a summary judgment motion, objections are waived, and the court properly considers the evidence submitted" (In the United States Court of Appeals for the Eleventh Circuit, No. 88-5720, *Tony Avirgan and Martha Honey v. John Hull* et al., Brief of Appellants, 40–41).

[54]United States District Court, SD Florida, 86-1146-CIV-KING, *Avirgan and Honey v. John Hull* et al., Order Granting Motions for Costs and Attorneys' Fees, February 2, 1989, 1–3.

[55]Bradlee, *Guts and Glory*, 431.

[56]*Los Angeles Times*, January 27, 1987; Sheila Ryan, "Palestinian Deportation Case Continues," *Mideast Monitor*, IV, 2 (1987), 1.

[57]"Alien Terrorists and Undesirables: A Contingency Plan," 7: "routinely hold any alien so charged without bond, as a danger to the national security and public safety; vigorously oppose granting of any bond by immigration judges."

[58]Judge Stephen Wilson, quoted in Ryan, "Palestinian Deportation," 3. The proceedings also drew public protest from a number of sources, including an ad placed by six Jewish organizations.

[59]*National Catholic Reporter*, November 27, 1987, 17; cf. *San Francisco Chronicle*, December 12, 1987. This FBI application of the terrorist label to peaceful protesters was not unprecedented. In January 1985, FBI agents in Buffalo and Washington had "questioned whether 'terrorism'

investigations of peaceful demonstrators against contra aid were 'warranted' and 'necessary,' according to FBI documents obtained under the Freedom of Information Act" (*National Catholic Reporter*, November 27, 1987, 16).

⁶⁰See Eve Pell, "F.B.I. Files Protected: FOIAbles of the New Drug Law," *Nation*, December 13, 1986. The amendments were sponsored in the Senate by Senators Orrin Hatch and Jeremiah Denton (whose aide Joel Lisker was directly involved in Contra support operations). Senator Hatch was later a member of the Senate Iran-Contra Committee and Joel Lisker a member of its staff.

⁶¹FBI teletype of July 1986; *Iran-Contra Report*, Appendix A, Vol. 1, 861.

⁶²*Iran-Contra Report*, 106–8, 112, 116.

⁶³In 1988 someone leaked a copy to a major TV network.

⁶⁴An example is the report's studied avoidance of Enterprise activities in Africa. An Enterprise chart of its own operating and other companies showed that one of its "collecting" companies, Dolmy Business, Inc., was designated to operate in Africa. The report transmitted without rebuttal Albert Hakim's uncorroborated claim that "Africa was included because . . . Secord said—allegedly in jest—'who knows, if we do a good job, the President may send us to Angola' " (*Iran-Contra Report*, 333). But Dolmy Business was no jest; it was Dolmy that obtained the ship *Erria* on short order for a North African operation (*Iran-Contra Report*, 368). In addition, Dolmy had an offshore subsidiary chartered in Liberia, which is shown in censored form on the chart (*Iran-Contra Report*, 334; unnamed company "F"), but about which the report was silent (*Los Angeles Times*, January 21, 1987). North met with the rebel Angolan leader Jonas Savimbi in Washington (Shultz exhibit GPS-74-78) and allegedly once introduced himself at a meeting of United Methodist Church leaders as a "veteran of two wars—Vietnam and Angola" (*Philadelphia Inquirer*, March 15, 1987).

⁶⁵The Pike report, based largely on the CIA internal "family jewels" memo of CIA illegalities that had been prepared for Director William Colby, was leaked extensively to the press; much of it appeared, just before its official release, in the *Village Voice* (*New York Times*, February 12, 1976, 14). In the midst of the resulting furor, the House, in an action without precedent, voted to withhold the report until the executive branch had censored it (*New York Times*, January 30, 1976). At the time, Otis Pike told the House that the CIA special counsel had told his committee staff director, "Pike will pay for this, you wait and see—we'll destroy him for this." He also repeated an earlier charge that the CIA "could have been" the source of the leaks (*New York Times*, March 10, 1976; cf. February 14, 1976). There is no need to implicate CIA officers directly in Pike's electoral defeat; other powerful and affluent groups in the covert opera-

tions lobby were available to engineer it. The CIA liaison to the Pike Committee staff was Donald Gregg, who became national security adviser to Vice President George Bush; Gregg denies any involvement in the leaking of the report but attributes the Congressional suppression of it to "outrage" at "a sloppily researched piece of work" (telephone conversation, February 19, 1988).

[66]*Iran-Contra Report*, 99.

[67]Shultz exhibit GPS-82, 2.

[68]Peter Kornbluh, *Nicaragua: The Price of Intervention* (Washington, DC: Institute of Policy Studies, 1987), 198.

CHAPTER 10

[1]*Los Angeles Times*, February 18, 1987.

[2]*New York Times*, February 24, 1987.

[3]Kerry report, 126–28.

[4]Palmer says he invented stories of government protection and that once he became a government informant he stopped all illegal smuggling. See Kerry hearings, III, 231ff.

[5]*Boston Globe*, February 13, 1988.

[6]*Newark Star-Ledger*, June 6, 1989.

[7]*New York Times*, January 20, 1987.

[8]*Nation*, May 8, 1989, 626.

[9]Cockburn, *Out of Control*, 153–67.

[10]Ibid. 165–66; Kerry report, 45, 150, 362.

[11]Kerry report, 61.

[12]Owen memo to North, March 17, 1986.

[13]Kerry report, 122.

[14]Cockburn, *Out of Control*, 175, quoting Morales's partner Gary Betzner.

[15]Joseph Kelso deposition in *Avirgan and Honey v. John Hull* et al., civil action 86-1146-CIV-KING, 37, 42, 44ff. Kelso's prime source was Warren Wyant Treece, former deputy director of the Narcotics Administration of Public Security. See *La Nacion*, December 3, 1986. Cf. Kelso deposition, 83.

[16]*Iran-Contra Report*, 648.

[17]Ibid., 106; Kelso deposition, 131, 150.

[18]*Iran-Contra Report*, Appendix B, Vol. 20, 857–58.

[19]Ibid.; Kelso deposition, 162–75; *La Nacion*, December 3, 1986, and December 4, 1986.

[20]*Rocky Mountain News*, March 1, 1987.

[21]*Iran-Contra Report*, 648.

[22]Ibid., 106.

[23]Ibid., Appendix B, Vol. 20, 818–19. As several members of the House Iran-Contra committee declared, "If North and Owen were using the Customs Service to provide them with criminal case information in order that they might defend themselves in a civil lawsuit, it was a flagrant abuse of North's position at the NSC." See *Iran-Contra Report*, 648.

[24]Kelso deposition, 131; *La Nacion*, December 4, 1986.

[25]Joel Millman, "Dead Men Tell No Tales," *Mother Jones*, April 1987. Cf. *La Nacion*, November 25, 1986.

[26]Owen memo to North, April 1, 1985.

[27]*New York Times*, February 10, 1988; Blandón testimony, Kerry hearings, II, 118.

[28]Blandón testimony, Kerry hearings, II, 121.

[29]Letters reproduced in Kerry hearings, II, 393–97.

[30]Quoted in Walker, *Drug Control in the Americas*, 216–17.

[31]House Foreign Affairs Committee hearing, *Narcotics Review in Central America* (Washington, DC: U.S. Government Printing Office, 1988), 94–95.

[32]Carlton testimony, Kerry hearings, II, 211.

[33]Kempe, *Divorcing the Dictator*, 252.

[34]Levine, *Deep Cover*, 215–19, 232, 277–78.

[35]Ibid., 19, 16.

[36]Alan Block, "Toward a History of American Drug Policy," paper delivered at University of Wisconsin conference, May 11, 1990.

CHAPTER 11

[1]Agent of the U.S. Bureau of Narcotics and Dangerous Drugs, quoted in McCoy, *The Politics of Heroin*, p. 147. These claims were based on distortions: for examples see Peter Dale Scott, "Opium and Empire: McCoy and Southeast Asia," *Bulletin of Concerned Asian Scholars*, September 1973, 49–56; Krüger, *Great Heroin Coup*, 15–16.

[2]Shannon, *Desperados*, 160; *New York Times*, March 19, 1986.

[3]See Chapter 6.

[4]Shannon, *Desperados*, 156.

[5]*Washington Post*, May 6, 1987: "As a result of a congressional investigation into Korean influence-buying in the late 1970s—which concluded that Moon's church had "operational ties" with the South Korean CIA—critics have long suggested that the Times was bankrolled by one or more foreign governments, including South Korea or other anticommunist governments, such as South Africa. Times officials categorically deny such charges. However, they do acknowledge that virtually all of the paper's subsidies come from overseas."

[6]Kornbluh, *Nicaragua*, 77–79.

[7]For a rather more critical evaluation, see Millman, "Narco-Terrorism," 48–49.

[8]Example and discussion in Woodward, *Veil*, 458–63.

[9]Carl Bernstein wrote years ago in *Rolling Stone* that the CIA's "relationship with the *Times* was by far its most valuable among newspapers, according to CIA officials," just as "CBS was unquestionably the Agency's most valuable broadcasting asset" ("The CIA and the Media," *Rolling Stone*, October 20, 1977, 60–61). Bernstein was reporting on the use of the *Times'* overseas reporting network for CIA cover. But among the reasons for this collaboration were "the close personal ties between the men [such as the Oakes brothers] who ran both institutions." In 1977 their uncle C. L. Sulzberger of the *Times* was still regarded by the Agency as an "active asset." For the CIA and the *Washington Post*, see Deborah Davis, *Katharine the Great: Katharine Graham and the Washington Post* (New York: Harcourt Brace, Jovanovich, 1979; reissued and expanded, 1987).

[10]Quoted in Mark Hertsgaard, *On Bended Knee: The Press and the Reagan Presidency* (New York: Farrar, Straus & Giroux, 1988), 314.

[11]As Hertsgaard has pointed out, "Despite, or more likely because of, Woodward's extraordinary access to Casey and CIA officials, he too failed to uncover the arms deals to Iran or, for that matter, the Contra connection" (*On Bended Knee*, 304–5).

[12]Hersh's story appeared in *New York Times*, June 12, 1986. Two months earlier a former Reagan NSC staffer, Norman Bailey, had already testified publicly that Noriega was "widely suspected of drug dealings" (Kerry report, 91).

[13]*Boston Globe*, April 27, 1987; quoted in Cockburn, *Out of Control*, 184.

[14]*San Francisco Examiner*, March 16, 1986; reprinted in Kerry report, 432; cf. Chapter 7.

[15]*Milwaukee Journal*, July 9, 1987. The fugitive's name was Detlaf Thomas, whose sister and codefendant, Leticia Thomas Altamirano, told the court of her efforts to send medical supplies to the Contras. She also identified herself as "the ex-wife of Bayardo Jiron, a former vice president and national security chief of Nicaragua." Such stories continue to appear; see for example *The Arizona Republic* (Phoenix), April 26, 1990:

> A Colombian was helping an international fund-raising plan for Nicaraguan rebels, not planning to smuggle cocaine, when he was arrested in an alleged cocaine-importing conspiracy last fall, a friend has testified in federal court. Miami businessman Carlos Javier Marulanda was arranging to ship gold—not cocaine—into the United States from Colombia, said his friend, Jorge Alegria. Alegria, 41, of Honduras, was described by Marulanda's defense attorney as a major fund-raiser for the Nicaraguan contras. Marulanda, who is on trial before U.S. District Judge Charles

Hardy, is accused of conspiring to import more than 1,000 kilograms of cocaine into the United States from Colombia.

[16]*Washington Post*, December 27, 1985. For Barger and Parry's difficulties in publishing the story, see *Rolling Stone*, September 10, 1987.

[17]Millman, "Narco-Terrorism," 50; cf. Hertsgaard, 314–15.

[18]Unnamed Associated Press staff member, quoted in Millman, "Narco-Terrorism," 50.

[19]Martin A. Lee and Norman Solomon, *Unreliable Sources: A Guide to Detecting Bias in News Media* (New York: Lyle Stuart/Carol Publishing, 1990), 290–91.

[20]Millman, "Narco-Terrorism," 51. This looks like an allusion to the relationship between ARDE lieutenant Octaviano César and Jorge Morales, who (as noted in Chapter 6) was arrested three weeks later. Parry was quoted in *Rolling Stone* as saying that when he and Barger proposed to follow up North and the drug story in early 1986, Washington bureau chief Charles Lewis "took me aside and said, 'New York doesn't want to hear any more on the drug story. We think you shouldn't be doing any more on this' " (*Rolling Stone*, September 10, 1987; Hertsgaard, *On Bended Knee*, 315). Lewis denied making the statement.

[21]Millman, "Narco-Terrorism," 51.

[22]"Feudal landlords whose buildings are threatened with confiscation by the Taraki government [of Afghanistan] are bringing the produce from their poppy crops into Pakistan, and then use the proceeds to buy rifles, explosives, and other weapons. Pakistani arms merchants report that their new customers come in daily and business is booming" (*MacLeans*, April 30, 1979, quoted in Krüger, *Great Heroin Coup*, 221); Zbigniew Brzezinski, *Power and Principle* (New York: Farrar, Straus & Giroux, 1983), 427.

[23]J. H. Lowinson and David F. Musto, *New York Times*, May 22, 1980; quoted in Krüger, *Great Heroin Coup*, 226.

[24]*New York Times*, June 30, 1983 (cf. April 12, 1984); June 18, 1986.

[25]*Newsweek*, May 13, 1985, 41.

[26]*New York Times*, February 12, 1988.

[27]Edward Herman and Noam Chomsky, *Manufacturing Consent: The Political Economy of the Mass Media* (New York: Pantheon, 1988), 40–41. Hertsgaard has also commented on this discrepancy (*On Bended Knee*, 71).

[28]Herman and Chomsky, *Manufacturing Consent*, 306.

[29]Kerry report, 147, 159; cf. 631, 635, 694.

[30]Kerry report, 159.

[31]*Iran-Contra Report*, 631; Memorandum of July 23, 1987, from Robert A. Bermingham to House Iran-Contra Committee Chair Lee Hamilton.

[32]Kerry report, 59; Iran/Contra Testimony, Owen exhibit RWO-7, 801. See Chapter 5.

[33]*Washington Post*, July 22, 1987.

[34]*Washington Post*, July 24, 1987. Congressman Rangel later published his letter in the *Congressional Record*, August 6, 1987, Daily ed., E3297.

[35]*Boston Globe*, August 5, 1987.

[36]"After two years of investigations, even such an outspoken critic of the *contras* as New York Congressman Charles Rangel concluded that there was no evidence that the *contra* movement as such had been supported by narcotics trafficking . . . . Republicans hit on the idea of asking Nields's top investigator—Robert A. Bermingham—to look into the allegations of a *contra* drug network. His report, concluding that there was no such connection, was published as Appendix E to the *Report of the Congressional Committees*, Minority Report. Since it was written by the chief investigator for the majority, it carries considerable weight" (Ledeen, *Perilous Statecraft*, 266).

[37]Kerry report, 42, 75, 53–54. See Chapters 5 and 6.

[38]*New York Times*, April 14, 1989; *Washington Post*, April 14, 1989.

[39]*Washington Post*, June 29, 1987.

[40]*Los Angeles Times*, August 26, 1989.

[41]Robert Parry and Peter Kornbluh, "Iran-Contra's Untold Story," *Foreign Policy* (Fall 1988), 3–4.

[42]Parry and Kornbluh, "Iran-Contra's Untold Story," 12–18, citing North memo to McFarlane of March 20, 1985; S/LPD Report of February 8, 1985, to NSC. See also Lee and Solomon, *Unreliable Sources*, 131–39.

[43]Hertsgaard, *On Bended Knee,* 347.

[44]Bob Parry, interview with authors, 1990.

[45]Hertsgaard, *On Bended Knee*, 77.

[46]Herman and Chomsky, *Manufacturing Consent*, 14.

[47]Hertsgaard, *On Bended Knee*, 96–97.

CHAPTER 12

[1]Kerry report, 124.

[2]For a summary of past CIA connections to the drug trade, see Marshall, *Drug Wars*, Chapter 4.

[3]McCoy, *The Politics of Heroin*, 144–45.

[4]U.S. General Accounting Office, *Drug Control: U.S. Supported Efforts in Burma, Pakistan and Thailand*, GAO/NSIAD-88-94, February 1988; Lawrence Lifshultz, "Inside the Kingdom of Heroin," *Nation*, November 14, 1988; see also Marshall, *Drug Wars*.

[5]*Los Angeles Times*, April 13, 1989; *Miami Herald*, April 30, 1990; *San Francisco Examiner*, October 8, 1989.

[6]*Central American Report*, August 11, 1989; *New York Times*, October 1, 1989.

[7]*San Francisco Chronicle*, July 8, 1989; Pacific News Service, October 9, 1989.

[8]*Los Angeles Times*, May 7, 1990.

[9]*San Francisco Chronicle*, July 8, 1990.

[10]*Prensa Libre* (Guatemala City), March 14, 1990; ACAN, March 15, 1990; *Central America Report*, March 30, 1990.

[11]*Cerigua Weekly Briefs*, May 7–13, 1990; *Los Angeles Times*, August 30, 1989 (Gen. Roberto Matta).

[12]*New York Times*, July 5, 1990.

[13]*Los Angeles Times*, May 7, 1990.

[14]*Christian Science Monitor*, March 7, 1990; *Central America Report*, August 11, 1989; *Report on Guatemala*, July–August 1987.

[15]*Miami Herald*, April 30, 1990.

[16]*Los Angeles Times*, April 14, 1990.

[17]*Central America Report*, January 12, 1990; *Los Angeles Times*, April 14, 1990.

[18]*Latin America Regional Reports*, RM-90-04, May 10, 1990.

[19]*Central America Report*, March 16, 1990.

[20]*Central America Report*, May 19, 1989; Julio Godoy, "Return to Guatemala," *Nation*, March 5, 1990.

[21]For a more thorough discussion of this problem, see Marshall, *Drug Wars*, passim.

[22]Jo Ann Kawell, "Drug Wars: The Rules of the Game," *NACLA Report on the Americas*, XXIII, 6 (April 1990), 10. In September 1990, the Peruvian government rejected the U.S. offer of drug aid, but negotiations will no doubt continue. The total Andean initiative aid package will come to $2.2 billion over five years (*New York Times,* November 25, 1990).

[23]*Miami Herald*, November 30, 1989.

[24]*Washington Post*, November 13, 1989.

[25]Americas Watch, *The Killings in Colombia* (New York: Americas Watch Committee, 1989), 4–5.

[26]*Wall Street Journal*, May 18, 1990.

[27]Memo from Blandón to Kerry subcommittee, February 8, 1988; reprinted in Kerry report, 493.

[28]Mills, *Underground Empire*, 584, 862, 876–79.

[29]*El Nacional*, October 12, 1987; *Latin America Weekly Report*, August 16, 1985; Lee, *White Labyrinth*, 106.

[30]*Washington Post*, December 29, 1984.

[31]Lee, *White Labyrinth*, 177.

[32]*New York Times*, June 21, 1990.

[33]Senate Government Operations Committee, Permanent Subcommittee on Investigations, hearing, *U.S. Government Anti-Narcotics Activ-*

*ities in the Andean Region of South America* (Washington, DC: U.S. Government Printing Office, 1989), 170.

[34]Lee, *White Labyrinth*, 119–120.

[35]Marshall, *Drug Wars*.

[36]Ibid.

[37]*Los Angeles Times*, July 14, 1990.

# Names and Organizations

ARDE (Alianza Revolucionaria Democratica): The Costa Rica Contra faction launched by Edén Pastora in 1983

Álvarez Martínez, Gustavo: Honduran army officer who helped launch the Contras

BNDD: Bureau of Narcotics and Dangerous Drugs, which in 1973 became the Drug Enforcement Administration (DEA)

Barger, Brian: Journalist with Associated Press who helped break the Contra drug story

Blum, Jack: Counsel to the Senate Foreign Relations Committee for the drug investigation of the Kerry subcommittee

Bueso Rosa, José: Honduran general convicted in drug-financed plot to assassinate the president of Honduras

CAL: Latin American Anticommunist Confederation (Confederación Anticomunista Latina), the Argentine-dominated Latin American chapter of the World Anti-Communist League (WACL)

CORU (Commando of United Revolutionary Organizations): An umbrella organization of Cuban anti-Castro terrorist groups, led by Orlando Bosch, Frank Castro, Luis Posada, and others

Carlton, Floyd: Panamanian drug trafficker using DIACSA as cover; after conviction he became the major U.S. government witness in the indictment of Noriega

Caro Quintero, Rafael: Mexican drug trafficker implicated in the killing of DEA agent Enrique Camarena

Carr, Steven: Witness who said he saw cocaine stored with arms for the Contras and who died mysteriously shortly after his story became public

César, Octaviano: An aide to Contra leader Edén Pastora; arranged for drug trafficker Jorge Morales to provide support for the Contras in Costa Rica

Chanes, Francisco: Official of Frigorificos de Puntarenas who participated in Contra military assistance operations

Clarridge, Duane "Dewey": CIA officer responsible for Contra operations from 1982 to 1984, when direct CIA aid was terminated by the
Boland Amendment

Corvo, Rene: Miami Cuban who arranged illegal arms shipment to the
Contras; his 1988 indictment on antineutrality charges was dropped

Currier, Kevin: A Miami FBI agent who investigated allegations of arms
and drug smuggling by Corvo and others on behalf of the Contras

DIACSA: An aircraft and parts supply company that came under DEA
investigation for cocaine trafficking and money laundering; chosen by
the State Department to supply humanitarian aid for the Contras

Escobar Gaviria, Pablo: Major Colombian trafficker in Medellín cartel

FDN (Frente Democratico Nicaraguense): The leading Contra faction
in Honduras

Félix Gallardo, Miguel Angel: Mexican trafficker suspected of shipping
cocaine to the U.S.

Fernandez, Joseph ("Tómas Castillo"): CIA station chief in Costa Rica

Frigorificos de Puntarenas: A shrimp company in Costa Rica allegedly
created as a cover for the laundering of drug money; it was involved
in North's Contra support operations and used by the State Department to deliver humanitarian Contra aid

García Meza, Luis: Bolivian general who organized and came to power
through 1980 Cocaine Coup; CAL conference participant the same
year

González, Sebastián "Guachan": ARDE Contra official who fled Costa
Rica in 1984 after indictment for drug trafficking

Harari, Michael: Former Israeli Mossad agent who trained Manuel Noriega's bodyguards and arranged arms shipments in the region

Hondu Carib: A small air freight company, suspected of drug smuggling, which flew supplies to the Contras

Hull, John: American rancher in Costa Rica who backed Contras in
conjunction with the local CIA station and whose airfield received
Contra supply flights and allegedly drug shipments

Kalish, Steven: American marijuana trafficker close to Noriega in Panama

Kattan Kassin, Isaac: Major Colombian money launderer for Cali cartel

Kiszynski, George: Veteran Miami counterterrorism agent for the FBI
who investigated Corvo case with Kevin Currier and forwarded copies
of his cables to Washington for Oliver North

Latchinian, Gerard: International arms dealer, former business partner
of Felix Rodriguez and Mossad agent Pesakh Ben-Or, convicted for
his part in 1984 Bueso Rosa cocaine plot

Lehder, Carlos: Colombian drug trafficker and admirer of Hitler, extradited to United States and convicted

MAS (Muerte a Secuestradores): "Death to Kidnappers," Colombian antiguerrilla death squad organization founded in December 1981 by members of Medellín cartel, Cali cartel, and Colombia military

Matta Ballesteros, Juan Ramón: Honduran drug trafficker with important drug connections in Mexico, Cali, and the Honduran army

Morales, George (Jorge): Convicted Colombian drug smuggler; testified to shipping arms to Contras for drugs in return for alleged promises of official protection

NHAO (Nicaraguan Humanitarian Assistance Organization): State Department office established to deliver humanitarian aid to the Contras

NNBIS (National Narcotics Border Interdiction System): Coordinated U.S. interagency antidrug effort launched in 1983 under Vice President George Bush

Nazar Haro, Miguel: Head of Mexican DFS (Direccion Federal de Seguridad), important CIA asset and known protector of Mexican drug traffickers

Noriega, Manuel: Panamanian general and dictator indicted for protecting drug shipments and laundering money; involved with Floyd Carlton, Oliver North, the Contras, and the CIA

Nuñez, Moisés Dagoberto: Officer of Frigorificos de Puntarenas who worked with Joe Fernandez and Robert Owen on anti-Sandinista operation for North

OSG-TIWG (Operations Sub-Group/Terrorist International Working Group): Secret counterterrorist working group cochaired by Oliver North in the National Security Council and used by him against drug witness Jack Terrell

Ocampo Zuluaga, Santiago: Associate of Cali cartel kingpin Gilberto Rodríguez Orejuela; president of MAS; indicted in 1980

Ochoa Vásquez, Jorge Luis: Leader of Medellín cartel, indicted in United States in 1984 and 1986; arrested in Spain in 1984 and extradited to Colombia, freed on $10,500 bail

Owen, Robert: Intermediary between Oliver North, the Contras, and their supporters in Latin America, like John Hull

Pastora, Edén: Contra leader in Costa Rica opposed by John Hull and FDN

PIP (Peruvian Investigative Police): Peru's elite, and corrupt, police agency assigned to combat drug trafficking but penetrated by drug traffickers; responsible for atrocities against peasants and human rights workers

Parry, Robert: Associated Press journalist who helped break the Contra drug story

Posey, Tom: American mercenary who collaborated briefly with John Hull, Robert Owen, and Jack Terrell on Contra support operations

Revell, Oliver:   Executive Assistant Director of the FBI with responsibility for counterterrorism matters; regularly attended OSG-TIWG meetings

Robinette, Glenn:   Ex-CIA private investigator engaged by Richard Secord and paid with proceeds from Iran-Contra arms sales to investigate Christic Institute witnesses such as Jack Terrell; worked with Moisés Nuñez and Robert Owen

Rodríguez, César:   Panamanian arms and drugs trafficker under Omar Torrijos and Manuel Noriega; killed in Colombia in 1986

Rodríguez, Félix:   Ex-CIA agent and former business partner of Gerard Latchinian; given Contra support role at Ilopango Air Force base in El Salvador after intervention by former CIA colleague Donald Gregg of Vice President Bush's office

Rodríguez, Luis:   Owner of Frigorificos de Puntarenas, indicted on drug charges that were later dropped

Rodríguez Gacha, Gonzalo:   Drug trafficker in Medellín cartel; killed in 1990

Rodríguez Orejuela, Gilberto:   Kingpin of Colombian Cali cartel; arrested with Jorge Ochoa in Spain in 1984 and extradited to Colombia, where he was later freed

SETCO (Servicios Turisticos):   Airline established by Honduran cocaine trafficker Juan Matta Ballesteros and used by the FDN and State Department to deliver supplies to the Contras

Sánchez, Aristides:   Contra leader whose relatives supplied cocaine in the San Francisco Frogman case

Seal, Adler Berriman ("Barry"):   Convicted drug smuggler who took photographs allegedly showing Sandinista official Federico Vaughan and Colombian kingpin Pablo Escobar loading cocaine onto Seal's plane

Sicilia Falcón, Alberto:   Miami Cuban, allegedly trained as a U.S. government agent, who in 1972 emerged as a trafficker of drugs through Mexico

Singlaub, John:   Ex-OSS and CIA officer, later a U.S. army general, who became head of the U.S. chapter of WACL and a supplier to the Contras

Spadafora, Hugo:   Panamanian enemy of Noriega who was murdered in 1985 after talking to U.S. officials about drug trafficking in Costa Rica

Suarez Gómez, Roberto:   Bolivian cocaine trafficker until arrested in 1988 after falling out with Colombian cartels

Suarez Mason, Carlos Guillermo:   Argentine general and P2 member who oversaw Argentine death squads and drug-financed activities that were coordinated through CAL

Tambs, Lewis:   U.S. Ambassador to Colombia and later Costa Rica; presented case, later discredited, that left-wing narcoguerrillas defended Tranquilandia cocaine base in Colombia

Tascón Morán, Eduardo:  1970s Cali arms and drug trafficker with alleged links to Torrijos family in Panama

Terrell, Jack:  Former U.S. mercenary and Contra supporter who was persecuted by North and OSG after he began talking to DEA and FBI about Contra smuggling activities; later indicted on antineutrality charges that were eventually dropped

Torrijos, Omar:  Panamanian strongman in 1970s whose family allegedly included drug traffickers; killed in 1981 plane crash

UNO (United Nicaraguan Opposition):  Contra political coalition created under CIA pressure to facilitate Congressional support

Vaughan, Federico:  Official of Nicaraguan Sandinistas whose picture was allegedly taken with Pablo Escobar by Barry Seal as part of a U.S. Government-financed sting operation

Vidal, Felipe ("Morgan"):  Miami Cuban and alleged CIA agent who took over small Costa Rica Contra faction after the drug indictment of Sebastián González

Villoldo, Gustavo:  Miami Cuban, former CIA officer sent, like Félix Rodríguez, to support Contra operations at Ilopango Air Force Base in El Salvador after intervention by Vice President Bush's office; accused of drug involvement

WACL (World Anti-Communist League):  An umbrella group of anticommunist organizations that has linked many suspected drug traffickers

# Index

| | |
|---:|:---|
| Compositor: | Impressions |
| Text: | 10 / 13 Galliard |
| Display: | Galliard |
| Printer: | Maple-Vail Book Mfg. Group |
| Binder: | Maple-Vail Book Mfg. Group |